في ذكرى

مارك لينز

INTERFAITH SERIES

Series Editor
Joshua Ralston

The Other Prophet

Jesus in the Qur'an

Mouhanad Khorchide
Klaus von Stosch

Translated by Simon Pare

GINGKO

First English edition published in 2019 by
Gingko
4 Molasses Row
London SW11 3UX

First published in the German by Verlag Herder GmbH in 2018

A CIP catalogue record for this book is available from the British Library.

ISBN 978-1-909942-36-3
e-ISBN 978-1-909942-37-0

Typeset in Times by MacGuru Ltd
Printed in the United Kingdom

www.gingko.org.uk
@GingkoLibrary

Contents

1 **Introduction**   1

2 **The State of Christology in the Seventh Century**   8
- 2.1 The Chalcedon controversy   9
- 2.2 A political compromise on dogma   13
- 2.3 The Neo-Chalcedonian doctrine of enhypostasis   16
- 2.4 Christological debates among non-Chalcedonians   20
- 2.5 The Arabian Peninsula as a confluence of heresies?   27
- 2.6 The situation in the Arabian Peninsula in the seventh century   33

3 **New Developments in Modern Christology**   42
- 3.1 The starting point of consciousness Christology   44
- 3.2 The modern paradigm shift in relational ontology and its impact on Christology   48
- 3.3 Testing against the historical Jesus   53
- 3.4 Multiple incarnations?   58

4 **A Holistic Reading of Surahs 19, 3 and 5 in the Context of a Diachronic Reading of the Qur'an's Verses about Jesus**   62
- 4.1 Jesus in Surah Maryam   65
  - 4.1.1 Zachariah and John   65
  - 4.1.2 Mary and her child   67
  - 4.1.3 Jesus's self-image   71
  - 4.1.4 An anti-Christological intervention in Q 19:34–40?   75
  - 4.1.5 Further themes in Surah Maryam   80
  - 4.1.6 Prophetological consolidation in the late Meccan and early Medinan periods   82
- 4.2 Surah Al 'Imran   85
  - 4.2.1 Prologue (verses 1–32)   86
  - 4.2.2 Narrative core (verses 33–62)   88

	4.2.3	Religio-political arguments (verses 63–99)	96
	4.2.4	Self-assurance of the Muslim community (verses 100–200)	98
	4.2.5	Jesus crucified?	99
4.3	Surah al-Ma'ida		105
	4.3.1	Structure and themes of the surah	106
	4.3.2	Criticism of any deification of human beings	109
	4.3.3	A break with Christianity?	114

5 Jesus's Position in Qur'anic Prophetology   119
(Zishan Ghaffar)

5.1	The early Meccan surahs: eschatological prophecy	121
	5.1.1 Imminent eschatological expectation?	125
5.2	The middle Meccan surahs: prophetology as a combination of salvation, election and mercy	129
	5.2.1 The new context of the proclamation in the middle Meccan period and its central topoi	130
	5.2.2 The Qur'an's apostolic doctrine in the middle Meccan period	132
	5.2.3 The birth of prophecy out of God's mercy	139
	5.2.4 Muhammad as *Moses redivivus* – the consolidation of Qur'anic prophetology in the middle Meccan period	141
5.3	Late Meccan prophetology: the apology of the messengers	143
5.4	Qur'anic prophetology in Medina	146
	5.4.1 From existential to textual typology	147
	5.4.2 From community of fate to the universal community of the covenant: Qur'anic prophetology between universality and exclusivity	148
	5.4.3 The Messenger Muhammad as lawmaker and his special prestige as a prophetic dignitary	151
	5.4.4 Prophetology as a counter-discourse to Christology?	152

6 The Work of Jesus Christ and the Qur'an: A Forensic Search for Functional Equivalents   157

6.1	God's self-revelation in the Islamic tradition (with the involvement of Darius Asghar-Zadeh)	159
6.2	The relation between God and humans as a liberating relationship	167
6.3	On the soteriological relevance of the Qur'an (with the involvement of Darius Asghar-Zadeh)	176
6.4	Can God suffer?	184

6.5   Qur'anic stimuli for conceiving of emotions in God   192

7 New Perspectives on the Qur'an   202
    7.1   Systematic conclusions from a Christian perspective   202
    7.2   Systematic conclusions from a Muslim perspective   206

Bibliography   211
Reference text   226

1

Introduction

In essence, the Christian faith is the belief that Jesus is Christ. As such, it is hard to overstate the importance for Christians of ascertaining how their counterparts from a different religion see Jesus Christ. Conversely, from a Muslim theological perspective it is extremely enriching to study Jesus outside of a purely Islamic context. In the past this often resulted in an apologetic attitude towards Christianity, insofar as the Qur'an was understood as wholly critical of Christianity. Discussions within Islam have so far neglected to take a broader account of how Christian views of Jesus have varied throughout Christian history, especially during the period of the formation of the Qur'an. Yet the Qur'an expressly invites Muslims to engage with Christian views and to discuss them on the basis of a common belief in one God. The Qur'an explicitly states: 'Say, "We believe in what was revealed to us and in what was revealed to you; our God and your God are one [and the same]; we are devoted to Him"' (Q 29:46).[1] The Qur'an in no way distances itself from Christians. Quite the contrary, in fact, it even promises them eternal bliss (Q 2:62; Q 5:69).

But how are Muslims to interpret this commitment to Christians in the light of intermittent disputes between the Qur'anic and biblical conceptions? How can an intensive theological analysis of Jesus in the Qur'an add to Muslim understanding of the one God Muslims and Christians share – as the Qur'an points out – and how does this analysis ultimately contribute to a better understanding of the Qur'an's statements about Jesus? This is where dialogue between Christians and Muslims becomes thorny, because Islam's very own record of revelation grapples in detail with the subject of Jesus the Messiah, Son of Mary. In total, Jesus is directly mentioned in 108 verses in fifteen different surahs of the Qur'an, and many other

---

1 Unless specified otherwise, quotations from the Qur'an are from the English translation by M.A.S. Abdel Haleem (OUP 2008).

passages allude to him. As we shall see, Christology is a central theme of the Qur'an, and one with which the proclaimer of the Qur'an[2] and the early Muslim community fully and critically engaged.

If one considers that the Qur'an represents an exchange between God and the first recipients of Muhammad's proclamation and that it was therefore of divine origin, then this finding constitutes an explosive combination in respect to Christian-Muslim cohabitation. It is obvious that the Qur'an diverges significantly from the usual Christian view of Jesus and, at first sight at least, contradicts some of the latter's core beliefs. One gets the impression at this point that the following choice is unavoidable: either one defends Christology against the Qur'an's criticism at the risk of appearing to attack Islam; or one agrees with the Qur'an's criticism of Christology, thereby potentially devaluing the Christian faith. For if the Qur'an is God-given, then God's critical objection must lead one to revise one's own religious views, but not to offer an apologetic reaction. The dispute over Jesus would appear to be a breaking point in Muslim-Christian coexistence, and repairing it would be one of the most urgent tasks facing theologians who wish to foster peaceful cohabitation between the religions.

Exploring Jesus's representation in the Qur'an is not only important for dialogue *between* the two religions, though; it also poses major challenges *within* the Christian and Muslim communities. From a Muslim perspective, it is extremely vexing that the Qur'an makes a series of – from the standpoint of Islamic scholastic theology – provocative statements recognising Jesus's special status. The Qur'an clearly honours the significance of Jesus Christ while also engaging critically with the Christian reception of this significance. A proper understanding of Qur'anic prophetology and Qur'anic self-reflection depends to a large extent on an analysis of its discursive engagement with Christology. That is why the manner in which Christ is acknowledged in the Qur'an is far more central to an adequate understanding of the Qur'an than has hitherto been recognised.

At the same time, the Qur'an's representation of Jesus Christ also contains many lessons for Christian theology. In any case, it is one of this book's principal objectives to demonstrate as much. Christians can gain a deeper insight into Jesus Christ and a better understanding of their own history by reading the Qur'an's pronouncements regarding Jesus. The Qur'an offers Christians a great deal of enduringly meaningful messages about Jesus Christ, and it is well worth

---

2 When we refer to the proclaimer of the Qur'an, we deliberately leave it open as whether this is God or Muhammad or both to ensure that a variety of readings of the book are possible.

listening closely to these, even for purely intra-Christian reasons. This is far from an obvious case to make and one that is impossible to argue in these few lines. Nonetheless, we present it here in this introduction as a kind of promise, and by the end of the book the reader will be in a better position to judge whether the authors have kept their side of the bargain.

So, in summary, this book has three goals. The first is to retrace the history of the dispute over Jesus in the Qur'an and to consider how coming to terms with it may contribute to fruitful coexistence between Christians and Muslims today. Second, it intends to show the considerable hermeneutic significance of Christological debate for a proper understanding of the Qur'an. And third, it wishes to suggest ways in which studying the Qur'an can help Christians to intensify and purify their belief in Jesus Christ.

In pursuit of these goals we shall use four principal innovative methodological steps, none of which has previously been applied in this form to the subject of Jesus's representation in the Qur'an. This is a particularly notable fact because countless books have been written on the subject and one might easily assume that everything that could be said about the questions that preoccupy us here has already been said. However, none of the books we are aware of uses a single one of the four distinctive methodological approaches that define our study.

For a start, this is the only book about Jesus in the Qur'an to date to have been co-authored by a Christian and a Muslim. This co-authorship should not be taken to mean that the Muslim author penned certain chapters while the Christian author wrote others. Instead, virtually all the chapters are the product of a joint creative process over a total of six years, and so both writers share responsibility for every one of them. A team of Muslim and Christian researchers assisted the authors, and we shall pay tribute in our subsequent acknowledgments to the precious support we received. The important point here is that we were able to call on exegetical skills that we ourselves will never possess and to take into account the views of other denominations within our respective religions. This allowed us to incorporate not just Sunni and Catholic opinions, but also Shi'ite, Protestant and Syriac Orthodox perspectives. We would never claim that we have taken adequate account of all these perspectives or accommodated every one of their concerns; but we did at least try our very best to avoid placing too much emphasis on any one denomination, and to develop a form of ecumenical cooperation that can percolate across the full spectrum of our two religions.

Despite all our efforts to be inclusive, this text is of course first and foremost a rapprochement between two authors, who describe, in separate chapters at the end of the book, the reflections about their own religion they have gleaned from this joint process. However, the final thoughts in the conclusion and the brief presentation of modern Christology in Chapter 3 aside, this is a joint text for which we bear equal responsibility. Accordingly, neither of us has ever worked on a text before in which we have wrestled with every single sentence. There were so many revisions, particularly to the section presenting an exegesis of the Qur'an, that we are ourselves amazed at how far our positions shifted over the course of our conversations and how much we learned from and with each other.

Our book's second methodological specificity is that we advance in strictly diachronic fashion during the whole description of Qur'anic exegesis and endeavour to provide a precise historical context for the evolution of the Qur'an's pronouncements about Jesus. There are already, of course, many historical classifications of this kind, but few classifications are combined with a diachronic history of the evolution of the Qur'an's messages. Above all, though, none has been conducted that does not include new revisionist conceptions of the Qur'an. This book therefore functions in a similar fashion to Angelika Neuwirth's Corpus Coranicum project,[3] taking as its starting point the heuristic assumption that the Qur'an was indeed largely written during the Prophet Muhammad's lifetime. It also traces the evolution of the Qur'an's statements about Jesus, son of Mary, in accordance with the same chronology as that laid out in the Corpus Coranicum.

This basic methodological assumption can certainly be questioned in terms of exegesis, and there are other options available. However, first, it strikes us as more historically plausible than contemporary revisionist models;[4] and second, it has the advantage of not contradicting any Muslim convictions, making it possible that the findings presented in this book can be accepted by Muslims too. At the very least, our methodological approach contains no hermeneutic premises that conflict with Muslim beliefs.

The third methodological specificity of our approach to Jesus in the Qur'an consists of reading at least the most important surahs about Jesus in a holistic fashion. We therefore strive to avoid the otherwise common fragmentation of the Qur'an, focusing instead on the relevant surahs as literary entities. Of course, given the limited space for this study, we cannot do this for every surah featuring verses about Jesus. We will, however, analyse in their entirety the main surahs that discuss Jesus in order to take into account in our interpretation the literary context of the respective deliberations.

---

3 See the introduction to Angelika Neuwirth, *The Qur'an and Late Antiquity: A Shared Heritage*, Oxford 2019.
4 For an overview and critique of these models see ibid, 91–104.

Our book's fourth and final methodological particularity is that it is guided by the principles of comparative theology.[5] For us both that means that we try to feel our way into the other's beliefs and help each other to formulate our respective faith as persuasively as possible. This eventually gives rise to an explicit reflection on our respective theological stances, which preserves the denominational dimension of our personal theological reflections.

At the same time, we would like to resist any agonal definition of the relationship between our two religions. Our aim is not to compete to determine who has the better perspective on Jesus of Nazareth, but rather to advance our perspectives by remaining faithful to the truths to which we are both committed. For that reason, we have worked historically and exegetically on the challenges and have tried to identify functional equivalents of Christology in the Qur'an. That is how we have gone about confronting the major challenges arising from our subject in philological, historical and systematic terms. In addition – as that all-important instance for comparative work, the third party – we have incorporated as many other perspectives as possible as a means of repeatedly testing our findings. However, we do not strive for an overarching, comprehensive result, but rather aim to produce separate yet interlinked theological conclusions.

To present our approach in detail: after offering an in-depth historical introduction to the state of Christology in the seventh century and to the presumed situation on the Arabian Peninsula (Chapter 2), we will proceed to reconstruct examples of Christological thought at the time (Chapter 3). This will serve on the one hand to clarify the tense situation in which the proclaimer of the Qur'an intervenes on discourses about Jesus. It should also, however, give some idea as to how those discourses have evolved to the present day and thereby highlight possible interpretations of the Qur'an in the light of the altered discursive situation. The systematic reconstruction provided in the third chapter is written entirely from a Christian point of view since it pursues the simple goal of surveying modern approaches to Christology and is designed to reveal the Christological perspective adopted by the Christian author of this book.

This is then followed by the real centrepiece of our book – the exegetical discussion of the Jesus verses in the Qur'an (Chapter 4). As already mentioned, this investigation will be conducted by studying the surahs in a holistic and diachronic manner, providing a set of exegetical findings that can be related in a very interesting

---

5 For our conception of the methodology of comparative theology, see Klaus von Stosch, 'Komparative Theologie als Wegweiser in der Welt der Religionen' (*Beiträge zur Komparativen Theologie*; 6), Paderborn 2012, 193–215.

way to the preceding presentation of the historical situation in the seventh century as well as opening up new potential for dialogue with contemporary Christological models. One of the most significant results of our exegetical and historical endeavours will show that the proclaimer of the Qur'an dissociates himself from the Christological discourses of his time and establishes his own prophetology. This prophetology, established by the Qur'an, is a subject of research in its own right, and it would take an additional book, at least, to give a proper record of it. We wanted to incorporate some initial points of reference from our considerations in this book and so we asked our Muslim project assistant Zishan Ghaffar to produce a first version of this prophetology. This is to be found in Chapter 5 and provides a more specific Qur'anic context for the statements about Jesus.

While our focus in the first five chapters is on the person of Christ, Chapter 6 aims to provide an outline of Jesus Christ's work. To be more precise, the aim of this chapter is to discuss the revelation-theological and soteriological role of Christ. In these matters, it is clear that the Qur'an does not concord with Christian explanations, because it is not Christ who is at the heart of its conception of revelation but the Qur'an itself. Here, we need to clarify whether, as a result, the Qur'anic discourse sees itself as the functional equivalent of the salvific work of Jesus Christ. As we have already noted, our book will conclude with separate final thoughts from the two authors, and we will summarise the historical and exegetical work we have done in our own systematic conclusions.

Before we plunge into the contents of our book, we would like to use this introduction to thank all those who made this project possible. First and foremost, we ought to mention the *Deutsche Forschungsgemeinschaft* (DFG; the German Research Foundation), which funded several posts for four years, enabling us to proceed with our research. The DFG also funded three conferences – two in Germany, one in the United States – which, along with a research trip to the USA, allowed us to test our ideas against scientific discourse and develop them further. This book would never have come about without their support and encouragement.

We would also like to thank our project assistants who not only actively contributed to this book but also helped us with their exegetical, historical and methodological knowledge. Deserving of special mention on the Muslim side are Hamideh Mohagheghi and Dr Zishan Ghaffar, who tirelessly urged us to carry out more precise philological studies and assisted us most effectively. Dr Zishan Ghaffar also ensured an essential link to the work of the Corpus Coranicum project and to Professor Angelika Neuwirth, whose many and varied interventions advanced our studies and, time after time, gave us fresh inspiration. Without their cooperation, we would not have come close to being able to provide the exegetical and philological accuracy that we now hope to demonstrate. We are especially grateful to our Christian project assistant Cornelia Dockter, who maintained a firm grip on our project and did us an invaluable service at countless stages of our work, research and enquiries. This book would not have been possible without her unstinting aid. Last but not least, we acknowledge our project assistant Dr Darius Asghar-Zadeh, who was of great help regarding important sections of Chapter 6.

Alongside these staff members, whom the DFG's funding allowed us to employ, there is a long list of other staff who have made major contributions to our project's success. Dr Dina El Omari continually helped us out with her exegetical skills, Martina Aras made sure that the Syriac Orthodox perspective was represented, Professor Muna Tatari and Tolou Khademalsharieh provided precious assistance particularly at the beginning of the project, and Christine Schlichtig shared the burden of our work throughout its duration. Eva-Maria Leifeld and Lena Steindl worked on the project for a long time as student assistants. In the latter stages, Katharina Holtmann was central to supervising the publishing procedure of the German edition of the book.

Finally, we would like to present our thanks to all those who advised and assisted our project and who offered us valuable tips as we reviewed our manuscript. We would like to mention by name: Professor Reinhold Bernhardt, Professor Lejla Demiri, Professor Georg Essen, Professor Hans-Peter Großhans, Dirk Hartwig, Narjes Javandel, Professor Milad Karimi, Professor Elisa Klapheck, Professor Wolf Krötke, Professor Leo Lefebure, Professor Hajj Muhammad Legenhausen, Professor Bernhard Nitsche, Professor Ömer Özsoy, Professor Ahmad Pakatchi, Professor Peter C. Phan, Professor Aho Shemunkasho, Professor Angelika Strotmann, Professor Georges Tamer and Professor Holger Zellentin.

We particularly wish to thank Professor Sidney Griffith and Professor Jürgen Werbick. During the Christian author's research sabbatical in Georgetown, Sidney Griffith gave him the chance to discuss the first draft of this book sentence by sentence in a series of weekly conversations and provided countless stimulating comments on the topic. He was also the American host of a joint conference on the subject of this book at the Catholic University of America, which was of great assistance to both authors. As part of the Münster-based cluster of excellence on the topic of religion and politics, Jürgen Werbick helped the two authors to intensify their dialogue while assisting with the process by which this book came into being. His proposals have been, and still are, a special source of inspiration to both authors.

Paderborn/Münster on the feast of Jesus's birth 2017
Klaus von Stosch and Mouhanad Khorchide

2

On the State of Christology in the Seventh Century

If we are to assess which forms of Christology were in circulation at the time the Qur'an was written, we need to examine the development of Christology after the Council of Chalcedon in 451, as the dispute surrounding the decisions made at this council had a significant effect on eastern Christianity, lasting well into the seventh century. We can therefore assume that these arguments had an impact on the forms of Christianity present on the Arabian Peninsula in the seventh century.

In the run-up to the Council, Christology was influenced by a wide-ranging dispute between two schools of theology called the *School of Antioch* and the *School of Alexandria* after the provenance of their main advocates. The School of Antioch had the tendency to define the union of the human and the divine in Jesus Christ as a functional union in will or action. It thus preserved the integrity of Jesus Christ's human and divine natures without providing an adequate definition of the union of these two aspects. It ran the risk of assuming a purely external togetherness of the two natures in Jesus Christ that did not conceptually circumscribe the unity of his person. The School was accused of ultimately assuming that there were two Sons of God, a divine Christ and a human Jesus, without being able to explain how the two could be unified in one person.

On the other side of the debate stood the School of Alexandria, which emphasised the unity of the person of Jesus Christ to such a degree that it would not hear of his dual nature. It was not satisfied with talking of a purely functional union of the divine and the human in Jesus, but stressed the essential bond between these two aspects. This put it in danger of being unable properly to explain how Jesus's human nature could remain intact if it was encompassed by his divine nature.

The Council of Ephesus had adjudged this dispute in Alexandria's favour in 431 by removing the leading advocate of Antioch's case and the then Patriarch of

Constantinople, Nestorius (386–451), from office. Hence, in his dispute with the leader of the opposing Alexandrian school, the Patriarch of Alexandria, Cyril (c. 375/380–412), it became clear that Mary was not only the mother of Christ but also the Mother of God.[1]

The main reason that this decision did not immediately result in a schism was because Nestorius himself accepted the ruling and his followers initially campaigned within the Church for greater consideration of their theology. And it is clear that the following council did indeed attempt to reconcile the interests and ideas of both schools.

2.1 The Chalcedon controversy

The Catholic, Protestant and Byzantine-Orthodox churches regard the Council of Chalcedon as a decisive and still valid 'dogma-political' compromise which ruled out the extreme positions of the clashing theological schools and established principles for all forms of Christology. On the other hand, the Council of Chalcedon was, for the Oriental Orthodox Churches, the primary reason for their separation from the Byzantine-Roman Church,[2] and therefore the compromise forged there was also the cause of the first great schism in the history of Christianity, the significance of which can hardly be overstated for a region where Islam was emerging.[3]

---

1 See Alois Grillmeier, *Christ in Christian Tradition. Vol. 1: From the Apostolic Age to Chalcedon*, tr. John Bowden, Louisville, KY 1975, 392–414.

2 From an Oriental-Orthodox standpoint, it is not the case that the Eastern Churches broke away from the main church, but rather that the reforms of the Council of Chalcedon destroyed the unity of the Church. See Alois Grillmeier, *Christ in Christian Tradition. Vol. 2/3: The Churches of Jerusalem and Antioch from 451 to 600*, ed. Theresia Hainthaler, tr. Marianne Ehrhardt, Oxford 2013, 185: 'The opponents of Chalcedon, in the first place the Alexandrian patriarchs Dioscorus and Timothy Aelurus, then in the sixth-century Severus of Antioch and his followers, did not consider themselves as the innovators and dividers of unity. They regarded themselves as the genuine original stem of Christianity, as the continuers of the tradition. They attributed – and their successors today attribute – the destructive actions of a revolution in the faith to the Council of Chalcedon and its adherents...'

3 Due to the decisions made at Chalcedon, the patriarchate of Antioch and that of Alexandria were divided, the Armenian and Ethiopian Churches broke away from the main Church. See Wilhelm de Vries, *Die Gründe der Ablehnung des Konzils von Chalzedon durch die altorientalischen Kirchen*, in Rudolf Kirchschläger & Alfred Stirnemann (eds.), 'Chalzedon und die Folgen. 1. Wiener Konsultation mit der Orientalischen Orthodoxie. Dokumentation des Dialogs zwischen der armenisch-apostolischen und der römisch-katholischen Kirche sowie des Dialogs zwischen chalzedonischer und nicht chalzedonischer Orthodoxie', FS 60th birthday of Bischof Mesrob K. Krikorian (*Pro Oriente*; 14), Vienna 1992, 124–31, here 124.

In other ways too, we feel that it is appropriate to call the effect of this schism on contemporary Christianity traumatic. When one considers that large swathes of Europe had not yet been Christianised by late antiquity – there was, of course, no inkling of the Christianisation of America as yet – then it soon becomes clear that this schism shook Christendom to the core and struck at its very heart.

This split obviously did not happen overnight. The tussle over the reception of the Council of Chalcedon's decision continued well into the sixth century. Initially, the Council of Chalcedon was received very differently in various regions, and the Byzantine Empire contained, in direct proximity to one another, some bishops who rejected the council and others who defended it. The emperors too took differing stances. For example, Emperor Zeno and his patriarch Akakios of Constantinople were so keen to integrate Christians influenced by Alexandria into the empire that he effectively overrode the Council of Chalcedon. This, however, resulted in a temporary schism with Rome, known as the Acacian schism (484–519), which only came to an end when Emperor Justin I accepted Rome's position and actively campaigned for the empire to swing behind Chalcedon.

Many view his successor Justinian (527–565) as the first emperor who truly attempted to implement Chalcedon, using professions of faith as his guiding principle, under duress if required.[4] Indeed, Justinian tried to stylise himself as a great and particularly orthodox theologian, penning his own theological treatises and attempting to persuade anti-Chalcedonians of the merits of the Council in court debates. He was therefore regarded as an extremely pious and devoted follower of the united church, living an ascetic life and trying hard to be seen as a paragon of faith. He eagerly set about Christianising the whole empire and as early as 529 closed down the Neoplatonic school of philosophy in Athens. Yet despite, or perhaps due to, his endeavours, at an early stage in his reign a separate non-Chalcedonian hierarchy emerged, largely due to the influence of John of Ephesus and Severus of Antioch, forcing Justinian to change policy at the beginning of the 530s and sue for reconciliation between the opposing parties.[5]

Even before he came to power, Justinian was the force behind the throne during the Theopaschite Controversy and attempted to reconcile the position of Scythian monks, who maintained that one of the Trinity had suffered on the cross, with

---

4 See W. H. C. Frend, *The Rise of the Monophysite Movement. Chapters in the History of the Church in the Fifth and Sixth Centuries*, Cambridge 1972, 255–95.
5 See Volker Menzel, *Justinian and the Making of the Syrian Orthodox Church*, Oxford 2008, 186–91.

the Roman Catholic interpretation of Chalcedon.[6] He was clearly following John Maxentius, the leader of the Scythian monks, who insisted that it was possible not only to say that Jesus was the God-Logos, but also that, conversely, the God-Logos was also Jesus[7] – a highly unusual statement to which we shall return in our exegesis of the Qur'an. In 533 Justinian decreed that the statement about 'one of the Trinity' – which is a title for Christ also discussed in the Qur'an – being crucified was applicable throughout the empire and gained Rome's support for this formulation in 534.[8]

In general, Justinian did all he could to reconcile the concerns of Alexandrian theologians with Chalcedon and prevent a schism. When endeavours to bring about a rapprochement were halted by Pope Agapetus – the background being his attempt to exert indirect criticism of Chalcedon via a personal appointee as Patriarch of Constantinople – his wife Theodora (c. 500–548) took on the role of providing a glimmer of hope to the anti-Chalcedonians at court by professing to be a non-Chalcedonian in 535 or 536.[9] Researchers are divided as to whether Theodora's opposition was tactical or whether she really did entertain a theological disagreement with her husband.[10] Although sources frequently cite her as a passionate opponent of Chalcedon, most modern researchers suspect that she and her husband had made a political arrangement and that this was a ploy by the imperial couple to integrate opponents of Chalcedon into the empire.[11] In 542 Justinian laid down a symbolic marker of reconciliation by supporting the official appointment of two anti-Chalcedonian bishops, Jacob Baradaeus and Theodore, although this symbolic act served only to further institutionalise the split.[12] However, to this day the Syriac Orthodox church regards the schism as an essential move for defending Syriac thought against the imperialist and intolerant policies of the Byzantine court.

In view of the looming, now institutionalised schism, the task of reconciling the two opposing theological camps became a matter of the utmost urgency for the imperial couple. The emperor therefore deliberately planned the Second

---

6 See Karl-Heinz Uthemann, 'Kaiser Justinian als Kirchenpolitiker und Theologe', in *Augustinianum* 33 (1999) 5–83, here 21–3.

7 Ibid. 20.

8 Uthemann, op. cit. 34–5.

9 Menzel, op. cit. 208.

10 Ibid. 209.

11 Ibid. 227–8 for example.

12 See Richard Bell, 'The Origin of Islam in its Christian Environment', The Gunning Lectures, Edinburgh University 1925, London 1968, 21.

Council of Constantinople in 553 as an attempt to forge unity. He did in fact achieve a partial revision of Chalcedon by condemning some theological writings on the Antiochian side, including the letter from Ibas of Edessa to the Persian Mari and some of the dogmatic texts by Theodore of Mopsuestia and writings by the church historian Theodoret of Cyrus.[13] He even compelled the pope to support these condemnations. Yet none of these moves satisfied the anti-Chalcedonians.[14] The emperor may have managed to bring many of them to Constantinople, but they refused to take part in the Council and seek a settlement because they had already made so many sacrifices in their opposition to Chalcedon.[15] They no longer demanded the simple hollowing out of the Council; they wanted it to be formally withdrawn. At the same time, their missionary successes in the East filled them with sufficient self-confidence to avoid being boxed in.[16]

We can therefore assume that the whole sixth century still bore deep scars from the controversy between the Chalcedonians and the non-Chalcedonians, and that the emerging schism only gradually crystallised in the institutions.[17] During Justinian's rule, however, it came to a situation where more and more cities had both a Chalcedonian and a non-Chalcedonian bishop who were at political logger-heads. In the decades after Justinian, the increasingly institutionalised schism and the disagreement over Christology at its root remained the predominant subject of all theological debate. This means that Christendom remained in a state of severe conflict over the correct form of Christology during Muhammad's lifetime, and this dispute filtered down to the level of local churches and had particularly

13 Menzel, *Justinian*, 265 with reference to Uthemann, *Emperor Justinian*, 48–76.
14 Menzel, ibid. 266.
15 Ibid. 269.
16 Justinian judged it to be an astute tactical move to act as patron of these missionary efforts led by John of Ephesus in order to tie these groups directly to himself. At the same time, the Chalcedonians could hardly condemn him for attacking heathens (see Menzel, 263–5).
17 Although Justinian's successor Justin II (565–578) continued attempts to make peace with the miaphysites to prevent Christendom splitting in two, and although the religious policies of his successors Tiberius II Constantine (578–582) and Maurice (582–602) were initially characterised by a quest for compromise, over time his policy became increasingly uncompromising towards the opponents of Chalcedon so that the overwhelmingly miaphysite population of Syria and North Africa hardened its opposition to the emperor and later welcomed the Muslims as liberators (see Frend, *The Rise of the Monophysite Movement*, 316–25). What stands out particularly is the hostility towards the anti-Chalcedonians in the final years of Maurice's rule (ibid. 329–36). We can therefore assume that the schism was institutionally consolidated across the spectrum in the 580s on this, see Aziz al-Azmeh, *The Emergence of Islam in Late Antiquity. Allah and His People*, Cambridge 2014, 264.

traumatic consequences in the East. It can certainly be assumed that this Christological controversy was also present on the Arabian Peninsula when the Qur'an emerged.

2.2 A political compromise on dogma?

But let us look beyond the political condemnations at the actual theological nub of the controversy. The decisive wording of the Council of Chalcedon says of Jesus Christ:

> [T]hat he is perfect in Godhead and perfect in manhood, very God and very man, of a reasonable soul and [human] body consisting, consubstantial with the Father as touching his Godhead, and consubstantial with us as touching his manhood; made in all things like unto us, sin only excepted (see Hebrews 4:15) ... This one and the same Jesus Christ, the only-begotten Son [of God] must be confessed to be in two natures, unconfusedly, immutably, indivisibly, inseparably [united], and that without the distinction of natures being taken away by such union, but rather the peculiar property of each nature being preserved and being united in *one* Person and *one* subsistence.[18]

In view of the controversy with the later Oriental churches, the especially contentious question was whether the unity in one person of Jesus Christ consists *of* two natures or was forged *from* two natures. If, like the Council of Chalcedon, one speaks of the unity *of* two natures, then the emphasis is on the integrity of the human nature of Jesus, this being implicitly at odds with the Christology of the School of Alexandria that had prevailed at the Council of Ephesus. This explains the use of the adverbs 'unconfusedly' and 'immutably' against possible misunderstanding of this form of Christology. That is because – and this was the argument of the Chalcedonian theologians at this point – if Jesus's divine nature is too closely interwoven with his human nature, then the human nature will be destroyed because the limited cannot exist within the limitless, just as a drop of honey in the sea will no longer taste of honey and can no longer be recognised as such, to cite a classic example quoted in debates on the matter in late antiquity. And if, through its absorption into the Logos, Jesus's human nature remains unchanged or no longer exists as something truly human, then it cannot be our ordinary humanity that is redeemed by Jesus Christ and raised into communion with God.

---

18 *The Seven Ecumenical Councils*, in NPNF, Second Series, vol. 14, 264–5.

That is why Christology of the Alexandrian school runs the risk – this is the fear of non-Oriental churches to this day – of diminishing Jesus's mortality or his human nature. One classic example of a theologian who overstepped orthodox Christology's red line long before Chalcedon is Apollinaris of Laodicea (315–390), who declared that the soul or divine spark (NOUS) was replaced by the divine Logos;[19] thus, in Apollinarianism, the Logos – just as the soul, for other people – was united with the body in a single nature (MIA PHYSIS). A further example of a clearly heretical Monophysite Christology is the position of Eutyches, who also coined the aforementioned phrase that Christ's humanity was absorbed by the divinity of the Word like a drop of honey in the sea.[20] He not only refuses to discuss two natures in Jesus Christ, but also assumes that Jesus is not consubstantial with us humans – a position that strikes at the heart of Christian soteriology. That is because according to a dictum of the early Christian church, which was repeatedly advanced by Gregory of Nazianzus, only that which was shared by God could be saved.[21] Hence if Jesus Christ did not truly share our human nature and did not truly make human nature immutably his own, we cannot be touched and changed by him – this was the conviction of the early Christian church.

It was therefore a scandal in the eyes of the Latin Church that Patriarch Dioscoros of Alexandria convened a synod in Ephesus in 449 at which he not only rehabilitated the Monophysite Eutyches, who had earlier been condemned by Patriarch Flavian of Constantinople, but also prevented the reading of the so-called *Tomus Leonis*, which was later to prove so significant at Chalcedon. This dogmatic text, which adopts a clear stance against an exaggerated Alexandrian Christology and was written in support of Flavian by Pope Leo, was only recognised upon the death of Emperor Theodosius II, who had sided with Dioscorus. The Christological thinking of Pope Leo was an important factor in the Council of Chalcedon's decision-making, stoking the ire of those who interpreted this as a resurgence of 'Nestorianism'.[22]

---

19 Grillmeier, *Christ in Christian Tradition*, vol. 1, 329–37.
20 Following the Council of Ephesus in 431, Eutyches pushed the Alexandrian tendency represented there too far, committing heresy and prompting his excommunication. See Karl-Heinz Menke, *Jesus ist Gott der Sohn. Denkformen und Brennpunkte der Christologie*, Regensburg 2008, 257–8.
21 Literally what he says is: '[...] car ce qui n'a pas été assumé n'a pas été guéri, mais c'est ce qui est uni à Dieu qui est sauvé' or in translation: 'What has not been assumed has not been healed; it is what is united to His divinity that is saved' (Ep 101:32; SC 208:50).
22 Grillmeier, op. cit. 520–36, 526–30. See also De Vries, op. cit. 124–6.

Nestorianism, associated with the aforementioned Patriarch Nestorius, has been rejected as discriminatory by more recent research.[23] Mention of Nestorians generally refers to the East Syriac Church, which placed itself squarely in the tradition of Antiochian Christology and therefore shared Nestorius's basic theological ideas.

Yet it was not just the East Syriacs and the Chalcedonians who refused to stand up for a curtailing of Jesus's human nature, but also most of the Council's miaphysite opponents. One can therefore describe Eutychianism and Apollinarianism as monophysite heresies, and every modern Church rejects them. On the other hand, the term miaphysitism has become common in ecumenical discussion for those churches and theologies that, in line with the School of Alexandria, reject the Council of Chalcedon. They were criticised by the Council for entertaining a one-sided theology, but as we shall see, their theology should not be seen as antithetical to Chalcedon.

That is because the Council of Chalcedon criticised not only Alexandrian Christology – that was the conciliatory nature of the text – the adverbs 'indivisibly' and 'inseparably' were also intended to eliminate the threat of a Christology in the Antiochian tradition. For if the divine and human natures of Jesus Christ are regarded as only functionally united, there is a risk of an ontological split, and one would ultimately have to speak of two Sons of God. There would also be a danger that all the events of the life and death of Jesus would be experienced and suffered by the one Logos – a view that would put intense pressure on Christian soteriology. The concern among most Oriental Orthodox Churches in their fight against the Chalcedonian Definition, therefore, was that the Council's decision had reinforced precisely this entirely external coexistence of the two natures of Christ. They insisted upon the wording of Jesus Christ being *from* both natures (rather than *in* both natures).[24] They detected a risk of being unable to adequately describe Jesus Christ's unity in one person and to be no longer able to explain God's full presence in Jesus the man, if Jesus Christ was avowed to be present in both natures.

---

23 See Johannes Oeldemann, *Die Kirchen des christlichen Ostens. Orthodoxe, orientalische und mit Rom unierte Ostkirchen*, Kevelaer 2008, 27.

24 The wording 'in both natures' is derived from Pope Leo I's text, *Tomus ad Flavianum*, to Patriarch Flavian of Constantinople. This teaching was the essential text for the horos of Chalcedon and was aimed among other things at the heresies of Eutychus. The formulation 'of both natures' was coined in the theology of Patriarch Dioscorus of Alexandria, who adopted a formulation of the Eutychians, although he did distance himself from Eutyches himself. See De Vries, *Die Gründe der Ablehnung des Konzils von Chalzedon durch die altorientalischen Kirchen*, 124–6; Grillmeier, *Christ in Christian Tradition Vol. 1*, 523–6.

The council fathers were naturally aware of this danger. Their formulation expresses the one divine Logos as the subject of both the human and the divine attributes of Jesus Christ so that one subsistence, or hypostasis, is considered to bear two natures.[25] This was intended to rescue the unity of the person of Jesus Christ, yet it did not resolve the issue of how the relationship between Christ's divine and human natures is to be construed and what constitutes the unity of the person of Jesus Christ. The question that even Chalcedon does not address is therefore how one can talk of one subsistence without restricting the integrity of Jesus's human nature (the threat of *monophysitism*) and, on the other hand, how one can talk of two complete natures without endangering the unity of the person of Jesus Christ (the threat of *Nestorianism*). While the Syriac church fathers saw the influence of Nestorianism at the Council of Chalcedon, it was just as clear to the Latin and Greek church fathers that the positions of the Eastern Christians were bound to lead to monophysitism. This unfortunate history of mutual condemnation was only finally brought to an end by the Viennese Christological formula of 1971, and from a present-day perspective, there are no longer any grounds to brand people who believe in different Christological conceptions heretics.[26]

2.3 The Neo-Chalcedonian doctrine of enhypostasis

The early church undertook an intensive search for theological possibilities for reconciliation between the newly established Oriental Christian communities and the imperial church. Building on the intuitions of the School of Alexandria in the centuries after Chalcedon, for example, the neo-Chalcedonian teaching on enhypostasis (represented by Leontios of Byzantium and Leontios of Jerusalem) sought to solve the aforementioned difficulties by regarding divine hypostasis in the pre-existing Logos as the origin of, and reason for, the unity of Christ's two natures.[27] According to this theory, the pre-existing God-Logos is the sole enabling,

---

25 It was for reasons of vocabulary that the Council's Syriac opponents found it impossible to take this particular step. The Syriac words *kyana* (nature) and *qnuma* (hypostasis) are mutually dependent. Thus one can only talk meaningfully of one nature and one hypostasis, or of two natures and two hypostases. See Sebastian Brock, *The Hidden Pearl: The Aramaic Heritage*, vol. 2, Piscataway, NJ 2002, 27.

26 See 'The Dialogues of the Catholic Church with the Separated Eastern Churches' (*Pro Oriente*), Vienna 1977, 9–11.

27 See Menke, ibid. 266–73: Grillmeier, *Christ in Christian Tradition Vol. 2/2 The Church in Constantinople in the Sixth Century*, with Theresia Hainthaler, 181–315. Although the neo-Chalcedonian teaching developed in the first half of the sixth century in opposition to strict Chalcedonianism, it began, towards the end of Justinian's rule, to establish itself as the

ontological cause of the hypostatic union and thus the pillar of the unconfused unity of divine and human natures in Christ. This definition is designed to ensure that the incarnation is exclusively attributed to God's initiative and that discussion of Jesus Christ's human nature does not lead people to suddenly suggest that there are two Sons of God – one divine and one human, bound only loosely to each other.

This does, however, create a risk that too little attention is paid to the integrity of Jesus's humanity, for if it is claimed that human nature cannot be considered without its own hypostasis, the wholeness and integrity of Jesus's true humanity would appear to be endangered. How can a nature without its own hypostasis be simultaneously hypostatic, and thus exist as one person?

The answer of the neo-Chalcedonian enhypostasis theory to these questions consisted of defining hypostasis as restricted to its function of uniting the two natures. Leontios of Jerusalem, at the very latest, pushed the idea of enhypostasis so far that it came to define the henotic function that divine hypostasis exerts on the superior human nature of Jesus. *Enhypostasis* therefore designates the act in which and through which human nature derives its autonomy and *raison d'être* not from itself, but from a different, pre-existing hypostasis of the Logos. Applied to the nature of Jesus, this signifies that its creation and its absorption in the hypostasis are indistinguishable. Human nature originally and entirely exists as a nature that has been assumed by the Logos and enhypostasised by it. At the same time, the metaphysical anthropology based on Leontius's definition guarantees that the notion of nature encompasses the entire constitution of human beings including their physicality, consciousness and freedom. The concept of hypostasis merely denotes the metaphysical act by which an individual nature comes into existence and attains autonomy.

Maximus the Confessor (c. 580–662) therefore acted in keeping with the logic of the neo-Chalcedonian axiom of enhypostasis by insisting that Jesus's human will should be distinguished once more from the will of the divine Logos, as did the Third Council of Constantinople (680/681) when it repudiated the monotheletism that rejected this doctrine. That is because, following Chalcedonian logic, the integrity of Jesus's human nature is only secure if it can be assigned its own will.

The price of sustaining the wholeness and integrity of both natures, however, is the substanceless, abstract emptiness of the concept of hypostasis, which,

---

dominant diphysite doctrine. See John F. Haldon, *Byzantium in the Seventh Century. The Transformation of a Culture*, Cambridge 1990, 289.

according to Karl Rahner, makes it very hard for us to grasp the soteriological meaning of the hypostatic union, and which struggles to explain how the unity of the hypostatic union should be conceived.[28] Any attempt to flesh out the notion of hypostasis runs an immediate risk of endangering the integrity of Jesus's human nature and sliding into monophysitism. The neo-Chalcedonian doctrine of enhypostasis was by no means immune to this precise danger, insofar as this approach suggested a quest for illustrations of the notion of hypostasis.

Theological developments over the centuries after Chalcedon tended to blur the boundaries between major currents of the theology of the imperial church and non-Chalcedonian doctrines. Not only non-Chalcedonian theologies but also neo-Chalcedonian theologies may have been thoroughly convincing and also compatible in their pure, academic form, but in their popularising form both theologies flirted with underplaying Jesus's human nature and sliding into monophysitism. If one wishes to know how common these monophysite tendencies were in the seventh century, then one need only to recall that the Byzantine Emperor Heraclius (575–641; emperor from 610 onwards) attempted 'with the aid of the doctrine of monotheletism [...] to re-incorporate miaphysite Christians into the imperial church.'[29] There is of course a significant difference between *monotheletism* and *monophysitism*. From a Catholic standpoint, with reference to the Viennese Christological formula of 1971, it is admissible that there is a comprehensible possibility in miaphysite theology to speak of *one* will in Jesus Christ without lapsing into monophysitism. That is why heretical monophysitism has been differentiated from miaphysitism, which is a legitimate Christian belief, and one could also distinguish miatheletism from monotheletism by the same reasoning.

However, the logic of the Chalcedonian Definition's two-nature doctrine makes discussion of Jesus Christ's human nature having its own will inevitable. If Jesus Christ did not also possess a human will, it would hardly be possible to say that he was fully a man. It is therefore quite dramatic that both the emperor and the pope had a monotheletist mindset at the time the Qur'an's most

---

28 See, for example, Karl Rahner's article on Jesus Christ, *SM* 2 (1968) 900–57, here 928: 'If one uses the term ὑπόστασις [...] then the carrying and ownership capacity of hypostasis remains relatively formal and abstract or slips easily back into the simple basic statements of Christology in the face of attempts to clarify its meaning, so that all that comes of it is a verbal protection against the tendency to explain away these basic statements [...] A final, additional perspective would be that the unifying point "hypostasis" or "personhood" would describe or explain the soteriological meaning of this unity only with difficulty or at best indirectly.'
29 Oeldemann, ibid. 24.

important Medinan surahs were being written. The pope was condemned at the Third Council of Constantinople for espousing these distorted, heretical Christological views.[30] However, this condemnation had not yet been made by the time the Qur'an emerged, and the emperor had Maximus the Confessor tortured on account of his anti-monotheletist interventions.[31]

Historians view Emperor Heraclius as the last great ruler of late antiquity.[32] He initially lost territory to the Persians, who conquered Jerusalem in 614. From 622 to 628, however, he attacked the previously victorious Persians and gradually drove them back. He portrayed them as 'fire-worshippers' and portrayed himself as a defender of Christianity, among other things by ordering the forcible baptism of Jews, whom the Persians had treated well. It is easy to imagine that the conflicts between Jews and Christians – depicted at precisely this time in the Qur'an – were not confined to this one region. Constantinople was besieged in 626 and only saved in extremis. In 629/630 the two sides agreed a peace settlement favourable to the Eastern Roman Empire, and on 21 March 630 Heraclius returned the cross to Jerusalem. He is therefore not just another emperor but a symbol of contemporary Christianity, and his reputation may well have spread as far afield as the Arabian Peninsula.[33]

It is therefore significant that this same Heraclius saw monotheletism as a way of reunifying the broken religious politics of the empire. He clearly approached the matter according to the logic that however many natures Jesus had, he had only one will. It is precisely this indifference to the exact theological framing of talk of one will that makes his theology heretical. It could be said that it was

---

30 The pope's error was a major subject of discussion regarding papal infallibility, especially in the context of the dispute with the Old Catholics. See Georg Kreuzer, 'Die Honoriusfrage im Mittelalter und in der Neuzeit' (*Päpste und Papsttum*; 8), Stuttgart 1975, 229; Hubert Jedin, *Kleine Konzilsgeschichte*, Freiburg im Breisgau, new edition of the 8th reprint 1978, 122–6; Hubert Wolf, *Krypta. Unterdrückte Traditionen der Kirchengeschichte*, Munich 2015, 77–80.

31 On the Christology of Maximus, see the illuminating study by Raphael Weichlein, *Gottmenschliche Freiheit. Zum Verhältnis von Christologie und Willensfreiheit bei Maximus Confessor*, Saarbrücken 2013.

32 On this and what follows, see Walter E. Kaegi, *Heraclius, Emperor of Byzantium*, Cambridge 2004. Heraclius appears to have been born and raised in Armenia (ibid. 19–29) and his origins may have tinged his Christianity with Julianist beliefs.

33 The emperor never directly encountered the Muslims, but there does appear to have been a first clash with the Muslims as early as 629 to the east of the Dead Sea, and Heraclius's troops emerged victorious (ibid. 233). It is therefore possible that Byzantine theological ideas became a more pressing topic for the Qur'an during the latter stages of its proclamation by the Prophet.

the quest for a formula to reconcile the legitimate intuitions of the two dominant theological schools of the age that made any compromise between the estranged churches problematic. Unlike Chalcedon, which had defined the union in negative terms and excluded extreme positions, the aim this time was to forge church unity. This removed any room for complementary theologies, each plausible in itself, and a unitary theology was supposed to reduce differences between the various denominations of the Church.

Heraclius took the lead in these unification efforts. After his great victory in 630, people generally expected him to succeed in his attempt to unify Christendom, but given the existing hatred in both camps, this enterprise was doomed to fail.[34] This must have given non-Christians the impression that the Church did not take the integrity of Jesus Christ's human nature seriously, and it also rendered talk of the two natures of Jesus Christ unintelligible.

2.4 Christological debates among non-Chalcedonians

The non-Chalcedonian Oriental Orthodox Churches rejected any extreme form of monophysitism. For good reason, all Churches now view the Christological questions that were so controversial at the time as non-schismatic. One should not imagine that the non-Chalcedonian camp was a single monolithic bloc, but accept that there were also heterogeneous theological positions and accompanying discord within the movement itself.[35] So when the Qur'an repeatedly criticises discord among Christians, it is referring both to the dispute between supporters and opponents of the Council of Chalcedon and to arguments within the non-Chalcedonian camp.

For one thing, anti-Chalcedonians' Christology was characterised by opposition to the East Syriac Church and their Antiochian doctrine. Mary's title as the God-bearer and the Mother of God was so deeply embedded in the West Syriac and Egyptian Churches that they viewed East Syriac theology as an affront to the very foundations of their faith. Miaphysites' polemic resistance to this theology contains repeated formulations that run the risk of obscuring Jesus's human nature.[36]

This situation posed a particular threat to a variant of anti-Chalcedonian Christology that had a powerful influence in the emerging miaphysite churches in

---

34 See Frend, *The Rise of the Monophysite Movement*, 345–6.
35 Grillmeier, *Christ in Christian Tradition*, Vol. 2/3, 386.
36 Ibid. 655.

the sixth century and was a source of much controversy within the West Syriac Church of the time. It is referred to in scholarly literature as *Julianism* after the contemporary miaphysite bishop Julian of Halicarnassus. Surviving documents testify to his clashes with one of the principal representatives of West Syriac theology, Severus of Antioch. Their arguments revolved around the question of whether the body of Christ was perishable or corruptible (*phtartón*) before the Resurrection.[37] Julian defended the idea of the *incorruptibility* (*aphtarsia*) of the body of Christ in his very first letter to Severus. Since he was born free of sin, his body must also be free of any of the consequences of sin, and therefore free of the punishment of mortality.[38] His opponents had the impression from this that Julian was contesting Jesus's suffering on the cross, and so his position was vilified as *aphthartodocetism*.[39] The Julianists came under repeated attack from other miaphysites because their teaching of the incorruptibility of Jesus's body distracted people from the reality of his Crucifixion.[40]

But Julian did not wish to deny the reality of Jesus's suffering. It was absolutely clear to him that Jesus really had suffered and died on the cross. His only contention was that this suffering was freely chosen and in no way naturally predestined.[41] Julian's theology was ultimately grounded in the fact that any form of corruptibility of the body stemmed from sin. Man before the Fall experienced neither death nor suffering, neither hunger nor thirst. If Jesus was exposed to all of these phenomena all the same, it was not by nature but of his own free will. Julian does not see this as endangering the integrity of Jesus's human nature, since corruptibility is, in his view, as little part of human nature as sin is, so Jesus could be without either and still be a man.[42]

By contrast, Severus sees Christ as being free only of the spiritual effects of sin, while the mortality and corruptibility of his body remain. If Julian considers the

---

37 René Draguet, *Julien d'Harnicasse et sa controverse avec Sévère d'Antioche sur l'incorruptibilité du corps du Christ. Etude d'histoire littéraire et doctrinale suivie des fragments dogmatiques de Julien* (Texte syriaque et traduction grecque), Louvain 1924, 95.
38 Ibid. 96, 102.
39 See Aryeh Kofsky, 'The Miaphysite Monasticism of Gaza and Julian of Halicarnassus', in *Orientalia christiana periodica* 78 (2012) 81–96.
40 See Sidney Griffith, '*Al Naṣārā* in the Qur'ān. A hermeneutical reflection', in Gabriel Said Reynolds (ed.), *New Perspectives on the Qur'an. The Qur'an in Its Historical Context* 2, London 2011, 301–22, here 319. Hence researchers have repeatedly tried to understand Q 4:157 as if it showed the reception of aphthartodocetic views. We shall see later why this impression is erroneous.
41 René Draguet, *Julien d'Harnicasse*, 104.
42 Ibid. 119.

body of Jesus to be naturally incapable of suffering and dying, then for Severus this calls into question the passion, death and resurrection of Jesus Christ.[43] He employs the word *aphtasia* exclusively for the body of the resurrected Christ, and therefore the use of this term to describe the body of Christ prior to resurrection is, in his theological conception, exclusively associated with Valentinianism and Eutychianism, a charge he repeatedly levels at Julian.[44] First, Severus contends, hunger, thirst and tiredness have nothing to do with sin,[45] and hence he cannot understand why Julian will not concede that this is also true of the nature of Jesus (and for man before the Fall).[46]

Yet Julian is not denying that Jesus was tired or hungry and suffered repeatedly. In this sense, he is no docetist, and it is unfair to categorise him in the tradition of Valentinianist Gnosticism. Julian is in no way a Eutychist, because he sees Jesus as having all his bodily functions intact; Jesus sustains his body by eating and drinking, just as we do.[47] His incorruptible body assumes a truly human nature.[48] Thus, as has been mentioned before, Julian does not deny the reality of Jesus's suffering, merely insisting that even in his suffering, Christ decided of his own free will to suffer, i.e. his nature remains immune to suffering and he has to make a voluntary, sacrosanct act of will to be able to suffer.[49] Julian therefore insists on the complete freedom and sovereignty of Jesus, even during the passion. He agrees categorically that Jesus actually dies, but he emphasises the fact that death has no power over him, i.e. Jesus chooses death even though he could live.[50] Accordingly, Jesus is also famished after fasting for forty days, but only because Jesus wills it to be so, not because his human needs force him to be so.[51] Hence if Jesus suffers, dies, is hungry or thirsty or goes to the toilet and has to do these things, it is only because he chooses to.[52] For Julian, Jesus is only truly God if his human nature is without sin, concupiscence and corruption, because they cannot possibly have these three contingencies by virtue of their divinity.[53] His body is

---

43 Ibid. 97.
44 Ibid. 164.
45 René Draguet, *Julien d'Harnicasse*, 108.
46 Ibid. 112.
47 Ibid. 160.
48 Ibid. 161.
49 Ibid. 187.
50 Ibid. 190.
51 Ibid. 207–8.
52 Ibid. 111.
53 Ibid. 151.

God's body – an assertion that, ironically enough, even his miaphysite opponents would subscribe to.[54]

The essential difference between the two parties, therefore, is merely that Julian insists that fallen humankind are sinners prior to any decision of their own, while God in His holiness cannot share their fallen nature.[55] If one were to claim that there was any aspect of Christ that could truly share this suffering, then he would no longer be God, and Nestorianism would be at the door.[56] That is why Julian emphasises that Jesus was from the very beginning immune from sin and its consequences – because he was born of the Virgin Mary.[57]

Julian is thus the victim of an injustice when he is perceived as early as the sixth and seventh centuries, in the wake of Severus's allegations, as an arch-heretic by Syriac theologians.[58] Despite Severus's malicious claims, it is not true either that Julian sees the body of Christ as being identical before and after the resurrection.[59] It is therefore no wonder that Julian remained influential even after his death – for instance, for Philoxenos of Mabbug[60] – and that the controversy surrounding him continued for decades.

In 520, this controversy, which had first surfaced in Constantinople, was revived in Egypt.[61] Patriarch Gaianus of Alexandria defended Julianism from 535 onwards.[62] Julianism was so widespread in Constantinople that Leontios of Byzantium himself attacked it in writing, although he did adopt its core thesis of the imperishability of Jesus's body.[63] In an edict to the Romans published in late 564 or early 565, Emperor Justinian himself embraced the position that the body of Jesus Christ was immortal. The Syrian-born church historian of late antiquity, Evagrius Scholasticus (died circa 600) therefore writes of the emperor's espousal of the Julian heresy shortly before his death, stating how the emperor had maintained 'that the Kyrios ate before his Passion as he did after his resurrection'.[64] Modern scholars are divided as to whether the emperor really did engage in such

---

54 Ibid. 152.
55 René Draguet, op. cit. 152.
56 Ibid. 153.
57 Ibid. 154–6.
58 Ibid. 171.
59 Ibid. 214.
60 Ibid. 232–50.
61 Ibid. 257.
62 Ibid. 259.
63 Uthemann, op. cit. 80.
64 Cited in Uthemann, 79; see also the corresponding reception in Grillmeier, *Christ in Christian Tradition Vol. 2/2*, 480.

aphthartic activity, and yet there is broad evidence that Justinian's last act in the area of religious policy might be mistaken for docetic heresy and that it was also interpreted as such at the time.[65]

Nonetheless, it is more historically plausible that the emperor did not adopt Julianism but rather – in similar fashion to Leontios – one of its core ideas, probably in order to encourage appeasement in the area of religious politics. He had only recently negotiated with the Nestorians in an attempt to find some areas of compromise with them.[66] Maybe Justinian was now planning to approach the Armenians, who also espoused Julianism.[67] The incorruptibility of Christ's body was in any case an idea defended by other supporters of the Chalcedon Definition, as proven, for example, by the aforementioned text by Leontios of Byzantium. This position was attractive for religio-political reception because its doctrine offered a way of circumventing the anti-Chalcedonians' emphasis on the aporiae of the two-nature doctrine: the full divinity *and* the full humanity of Jesus Christ would appear to be preserved if Adam's humanity *prior* to the Fall was regarded as true humanity.[68] The Julianist position could thus be seen as a politically attractive mediation gambit, and it is conceivable that the theologically engaged emperor might have resorted to it. However, it might simply have been an absolutely unbearable thought for an ascetically inclined emperor that the terrestrial Jesus must have eaten and gone to the toilet as he did. His earthly body looks like the pneumatological body of the resurrected Christ, who the Gospels say can walk through walls and is therefore unconstrained by the same earthly barriers as those that restrict our own bodies.

Whatever one's judgement of Justinian's personal motives, his campaigning on behalf of the incorruptibility of the body of Jesus shows just how common Julianist views were in the second half of the sixth century. Julian's ideas also enjoyed substantial support in Syrian and Iraqi monasteries;[69] it even seems that Julianist ideas cropped up again and again in Syrian monasteries at the time of the Qur'an.[70] According to Michael the Syrian, many other countries including

---

65 See the letter from Bishop Nicetius of Trier in which he accuses the emperor of heresy in the summer of 565, 'becoming at the end of his life a supporter of Nestorius and Eutyches, both of whom would have denied the human nature of Christ' (Ibid. 494).

66 Uthemann, op. cit., 77–8.

67 See Michael van Esbroeck, 'The Aphthartodocetic Edict of Justinian and Its Armenian Background', in *Studia Patristica* 33 (1997) 578–85.

68 See Kate Adshead, 'Justinian and Aphthartodocetism', in Stephen Mitchell / Geoffrey B. Greatrex (eds.), *Ethnicity and Culture in Late Antiquity*, London 2000, 331–6, here 333.

69 Draguet, op. cit. 259.

70 We are grateful to Sidney Griffith for this insight.

Ethiopia, Armenia and Arabia were greatly influenced by Julianism.[71] There were supposedly even Julianists in Najran, with whom Muhammad had dealings.[72] The Julianist influence can be explained by the fact that Julian himself had found asylum in Ethiopia in 518,[73] and major missionary efforts were undertaken in the west of the Arabian Peninsula.

We do not know how widespread Julianism was on the Arabian Peninsula in the seventh century. However, we do know that its expansion gradually petered out over the course of the seventh and eighth centuries, and it is plausible that Julianism, and above all the controversy surrounding it, was prominent during the proclamation of the Qur'an. How and to what degree it influenced or even shaped the Qur'an's attitude to Christianity can only be revealed by a close reading of the Qur'an, and even that is unlikely to yield any unqualified certainties.

Several types of influence are conceivable, however. First, it could be that the attacks by the West Syriac church leaders on the Julianists gave the impression that Julianist views, distorted in the polemical retelling, really did accurately represent the positions of major Christian factions. Julianism was obviously widely accused of adopting the heresies of Valentinianist Gnosticism and presenting the peculiar view 'that there was no true digestion and excretion of food by Christ'.[74] This must have conveyed the impression that Jesus had not eaten properly, and this could then be used to question Christian views by referring to the fact that Jesus had indeed taken food.

Given the Mariological theologoumena behind the Julianist argument, one might also consider that Julian's ideas referred not only to Jesus but to Mary too. For as we have seen above, Julian explained Jesus's lack of original sin and the resulting corruptibility of his body in particular by his being born of the Virgin Mary. If, however, Mary's virginity is the principal reason for guaranteeing Christ's freedom from sin and corruptibility, it requires no great leap of the imagination to come to the conclusion that has been drawn many times throughout theological history and eventually led to the dogma of *Mary's immaculate conception* in 1854. Mary herself must have been conceived without original sin (and

71 Draguet, op. cit. 260.

72 See Hainthaler who reports on the 7th-century author Anastasius Sinaita, who clearly connects Julianism with Najran (see Hainthaler, *Christliche Araber vor dem Islam*, 133–4) See also, for a critical appraisal of the presence of Julianism in Najran, René Tardy, *Najrân. Chrétiens d'Arabie avant l'islam*, Beirut 1999, 177, 184.

73 See Al-Azmeh, *The Emergence of Islam in Late Antiquity*, 275.

74 Alois Grillmeier, *Christ in Christian Tradition Vol. I*, 133–4; see also the reference to Clement of Alexandria, *Stromata* III.7.59.3.

therefore, for Julian, without the resulting corruptibility of the body) if Jesus is truly to be present in God. Not just Jesus but also Mary would therefore be – to polemical opponents of Julianism – eating and drinking only *in appearance*, and the idea that Jesus and Mary ate normally became a plausible anti-Christian argument. We will discuss whether the relevant formulation in Q 5:75 is to be understood in this anti-Julianist interpretation in our exegesis of that surah.

Yet even if it was the polemical opposition to Julianism that first came up with the idea that Jesus and Mary did not eat normally, there is one highly problematic aspect of Julian's position which, without justifying the slanderous polemics directed at him, nevertheless provides ground for people to distance themselves from him. As we have explained in more detail above, Julian assumes that it is impossible for God to participate in Jesus's human nature after the Fall because God is immune to suffering and death. The backdrop here is Julian's image of God, which owes a great deal to Neoplatonism and does not admit that God is subject to change. In this philosophy, which exerted great influence within Islam and Christianity alike, God is always sovereign and powerful, can undergo no change He does not bring upon Himself, and can therefore never suffer if He does not will that suffering upon Himself.

Yet humankind's greatest problem is that we are again and again subjected to suffering and dying not of our own choosing. It is exactly from this unwanted hunger and thirst that we need to be saved. It is our confrontation with unwanted suffering from which we cannot escape that risks destroying our integrity; premature death alone leads us to despair. Hence it would be fatal to this explicit dictum of the Early Church that what is saved or healed in Christ is only that which he himself has also accepted, if Jesus did not experience the phenomenon of pain he had not freely chosen. He was not hungry after fasting in the desert simply because he kindly agreed to be hungry, but because it is a fact of human nature – even before the Fall (!) – that humans have to eat.

If God in Jesus Christ partakes of this nature, then this means, from a Christian point of view, that God is with us in our suffering and dying and therefore at every other time when we feel that we cannot go on and are faced with things not of our choosing. This is how God shows Himself to be a compassionate God who stands with humanity and allows Himself to be affected by their misery. We shall see later that the Qur'an can be read in the same way, that it preaches about precisely this kind of empathetic God and not the Neoplatonic ideal of God which Islamic and Christian scholastic theology unanimously wish – and wished – to see in Him (see Chapter 6).

Reviewing Julianism's fundamental departure from the basics of Christian soteriology and its challenge to the Bible and the Qur'an's shared conception of

God, it becomes easy to see why it might be important for the Qur'an to counter Julianism and adopt its opponents' arguments, however pointed their rhetoric. Furthermore, it seems possible to us to interpret statements such as the one in Q 5:75 as dissociating the Qur'an from Julianist-influenced Christianity. When one considers that the Arabic text mentions that Jesus and Mary 'ate food like other mortals', it becomes particularly clear that this distancing from Julianism might be not polemical, but extremely specific. Jesus – this would be the intention of this intervention by the Qur'an – did not need to kindly decide to eat as a sign of his solidarity with us; he had to eat because he was a man. We shall explore further in Chapter 4 whether this kind of theological assessment is reconcilable with the Qur'an's interventions on Christology.

2.5 The Arabian Peninsula as a confluence of heresies?

We are of the opinion that a study of Julianism, as a variant of Christianity, might help us to gain a better understanding of certain instances where the Qur'an dissociates itself from Christianity. We ought, however, to be wary of viewing the Qur'an's interventions as comments on heretical phenomena on the margins of Christianity. In fact, Julianism is not a marginal phenomenon but a doctrine that takes us into the heart of the Christology of its time and even influenced the official positions of the emperor and his most influential politicians. Unfortunately, though, there is a deplorable tradition in Western readings of the Qur'an that attempts to discredit Islam's holy scripture by portraying it as being over-interested in Christian splinter groups. What might emerge from the background here is a noble interest in reconciliation between Islam and Christianity by noting that the target of the Qur'an's statement is not Christianity itself but the heretical marginal phenomena alone.

From a Muslim perspective, however, this peace offer should be greeted with the greatest caution, because the proclaimer of the Qur'an himself explicitly stated that he was referring to Christians, and the whole Muslim theological tradition assumed that the Qur'an was critically pitted against Christianity. It would therefore be somewhat embarrassing for Muslims, to put it mildly, if they were forced to concede that the Muslim tradition in its entirety was wrong and that the proclaimer of the Qur'an had simply confused specific heresies on the Arabian Peninsula with Christianity.

Of course, this suggestion is by no means a religio-political argument, and in the following section we intend to discuss in depth the arguments by which we aim to prove that the Qur'an dissociates itself only from heretical splinter groups. After all, it is now standard for Western scholars to regard Arabia as a confluence of Christian heresies,[75] such that it is easy to reach for a particular Christian faction whenever a Qur'anic formulation requires explanation. The diagnosis that there was no generally accepted Christology anywhere in Arabia 'but various regional-national churchdoms and sects advocating sometimes very different forms of Christology and at permanent odds with each other, Christologically speaking'[76] is therefore no marginal academic position but indeed a fairly common one, even among scholars who think that by making this case they are doing Islam a favour. In the following section, we would like to study in detail the heretical Christian groupings whose presence on the Arabian Peninsula in the seventh century occurs most frequently in the literature: the Jewish Christians, the Mariamites and the Tritheists.

Let us start with perhaps the most influential idea mentioned in the literature – the claim that there were Jewish Christians on the Arabian Peninsula in the seventh century. The main driver behind such references was probably research conducted by Hans-Joachim Schoeps, who advanced a theory in the mid-twentieth century that Islam had adopted numerous elements of Jewish Christianity and was itself proof of their continued existence.[77] He primarily discusses subjects related to rites and religious laws, but he also sees major parallels in prophetology. Overall, he comes to the conclusion that 'the indirect dependence of Muhammad on sectarian Jewish Christians [is] beyond all doubt. [...] The Ebionite combination of Moses and Jesus culminates in Muhammad'.[78] Further to this, more recent research has repeatedly explored the thesis that elements of Jewish Christianity or Ebionite theology might have fed into the development of Islam.[79]

---

75 See Hainthaler, *Christliche Araber vor dem Islam*, 56.

76 Martin Bauschke, 'Jesus – Stein des Anstoßes. Die Christologie des Korans und die deutschsprachige Theologie' (*Kölner Veröffentlichungen zur Religionsgeschichte*; 29), Cologne 2000, 104.

77 See Hans-Joachim Schoeps, *Theologie und Geschichte des Judenchristentums*, Tübingen 1949, 334–42. Adolf von Harnack had already developed a theory on the influence of Jewish Christianity on Islam in his dogmatic history published in 1893 (see Adolf von Harnack, 'Dogmengeschichte' (*Grundriss der Theologischen Wissenschaften*; 4/3), Freiburg im Breisgau 1893, 48). More recently, Kurt Bangert has studied the possible influence of Jewish Christianity on Islam. See Kurt Bangert, 'Zeitgenössische Zeugnisse. Haben Koran und Islam judenchristliche Wurzeln?', in Bangert, *Muhammad. Eine historisch-kritische Studie zur Entstehung des Islams und seines Propheten*, Wiesbaden 2016, 587–652. Bangert refers primarily to Schoeps's studies, but also considers the work of Holger Zellentin, which we will examine more closely in the following section.

78 Schoeps, op. cit. 342.

79 See Jürgen Wehnert, 'Ebioniten', in *LThK* 3 (1995) 430–1, here 431; Georg Strecker,

But is the existence of parallels between Jewish Christian or Ebionite ideas and Muslim conceptions sufficient grounds for talk of a continuation of Jewish Christianity in Islam, or at least to be able to claim that there was a common history of traditions? This strikes us as a step too far. If one studies the evidence in the sources, then one can only conclude that all direct traces of Jewish Christianity vanish as early as the fifth century, so that any notion of its having any influence beyond this date must be deemed pure speculation.[80] When some more recent studies now claim that only part of Jewish Christians – the Nazarene Christians, to be precise – disappeared or were absorbed by the mainstream church in the fourth or fifth century, while a Jewish Christianity more closely bound to the synagogue – the Ebionites and Elcesaites – may have endured until the eighth century and may have influenced Islam, that too is sheer speculation. That is because we have no direct sources whatsoever to prove any such continued existence. If one takes the hallmarks of Jewish Christianity as evidence of its continued existence in Islam, then one must be able to point out not only the obvious similarities but also the great differences between the two – for instance, the practice of vegetarianism or rejection of Mary's virginity, which are to be found in Ebionite writings but not in the Qur'an.[81]

Holger Zellentin recently argued that by comparing the Qur'an with older Jewish Christian texts such as the *Epistles of Clement* and the *Didascalia Apostolorum*, one could recreate Jewish Christian legal culture, which is of particular significance for the longer surahs of the Qur'an.[82] Zellentin assumes not separate Jewish Christian communities but a special Jewish Christian impact on Syriac Christianity and Rabbinical Judaism.[83] He is able to pin this shared legal culture to common dietary guidelines, which are very similar in the Didascalia and the

---

'Judenchristentum', in TRE 17 (1988) 310–25, here 323; Francine E. Samuelson, 'Messianic Judaism: Church, Denomination, Sect or Cult?', in *Journal of Ecumenical Studies* 37 (2000) 161–86, here 162; Simon Claude Mimouni, *Le judéo-christianisme ancien. Essais historiques*, Paris 1998, 22.

80 See for example Ernst Dassmann, *Kirchengeschichte I. Ausbreitung, Leben und Lehre der Kirche in den ersten drei Jahrhunderten*, Stuttgart 1991, 63.

81 We know many of the hallmarks of the Ebionites only from polemical portrayals by the church fathers, which gives them only limited value as sources. It is, however, fairly unlikely that these portrayals are invented, and one should at least be able to explain why these kinds of polemic arose.

82 See Holger Michael Zellentin, *The Qur'an's Legal Culture. The Didascalia Apostolorum as a Point of Departure*, Tübingen 2013, X.

83 Ibid. 50.

Qur'an,[84] and to shared ritual rules.[85] He comes to the conclusion that there was a common legal culture between the fourth and the seventh centuries, which he characterises thus: 'Ritual washing after intercourse and before prayer, the prohibition of intercourse during the menses, the strict and expanded prohibition of carrion, and the avoidance of pork.'[86]

Yet even he cannot demonstrate that the (Greek!) sources he used influenced thinking on the Arabian Peninsula, especially as the legal guidelines he presents were by no means exclusive to Jewish Christians but were also, for instance, practised by the Jews themselves. Neither does the presence of Jewish Christian theologoumena necessarily require the wide-ranging theory of the continued existence of Jewish Christian groupings; it can also be explained by the fact that Ethiopian Christianity – which was very much present in Arabia – was highly influenced by Jewish Christian conceptions.[87] The Abyssinians seem to have been particularly theologically partial to the idea that the elected status of Israel had been passed on to them and that they were now God's chosen people.[88] They lay particular stress on Jesus's Messianic status in a way that suggests that for them the role of the title of Messiah is similar to that of the Logos in the Eastern Roman Empire.[89] Their theology and piety were defined in such a way that 'in specific cases, Mariology becomes so predominant that even a Eucharistic anaphora is expressed in Marian terms!'[90] Its existence is therefore quite sufficient evidence for Jewish Christianity's oft-cited role of midwife for certain Qur'anic ideas. It is therefore wildly speculative to conclude from recent studies that the Qur'an bears the mark of Jewish Christian beliefs.[91]

---

84 Ibid. 170.
85 Ibid. 178.
86 Ibid. 200.
87 See Hainthaler, *Christliche Araber vor dem Islam*, 139; Hainthaler, *La foi au Christ dans l'Église éthiopienne. Une synthèse des elements judéo-chrétiens et helléno-chrétiens. In: Revue des sciences religieuses* 71 (1997) 329–37, here 330–1. On the discussion about Jewish Christian influences on Islam, see details in Angelika Neuwirth, 'Imagining Mary – Disputing Jesus. Reading surat Maryam and related Meccan texts within the Qur'anic communication process', in Benjamin Jokisch / Ulrich Rebstock / Lawrence Conrad (eds.), *Fremde, Feinde und Kurioses. Innen und Außenansichten unseres muslimischen Nachbarn*, Berlin 2009, 383–416, here 412, which does not think much of the claim of a Jewish Christian influence on the Qur'an.
88 Grillmeier, *Christ in Christian Tradition. Vol. 2/4: The Church of Alexandria, with Nubia and Ethiopia After 451 AD*, with Theresia Hainthaler, New York 2001, 337.
89 Ibid. 336.
90 Ibid. 389.
91 Pace Zellentin, *The Qur'anic Legal Culture*, 197: 'Muhammad kept alive part of the

Scarcely less bold is the assertion that Mariamites existed at the time the Qur'an emerged. These were groups who saw Mary as one of the Trinity in lieu of the Holy Spirit. This gave rise to the notion of a divine family in heaven made up of a father, a mother and a child – a conception that can no longer really be considered monotheistic. Julius Wellhausen referenced these *Mariamites* or *Collyridians* over a century ago and linked them to Islam. He treats it as a foregone conclusion 'that the Collyridians made the goddess al-'Uzza, whom they had worshipped when they were pagan Arabs, into the goddess Mary after their conversion to Christianity, and transferred a rite from 'Uzza worship to Mary worship by offering KOLLURIDES (cake) to Mary'.[92] 'Uzza was regarded as Venus, whom Hebrew women worshipped as the queen of heaven. Most of the extant information about her, however, comes from her opponent, Epiphanius of Salamis, from the fourth century. Isaac of Antioch, to whom Wellhausen refers, died in 460, and it is therefore fairly daring, historically speaking, to conclude from these sources that there were Mariamites 200 years later roughly 1,000 miles away.

In more recent literature, scholars use for their arguments evidence no more convincing than Wellhausen's sources. Martin Bauschke, for example, argues in the following manner for the existence of Mariamite ideas on the Arabian Peninsula: 'This female – or better, maternal – pneumatology was already known to the Jewish Christians in Egypt, as documented in the *Gospel of the Hebrews*. Fragment 3 specifically names the Pneuma Hagión as the mother of Jesus.'[93] Another branch of Montanism regarded as Mariamite also thought that Mary, like Jesus, was divine.[94] This brings Bauschke to the following conclusion: 'From a point of view of religious history, there can be no doubt that Mary took the place of the cult of the mother goddesses in the Orient.'[95]

Whatever one's assessment of these religio-historical theories,[96] it is very

---

Jesus movement that Christianity did not.' This is as unconvincing as the similarly couched claim that the Nazarenes mentioned in the Qur'an (*al-Nasara*; Q 22:17) are identifiable as Jewish Christians; see the corresponding diagnosis, ibid. 189, but also earlier in François de Blois, 'Naṣrānī (Ναζωραῖος) and ḥanīf (ἐθνικός): Studies on the Religious Vocabulary of Christianity and of Islam', in *Bulletin of the School of Oriental and African Studies* 65 (2002) 1–30, here 27. For more detailed criticism, see Griffith, *Al-Naṣārā in the Qur'ān*, 312–9.

92 Julius Wellhausen, *Reste arabischen Heidentums*, Berlin 1897, 41.

93 Bauschke, *Stein des Anstosses*, 156–7: 'The Jewish-Christian Elcesaite sect believed in a female-maternal pneumatology.'

94 Ibid. 155.

95 Ibid. 155.

96 For criticism of them, see Karl-Heinz Menke, *Fleisch geworden aus Maria. Die Geschichte Israels und der Marienglaube der Kirche*, Regensburg 1999, 90–4.

difficult to prove the existence of Mariamites on the Arabian Peninsula. At the very least, the sources show no evidence of Jewish Christians or Montanists in the sixth or seventh century. The most important clue for the acceptance of Mariamite presence is often the letter to Jacob Baradaeus in 569/570, which on closer inspection turns out to provide no indication of the existence of Mariamites in the sixth or seventh century.[97] A far simpler explanation for the exaggerated veneration of Mary on the Arabian Peninsula than the presumption of an otherwise unknown heretical group, is, once again, the considerable Marian worship within the Ethiopian Church, which has long been known in Oriental studies as the Church within which 'Mary – as the heiress of Isis – enjoyed veneration unlike any afforded to her anywhere else in Christianity'.[98] The seemingly heretical Mariological variants are therefore less an indicator of a wide range of heresies and more the sign of dubious developments within the main churches themselves.

The oft-lamented distortions of the doctrine of the Trinity were by no means a marginal phenomenon at this time. Among the anti-Chalcedonians was a group known as the *Tritheists* who became particularly influential around the middle of the sixth century, 'whose ideas were given a philosophical foundation by John Philoponus'.[99] These Tritheist ideas appear to have been common among the anti-Chalcedonians in Syria at the time of the emergence of the Qur'an. Tritheism claimed, in contrast to today's church doctrine, that there were three Trinitarian hypostases, each of which had its own ousia, physis and divinity; 'another monk called Polycarp disseminated this "polytheism" in the territories of Asia and Caria. Even the imperial family was susceptible to such speculation, since Athaniasius, grandson of the empress Theodora, became an enthusiastic adherent of John.'[100] However, one should not confuse these Tritheist conceptions with Polytheism.

---

97 See al-Azmeh, *The Emergence of Islam in Late Antiquity*, 276, with reference to Greg Fisher, *Between Empires. Arabs, Romans and Sasanians in Late Antiquity*, Oxford 2011, 59: 'The existence of the tritheistic Kollyridian or Maryanist ideas, concerning belief in the theistic triad of God, Christ and Mary [...] is attested in a letter of 569–570 from a number of monasteries, presumably in the Syrian desert and northern Arabia, to Jacob Baradeus.' However, in this passage Fisher does not mention Mariamites but refers only to the known tritheistic groups we will discuss next.
98 Tor Andrae, *Der Ursprung des Islams und das Christentum*, Uppsala 1926, 205. We must of course be extremely careful with such characterisation because there are next to no genuinely reliable, surviving documents about the theology of the Ethiopian Christians at the time of the emergence of the Qur'an.
99 Hainthaler, *Christliche Araber vor dem Islam*, 32.
100 Grillmeier, *Christ in Christian Tradition Vol 2/3: The Churches of Jerusalem and Antioch*, from 451 to 600, 184–6, to the aforementioned Philoponus, 'Father, Son and Holy Spirit are three hypostases in the form of three concrete individual natures' (Ibid. 279).

In essence, this was nothing but a logical continuance of miaphysite Christology. If Jesus Christ is only one nature and one person, then the Trinity cannot be conceived of in any other terms than as three natures. Even Philoponus had no intention of challenging monotheism. It is thus extremely problematic to discredit these theological approaches by tracing them back to the influence of Ancient Egyptian triads of gods.[101]

However, there is no need to bring up these kinds of unknown heresies to understand the Qur'an's criticism of Christianity. A better path to understanding the Qur'an's invectives is by accepting only the generally acknowledged main currents of Christianity that existed at the time; we therefore assume that the proclaimer of the Qur'an engages with Byzantine, East Syriac and miaphysite Christians. In view of the sources, it is likely that the Julianists played a prominent role among the miaphysite Christians. Also, one will be able to take account of not only West Syriac but also the Ethiopian influences, yet it is unnecessary to take account of any other Christian groups. The proclaimer of the Qur'an pits his wits against the Christianity of his day, not marginal or peculiar heretical groups. If the positions of Christians referred to in the Qur'an seem dubious to us, it is because Christianity itself was quite ambiguous, at least in its seventh-century guise.

2.6 On the situation in the Arabian Peninsula in the seventh century

The Arabian Peninsula has been surrounded by Christians on all sides for centuries,[102] and we can assume that there was a clear and longstanding Christian presence in the country's main trading centres at the time of the emergence of the Qur'an. Christian ideas and controversies within Christianity must also have been noticeable in Mecca and Medina.

The main missionary impact on Mecca and Medina probably came from miaphysite-influenced Christians from South Arabia. We researchers have long known of Christian settlements in South Arabia.[103] As far as the sixth century is concerned, there is evidence of Christian influences via the king of Himyar. The kings of this South Arabian kingdom had shown favour to Judaism since 320, as

---

101 Against Bauschke, op. cit. 154, which explains the alleged tritheist bias of Oriental Christian piety by the continuing influence of ancient Egyptian conceptions of triads of gods.
102 See Griffith, op. cit., 301–22; al-Azmeh, *The Emergence of Islam in Late Antiquity*, 263.
103 See Horst Bürkle, 'Jesus und Maria im Koran', in Günter Risse / Heino Sonnemans / Burkhard Thess (eds.), *Wege der Theologie an der Schwelle zum dritten Jahrtausend, FS Hans Waldenfels*, Paderborn 1996, 575–86.

recent finds of inscriptions have proved. There were no further pagan inscriptions after 380,[104] and until 530 the only inscriptions were made by Jews and by the new faith of the devout promoted by the monarchy[105] – a form of monotheism inspired by Judaism, known in the Islamic tradition as that of the *hanife*. The kingdom of Himyar is of great importance to us because it conquered large areas of central and western Arabia, including Mecca and Medina, between 420 and 445.[106] It probably controlled the whole Arabian Peninsula around 500.[107] Over time, the king of Himyar appears to have converted to Judaism too.

Yet soon afterwards – probably during the rule of Maʿdikarib Yaʾfur (519–522) – Himyar was taken over by the Ethiopian Christian kingdom of Aksum.[108] One potential explanation is the geopolitical interests of the Eastern Roman Empire, which regarded this Jewish kingdom as part of the sphere of influence of the Jewish-friendly Persians and thus a hostile power. The empire therefore seems to have incited the Ethiopian Negus to act in order to counter Jewish – and thus Persian – influence.[109] Yet the very next king of Himyar, Joseph, led an attempted insurgency and brought South Arabia back under Himyar's control. The Christians of Najran did put up considerable resistance, though, and a massacre of Christians probably took place in the city in the year 523.[110]

Naturally this massacre provoked Ethiopian reprisals, and in 525 Joseph was killed and the area returned to Ethiopian control.[111] The Ethiopians immediately began to Christianise the population and to persecute the Jews.[112] But the Christian prince the Ethiopians had installed on the throne quickly lost control of the Arabian heartland because Abraha, the commander of his army in Arabia, turned against him and made himself king of Himyar, probably from 535 to 565.[113]

---

104 See Christian Julien Robin, 'Ḥimyar, Aksūm, and *Arabia Deserta* in Late Antiquity. The Epigraphic Evidence', in Greg Fisher (ed.), *Arabs and Empires Before Islam*, Oxford 2015, 127–71, here 129. Of course, one is not entitled to conclude – as Robin himself stresses – from this disappearance of polytheistic references in grave inscriptions that there were no longer any polytheists in South Arabia. However, their disappearance from the public sphere indicates that they had lost a great deal of their influence.
105 Ibid. 129–30.
106 Ibid. 138.
107 Ibid. 145–6.
108 Ibid. 146.
109 See Jonathan Berkey, *The Formation of Islam. Religion and Society in the Near East, 600–1800*, Cambridge 2003, 47.
110 See Robin, 'Ḥimyar', 148; al-Amzeh, *The Emergence of Islam in Late Antiquity*, 265.
111 Robin, 'Ḥimyar', 149.
112 Ibid.
113 Ibid. 150.

In an inscription carved shortly after 552, Abraha rejoices that Himyarite authority has been re-established over the whole of *Arabia deserta* including Medina.
Christianity was the official religion under his rule, as is proved by several of his
inscriptions.[114] He soon rejected Ethiopian Christianity and turned increasingly to
the Syriac rite for inspiration. Robin suspects that Abraha was a Julianist – in any
case, he assumes that Himyar became a refuge for several Julianist bishops during
his reign.[115] If this statement is correct, we would have proof that in the region of
Medina at least, there were Julianist missionary ventures, with the king's protection, until shortly before the birth of Muhammad.

Mecca too must have been affected by these efforts, even if the king clearly did
not succeed in subjugating the area ruled by the Quraysh. He does appear to have
tried, however. According to Muslim tradition at least, the Quraysh were known
as 'God's people' because they defeated Abraha.[116] There is a celebration of his
repelled attack in the surah The Elephant (Q 105). The reason for his attempted
conquest may well have been a desire to make the temple of Sana'a, which he
had built, the most important pilgrimage centre in Arabia and therefore eliminate
Mecca as a rival.[117]

We do not know this for sure, though. Whatever the exact situation, its influence shows just how widespread Christianity was on the Arabian Peninsula until
shortly before the birth of Muhammad, and how strong miaphysitism must have
been in either its West Syriac or Ethiopian form. Abraha clearly could not promul-
gate Christianity without some losses, and he was therefore forced to make compromises with the still influential Jewish elites. That, in any case, is how Robin
explains the fact that Abraha repeatedly mentions the power of the merciful God
and of his Messiah in his inscriptions – a wording that is entirely compatible with
the Qur'an and therefore adds further weight to the plausibility of the presence of
the Christianity he propagated in Medina.[118]

At any rate, most scholars assume that the Jews retained solid roots on the Arabian
Peninsula.[119] The Jews were presumably well integrated into their surroundings and
had probably arrived on the Arabian Peninsula after having been chased out of Palestine.[120] They may also have been better organised and scattered more widely than

---

114 Ibid. 153.
115 Ibid. 154.
116 Ibid. 152.
117 See Bell, *The Origin of Islam*, 40.
118 Robin, 'Ḥimyar', 153.
119 See Berkey, *The Formation of Islam*, 46.
120 Ibid. 42.

the Christians. Ultimately, though, these ideas remain as speculative as the suspicion that, in spite of everything, Arabia remained predominantly polytheistic.

The only thing we know for certain is that Abraha's kingdom collapsed in the 570s when his sons were on the throne,[121] and with this the Eastern Roman Empire lost one of its most important allies. Its South Arabian territories were conquered by the Sassanids in 570 and were henceforth under Persian control. Both the Jews and the East Syriac Christians saw the Sassanids as their protectors, and one can therefore assume that Christianity continued to hold considerable sway under Persian rule, albeit in its East Syriac version. In the sixth and early seventh centuries, the East Syriac Christians were present not only in the ports of Yemen but in the islands of the Persian Gulf as well as in al-Hira (south of Baghdad, on the border of the Sassanid Empire)[122] – precisely where one source tells us that Julianism was influential. So the East Syriac Christians exerted an influence not only on the Persians but also on their Lakhmid vassal state in the north-east of the Arabian peninsula.[123] What we do know for sure is that the East Syriac Christians got a toehold in Sana'a at least following the Persian occupation of South Arabia.[124] Theresia Hainthaler concludes from this that they 'could almost certainly be found in the cities and in particular in the ports of Yemen, but there is no evidence that they took root among the rural population'.[125] It is therefore pure speculation to claim that the East Syriac Church had any influence on the Qur'an.[126]

On the other hand, the considerable influence of West Syriac theology is evident from more examples than simply the influence of the kingdom of Himyar. In the Arab north-west of the Arabian Peninsula resided the equally West-Syriac-influenced Ghassanids, or the Jafnid kingdom, as more recent literature refers to it. Despite miaphysite tendencies, this dynasty was a loyal ally of the Eastern Roman Empire.[127] The Ghassanids or Jafnids obviously aligned themselves with

---

121 Robin, op. cit. 152.
122 See Hainthaler, *Christliche Araber vor dem Islam*, 110, 134–5.
123 The Lakhmids were not Christians, however. As late as the beginning of the sixth century, the Arab king of al-Hirah sacrificed a group of Christian nuns (see Bell, op. cit. 27).
124 The influence of the East Syriac Church should not be overestimated, though, because the Persians took an extremely pragmatic approach and supported the miaphysite majority in places such as Palestine and Syria, recognising it as the dominant religion (see Frend, *The Rise of the Monophysite Movement*, 337).
125 Bell, *The Origin of Islam*, 134.
126 See Tardy, *Najrân*, 165–6, who considers Nestorianism to have been a marginal phenomenon on the Arabian Peninsula and also assumes that monophysitism was influenced by Julianism (ibid. 172).
127 See Greg Fisher, *Between Empires*, 60–1.

whichever religious positions was dominant inside their territory.[128] The form of Christianity that was prevalent on their territory was therefore miaphysite and anti-Chalcedonian in nature; this influence is recognisable, for example, in the fact that it was the Ghassanid or Jafnid king al-Harith who requested three bishops from the emperor's wife Theodora.[129] Even if the anti-Chalcedonians had only a very weak religious hierarchy on the Arabian peninsula, they do nevertheless appear to have been very popular among the faithful.[130] It is not solely the afore-mentioned religio-political activities of the Ghassanid or Jafnid kings that testify to this, but also the foundation of miaphysite monasteries in the north-western part of Arabia.[131] In general, it seems to have been predominantly monks including a number of influential miaphysites – Hainthaler cites Saint Sergius as an example – who exerted an influence on Arab Christians, and this observation appears plausible, given the Qur'an's repeated disputes with monks.[132]

The Arabs on Ghassanid territory were therefore clearly of a miaphysite tendency, and it is completely possible that their influence stretched as far as Medina.[133] If one can assume that Abraha was successful in his missionary work in Medina, then it is easy to conclude that the West Syriac Christians were in contact with their fellow believers there. It was not until 613/614 that the kingdom was overrun by the Persians and ceased to exist.[134] That does not, however, detract from the plausibility of a pre-existing Christian influence in Medina.

There is an increasing realisation that, even in the seventh century, the majority of the Christians on the Arabian Peninsula were miaphysite-leaning opponents of the Council of Chalcedon.[135] It is not only in the north of Arab territory that the Christians seem to have adopted an anti-Chalcedonian position but in the south too,[136] as we saw above. The city of Najran played a special role in this, as Christianity had gained a toehold there as far back as the middle of the fifth century. The city was regarded as one of the main centres of Christianity on the Arabian

---

128 Ibid. 63.
129 Al-Azmeh, *The Emergence of Islam in Late Antiquity*, 264.
130 See on this and what follows Hainthaler, *Christliche Araber vor dem Islam*, 67–80.
131 Ibid. 72–75, 77.
132 Hainthaler, op. cit. 61–2.
133 Bell, *The Origin of Islam*, 22–3.
134 Ibid. 23.
135 Thus Hainthaler, following Grillmeier, speaks of a strong anti-Chalcedonian strain already in the 5th century in the Arab tribes and bishops after the Council, 'whose leading representatives were Peter the Iberian, his biographer and the later bishop of Maiuma John Rufus, Romanus and Gerontius.' (Grillmeier, *Christ in Christian Tradition. Vol. 2/3*, 151).
136 On this and what follows, see Hainthaler, *Christliche Araber vor dem Islam*, 111–36.

Peninsula,[137] and it is of great importance for the Qur'an with regard to the revelation of Q 3:61–62, which the Muslim tradition views as having been motivated by Muhammad's dispute with Christians from Najran.[138] It is assumed that there was also an anti-Chalcedonian hierarchy in Najran, even though it is thought that the anti-Chalcedonian tendency on the Arabian Peninsula never had a proper hierarchy of its own.[139] According to Norbert Nebes, a markedly anti-Chalcedonian form of Christianity took hold in Najran during the sixth century.[140]

Yet even without taking Najran into account, we can assume the presence of miaphysite influences on the western and southern edges of the Arabian Peninsula. Ethiopia, which had entirely converted to Christianity in the fourth century,[141] clearly served as a protector for the Christians in South Arabia,[142] as the campaign against the kingdom of Himyar described above attests. A second wave of missionary efforts won Ethiopia for the anti-Chalcedonian movement, and so we can assume that South Arabia was for the time being predominantly anti-Chalcedonian.

We began our remarks in this section with the observation that by the seventh century the Arabian Peninsula had already been completely surrounded by Christians for some time. We have not yet mentioned Sinai, where the Copts were present, although there is no sign of their having exerted any influence on Mecca or Medina. Travelling south from Sinai, one can establish the Ethiopian Christian influence on the west coast of the Arabian Peninsula, since the Ethiopians had proselytised there again and again, and their ideas had spread. This area was connected with the spheres of influence of the West Syriac Christians to the south and north-west, and those of the East Syriac Church to the east and north-east. This all goes to show just how prevalent Christianity was on the Arabian Peninsula.

Nevertheless, the non-Qur'anic sources offer only very few clues as to the

---

137 Ibid. 120.
138 On the importance of Najran, see also Grillmeier, *Christ in Christian Tradition Vol. 2/4: The Church of Alexandria with Nubia and Ethiopia after 451*, tr. O. C. Dean Jr, 305; Werner Schmucker, 'Die christliche Minderheit von Nāǧran und die Problematik ihrer Beziehungen zum frühen Islam', in *Studien zum Minderheitenproblem im Islam* 1 (1973) 183–281; Claus Schedl, *Muhammad und Jesus. Die christologisch relevanten Texte des Korans*, Freiburg 1978, 374–97; Gordon Nickel, '"We will make peace with you": the Christians of Najrān in Muqātil's "Tafsīr"', in *Collectanea Christiana Orientalia* 3 (2006) 171–88; Tardy, *Najrân*.
139 Hainthaler, op. cit. 129.
140 See Norbert Nebes, 'The Martyrs of Najran and the End of the Heryar. On the Political History of South Arabia in the Early Sixth Century', in Angelika Neuwirth / Nicolai Sinai / Michael Marx (eds.), *The Qur'an in Context. Historical and Literary Investigations into the Qur'anic Milieu*, Leiden 2009, 25–60, here 46–8.
141 Grillmeier, *Christ in Christian Tradition. Vol. 2/4*, 295.
142 On this and what follows, ibid. 308–14.

actual prevalence of Christians in Mecca and Medina. One can at least assume that, being a trade centre, Mecca was in contact with Syria and that at least two caravans per year travelled back and forth between Mecca and Syria.[143] Christians seem to have enjoyed only very little influence in Mecca, though, and there is no evidence of church buildings. 'The Christians we know of were a number of slaves, adventurers, traders, wine merchants,'[144] although according to Henri Lammens there were also doctors, surgeons and dentists.[145] What is certain is that Christian merchants were at least sporadically active in Mecca.[146]

Lammens states that Mecca was intermittently occupied by Christian Abyssinians before the Hijrah. Mecca obviously also had intensive connections with Najran and other Christian centres in Yemen, as can be told from the Najranites' prominence in the *Al-sira* and early Qur'anic exegesis.[147] Of all the Quraysh clans it was primarily the Banu Asad who had affinities with Christianity,[148] since some of them were affiliated to the Ghassanids.[149] Nevertheless, Christians were extremely weakly represented in Mecca prior to the Hijrah,[150] and thus although Muhammad heard about them, he could not, or did not, want to undertake any specific theological distinctions.[151]

The circumstances were somewhat different in Medina as we set out earlier while considering Abraha's influence, and yet most Western historians continue to claim that there were almost no Christians in Medina. Hainthaler, for instance, writes: 'There were very few Christians in Medina, their names virtually unknown, and definitely no organised Christianity.'[152] It is generally assumed that

---

143 Hainthaler, *Christliche Araber vor dem Islam*, 137, n. 2.

144 Ibid. 138.

145 Ibid. 140, with reference to Henri Lammens, 'Les chrétiens à la Mecque à la veille de l'hégire', in Lammens, *L'Arabie occidentale avant l'hégire*, Beirut 1928, 1–49, here 29, which Hainthaler considers the best and most comprehensive source to date about Christians in Mecca.

146 See J. Spencer Trimingham, *Christianity among the Arabs in Pre-Islamic Times*, London 1979, 260. As Mecca was a slave-trading centre, it is highly likely that there were also Christian slaves there (see Lammens, op. cit. 12).

147 Lammens, op. cit. 16.

148 Ibid. 37.

149 Ibid. 38.

150 Ibid. 47.

151 It may of course also be the case that Muhammad did not initiate any precise theological dissociations in these early days of the proclamation for strategic reasons so as to encourage open debate at first.

152 Hainthaler, *Christliche Araber vor dem Islam*, 140.

the image of Christians was largely shaped by the presence of Jews.[153] However, in conflicts between Jews and Christians, the Qur'an always comes down on the Christian side, and so we should test this judgement again when we come to look at the Qur'anic statements in detail. We shall need to examine with particular care whether Julianist-inspired Christianity may have been present in Medina.

Although the existence of Ethiopian, West Syriac and East Syriac versions of Christianity on the Arabian Peninsula is largely a matter of historical record, it is unclear to what extent pro-Chalcedonian Christianity was also present there. In the Arab world, Chalcedonians were considered to be loyal to the emperor, earning them the not exactly flattering nickname of Melkites, meaning 'the Emperor's Men'. Interestingly, these Melkites were the first Christians to assert Arabic as their mother tongue, and so soon after the death of Muhammad they became the Muslims' main interlocutors.[154] Yet their readiness to communicate in Arabic does not necessarily demonstrate that they were especially numerous on the Arabian Peninsula. It is easy to explain their Arabisation after the split of the Greek Empire by the fact that the liturgical language was not a symbol of ethnic identity, meaning that they had a greater capacity to adapt than Christians informed by Aramaic.

The Melkites repeatedly tried to show that the doctrine of the Trinity and Christology could certainly be construed from the Qur'an, especially with reference to Q 4:171.[155] This suggests that they did not interpret the Qur'an's explicit statements opposing the Trinity doctrine and Christology as an attack on their own positions. It also explains why Muslims began at a very early stage to counter such Christian attempts at appropriation by insisting that the verdicts of the Qur'an were indeed directed at the Christian faith as a whole. This is a very understandable polemical stance from an emerging religion seeking to establish its identity, but it nonetheless provides very little information about the extent to which the proclaimer of the Qur'an had Melkite theology in mind at the time of the emergence of the Qur'an. It is interesting, in any case, that the Melkites felt only marginally attacked by the Qur'an.

Instead it appears to be the Syriac version of Christianity that the Qur'an has

---

153 Lammens, op. cit. 48. In similar fashion, Barbara Finster stresses that Yathrib was also Jewish at the time of Muhammad. See Barbara Finster, 'Arabia in Late Antiquity. An Outline of the Cultural Situation in the Peninsula at the Time of Muhammad', in Neuwirth / Sinai / Marx (eds.), *The Qur'an in Context*, 61–114, here 72.

154 See Sidney H. Griffith, 'The Melkites and the Muslims. The Qur'an, Christology and Arab Orthodoxy', *Al-Qantara* 33 (2012) 413–42, here 423.

155 Ibid. 433, 438.

in its sights. What is worth noting in this context are the considerable formal similarities between the Syriac *mêmrê* (verse homilies) and the Qur'an. They too have
cadences, are proclaimed orally, tackle didactic and ethical issues, are addressed
to both the individual and the community, and have a 'composer' and a specific
audience. This leads Sidney Griffith to conclude that the surahs of the Qur'an
arose from the same cultural milieu as the Syriac *mêmrê*.[156] In his opinion, what
connects the two is a preference for verse and recitation in religious speech.[157] In
their *mêmrê*, the Syriac church fathers proceed from the assumption that signs
of God's pledge – the so-called *roze* – are to be found everywhere in Scripture
and in Creation, all of them pointing to Christ.[158] Equally, the proclaimer of the
Qur'an sees in all the *'āyāt* signs of the Word made reality in the Qur'an. We shall
explore the relationship between these two basic conceptions in more detail, but
what should be clear at this point is that both our historical knowledge and an
examination of the stylistic characteristics of the writings of the Syriac church
fathers suggest that the proclaimer of the Qur'an was predominantly exercised by
this and similar miaphysite forms of Christianity.[159]

This is not to say that the proclaimer of the Qur'an was unaware of other variants, of course. A large part of the Arab population was Bedouin and they travelled
widely for their living. They followed their flocks as far as central Iraq, which
strongly suggests that the Arabs knew not only of miaphysite but also of Melkite
and East Syriac forms of Christianity and were aware of the quarrels between
these groups.

---

156 See Sidney H. Griffith, 'The Poetics of Scriptural Reasoning: Syriac Mêmrê at Work',
in Jeffrey Wicks / Kristian S. Heal (eds.), *Literature, Rhetoric, and Exegesis in Syriac Verse*
(*Studia Patristica*; 78), Louvain 2017, 5–25, here 25.
157 Ibid. 2.
158 Ibid. 18. Strange as such typological representations may appear to us today, they are
deeply rooted in the Christian tradition and were self-evident to the church fathers. We shall
return to this link in more detail during our discussion of prophetology.
159 No genre equivalent to the *mêmrê* exists in either the Ethiopian or the Coptic tradition.
The Ethiopian tradition does feature the originally Syriac *suggiothe*, dialogical scriptural
texts, e.g. about Adam and Eve, or body and soul. Of course, the Ethiopian Church was so
influenced by the Syriac rite that there would seem to be no point in pitting the influences
of these two churches on the Qur'an against each other. The Copts are also closely related to
them theologically and, like the West Syriac Church, inspired by Severus of Antioch, who
lived in exile in Egypt.

3

New Developments in Modern Christology

In seeking to clarify the relationship that Qur'anic statements about Jesus Christ bear to Christology, it is now important, after our preceding historical review, to turn our gaze to modern developments in Christology. This study can of course only scratch at the surface of these transformations, our aim here being merely to understand where they started and, from there, to present our own proposed Christology, which we will use in the rest of the book as the basis for a dialogue with the Qur'anic view of Jesus. The Christian author bases his Christological thinking on this approach, which he believes capable of fostering a dialogue with Muslims. In line with this book's objectives, his aim is not to lay out his own Christological approach but merely to present the intellectual foundations for this book's Christian theological argument.

It is worth stating in advance that we do not believe that watering down Christological positions to such a degree that they are no longer accepted by mainstream Christian theology is conducive to dialogue between Christians and Muslims. First, this kind of diluted Christology would not encourage the mainstreams of both religions to come together and reconcile their differences. Second, it is becoming ever clearer from recent exegetic research that high Christology was not somehow 'invented' by the fourth- and fifth-century Councils, but has been part of Christianity since its infancy. Liberal exegetes may have long believed that the Greek philosophical terminology of the Councils exaggerated the biblical evidence and unjustly deified Jesus,[1] but scholars are increasingly coming round

---

1 One only needs to consider Adolf von Harnack's famous demand for a de-Hellenisation of the Christian faith (see Adolf von Harnack, *Das Wesen des Christentums*, edited and with a commentary by Trutz Rendtorff, Gütersloh 1999, here especially 194–200, and also

to the position that the Councils did not 'invent' Jesus's divinity, they simply expressed in new terms something that had already been stated in the Bible. One must at least admit that solid foundations for later developments in Christological dogma were there in the early days of Christianity.[2] The fact that the development of dogma introduced terminology influenced by new Hellenist thinking into Christology is due to the rise of categories during the philosophical debates of the third and fourth centuries that threatened to obscure a faith based on biblical tenets. Precise philosophical interpretation of the mystery of Jesus Christ's person was therefore required to adequately circumscribe his singularity in the face of recent discussions. If we attempt to look back to the time before these clarifications and, as Martin Bauschke does, introduce a pre-Nicene Christology into the conversation with Muslims,[3] there is a risk that blurring the boundaries between the religions actually hinders dialogue and that the resulting rapprochement will be accepted only in extremely liberal Christian circles. It is therefore not an option to dilute Christology to such a degree that it loses all contentiousness; the aim should be to express it in new philosophical categories and ways of thinking in order to facilitate inter-religious dialogue. In this context, it strikes us that the contemporary Christology that has evolved since Schleiermacher offers some interesting points of reference.

We shall now curtail our discussion to focus on this starting point, not because we do not think that there are grounds for Christological reconstruction on the basis of the Bible, but solely because our aim in this section is to provide an overview of Christology's new approach in modern times and to explore its potential for promoting Christian-Muslim dialogue.

Harnack, *Lehrbuch der Dogmengeschichte. Vol 1: Die Entstehung des kirchlichen Dogmas*, Darmstadt 1964, here especially 243–91). For a discussion of this theory, see Christoph Markschies, 'Hellenisierung des Christentums. Sinn und Unsinn einer historischen Deutungskategorie' (*Forum Theologische Literaturzeitung*; 25), Leipzig 2012, 49–61.
2 On these new developments, see Richard Bauckham, *God Crucified. Monotheism and Christology in the New Testament*, Grand Rapids – Cambridge 1998; Larry W. Hurtado, *How on Earth Did Jesus Become a God? Historical Questions About Earliest Devotion to Jesus*, Grand Rapids – Cambridge 2005; and, in order to place these somewhat one-sided explanations in context, Stefan Schreiber, *Die Anfänge der Christologie. Deutungen Jesus im Neuen Testament*, Neukirchen 2015; Klaus von Stosch, *Trinität (Grundwissen Theologie)*, Paderborn 2017, 11–23.
3 See Bauschke, op. cit. 427–31; Bauschke, op. cit. 138–49.

3.1 The starting point of consciousness Christology

Friedrich Daniel Ernst Schleiermacher was the first influential theologian of the modern age to break radically with the two-nature doctrine and traditional Christology. One of his interpreters notes correctly that his Christology 'left not a single stone of traditional doctrine standing'.[4] His Christology was such a new formulation that the usual Muslim accusations against it initially miss their mark and it seems appropriate to revisit it – if, that is, one is minded to pursue his paradigm change.

Schleiermacher's decisive and novel contribution was to replace the two-person doctrine with the doctrine of the archetypal and historical nature of the person of Jesus Christ. While the latter emphasises his enduring historical reality, the archetypal nature is the legacy of the doctrine that emphasises Jesus's divinity. 'The archetypal nature of Jesus is the absolute strength of his consciousness of God.'[5] The feeling of complete dependency which, according to Schleiermacher, characterises every human being is, in this Christology, present to an unparalleled degree in Jesus. 'The formula that encapsulates the understanding of the person of Christ is: "The Saviour is therefore like all other humans by dint of the sameness of human nature, but he is distinguished from them all by the power of his consciousness of God, which was God's real existence within him" (§94).'[6] Schleiermacher excludes all other divine elements from his Christology and rejects in particular any form of Logos Christology. He makes no claims for any special or ideal character of Jesus's humanness; the only thing that is special about Jesus is his consciousness, which is indistinguishable from his proximity to God. The decisive aspect of this conception is that Jesus's singularity depends entirely on his impeccability, and his special consciousness of God is therefore able to spread its healing power because this consciousness is not separated from God by sin.

Schleiermacher's Christology was often criticised subsequently because it played down the historical aspect and was thus unable to provide any satisfactory answer to the historical criticism of Christological dogma voiced by David Friedrich Strauss.[7] Impeccability alone ultimately proved too tenuous a link to render it truly plausible that the historical archetype he had reconstructed can truly be associated with Jesus of Nazareth and with no other human being. Particularly in the Christian-Muslim dialogue, we will soon see that impeccability is considered

---

4 Hermann Fischer, *Friedrich Daniel Ernst Schleiermacher*, Munich 2001, 114.
5 Ibid. 113.
6 Ibid.
7 For an introduction to this topic, see Christian Danz, *Grundprobleme der Christologie*, Tübingen 2013, 118–41.

an accepted category by the classic Muslim scholastic theology of the Prophet, and it is therefore not particularly persuasive for our case to link the divine or archetypal nature of Jesus to it. Muslims will have few problems with Schleiermacher's conception, but they will ask why other prophets should not enjoy an equally strong consciousness of God and an equally special intimacy with God as Christ does. In addition, there is a need to be more explicit about what it is about this consciousness that is so salvific. If Christians wish to adhere to the uniqueness of Jesus Christ and continue to proclaim him the Saviour, then Schleiermacher's reasoning is flawed.[8]

We do not intend to build on Schleiermacher's own writings here but on modern attempts to interpret and base his Christology on a theology of history, while also pursuing his line of reasoning and arguing in terms of a theory of the subject. There have, for example, been attempts led by the Lutheran theologian Wolfhart Pannenberg to construct the original meaning of the story of Jesus from history using a *bottom-up Christology* and thereby to preserve it exegetically. The hermeneutic emphasis here is that faith should not read anything into history that is not already there. Although I am unable to say here and now whether this approach is likely to be successful, my objective is simply to elucidate its implications for the reconstruction of high Christology, i.e. *top-down Christology*, as this is what requires fresh interpretation for the purposes of Muslim-Christian dialogue.

In this brief reconstruction, we shall therefore focus on how Pannenberg's work has been received by a student of Thomas Pröpper whose work is very influential in Catholic theology – the Bochum-based dogmatist Georg Essen. In a similar vein to Schleiermacher and Pannenberg, he views the ontological specificity of Jesus's freedom as Jesus's consciousness of unmediated immediacy with the Father, unhindered by sin,[9] and attempts to provide a historical and exegetical basis for this approach. Jesus's singularity, he argues, consists therefore of his freedom to let himself be 'originally defined by the Father's unconditional affection'.[10]

---

8 For criticism, see also Wolf Krötke, 'Vorösterlicher Jesus – Nachösterlicher Christus. Dialogische Perspektiven in der Christologie', in Klaus von Stosch / Mouhanad Khorchide (eds.), 'Streit um Jesus. Muslimische und christliche Annäherungen' (*Beiträgen zur Komparativen Theologie*; 21), Paderborn 2016, 155–66, here 158.

9 See Georg Essen, 'Die Freiheit Jesu. Der Neuchalkedonische Enhypostasienbegriff im Horizont neuzeitlicher Subjekt und Personphilosophie' (*ratio fidei*; 5), Regensburg 2001, 289.

10 Essen, *Die Freiheit Jesu*, 308. Jesus is uniquely defined by the love of God and 'directly certain of his original and immediate relationship and united with His love' (ibid. 295); 'the self-consciousness of Jesus refers immediately not to the divine Logos as the second person of the Trinity but to God the Father, with whose will he knew himself to be one' (ibid. 283).

Regardless of its exegetical defensibility, what is questionable about this conception is how the immediate relationship with God claimed here can be reconciled with human freedom. If one considers humans' corporeal state and the fact
that they can only forge a relationship with God and the world through historical
signs, then the idea of immediacy is hard to comprehend.[11]

Adopting a subject-theoretical approach, the theory of pre-reflexive self-awareness of human self-consciousness, as in Dieter Henrich's discussion of Fichte,
might provide a means of understanding the idea of unmediated immediacy.[12] In
the same way that I am aware of myself prior to any reflexion and am therefore
to a degree pre-reflexively familiar with myself, one could say of Jesus of Nazareth's self-consciousness that, beyond any guarantees, he had always lived in an
unreflexive unmediated immediacy with the Father. In any case, the Bonn-based
dogmatist Karl-Heinz Menke appears to be thinking in this way when, taking up
Rahner's ideas, he explains that Jesus 'has always unreflexively and originally
[known] of his personal identicalness with the Son in the Trinity, because the
reason for his singular consciousness of God is the event of the hypostatic union'.[13]

We do find this an interesting analogy. Nevertheless, it still has a slight whiff of
a somewhat obscure metaphysical ad-hoc solution because we are deprived of any
vision or possibility of thinking of a self-consciousness referring pre-reflexively to
anything other than ourselves. Also, we find inconceivable the idea of any union
of the Logos and the Father in the Trinity without the Holy Spirit, and thus talk
of an unmediated relationship of one person with the other is also questionable in
the context of the Trinity. Furthermore, if one considers the biblical record, it is
worth reflecting if one may not speak of the special and unique intimacy of Jesus
with the Father and Jesus's familiarity with God's will as being facilitated by the
Holy Spirit. It must be possible to say that this intimacy encompassed Jesus at

---

11 See only the fundamental anthropological rule of unmediated immediacy in Helmuth
Plessner, *Mit anderen Augen. Aspekte einer philosophischen Anthropologie*, Stuttgart 1982,
31–55.
12 See Dieter Henrich's discussion of Fichte in Dieter Henrich, 'Selbstbewusstsein.
Kritische Einleitung in eine Theorie', in Rüdiger Burner / Konrad Cramer / Reiner Wiehl
(eds.), *Hermeneutik und Dialektik. Aufsätze I: Methode und Wissenschaft – Lebenswelt und
Geschichte*, Tübingen 1970, 257–84; see also Klaus Müller, 'Wenn ich "ich" sage. Studien
zur fundamentaltheologischen Relevanz selbstbewußter Subjektivität' (*Regensburger
Studien zur Theologie*; 46), Frankfurt 1994, 471–80.
13 Menke, *Jesus ist Gott der Sohn*, 352. Similarly to Magnus Striet in his subject theory,
Georg Essen combines Henrich's concept of the ego's pre-reflexive familiarity with Kring's
idea of the self-origination of freedom (see Essen, op. cit. 171–3). He does not seem to use
Henrich's concept to illustrate Jesus's original intimacy with the Father.

birth and determines his personality.[14] It was only during the course of his life that he gradually understood what this intimacy involved. We might even say that he never achieved understanding, since, as a man, he could not fully comprehend that he had been born into the secret of God and to owed his life to Him. Yet one could still say that at an ontological level he exists in his self-awareness in a unique and special intimacy with the Father, brought about by the Holy Spirit, and this is the divine aspect of his humanity.

At this point, however, Georg Essen would insist that this singular intimacy requires us to conceive of a formal and numerical identicalness of the freedom of Jesus with the freedom of the Logos of the Trinity. This threatens to render his Christology, informed by the theory of the subject, aporetic. That is because his approach is strongly informed by the philosophy of freedom and a libertarian conception of freedom, and so at least from a transcendental perspective, freedom requires the existence of alternative possibilities. Therefore if Jesus and the Son within the Trinity are formally and numerically identical, then the Son within the Trinity must have a real option to stand up to the Father if this possibility is assumed for the historical Jesus – at the very least, that is, if Essen takes the idea seriously that here God and man declare freedom with one voice. This leaves only two options: either Essen admits the idea of a dispute between gods, which to me appears to lead inevitably to polytheism; or Jesus forfeits the freedom to stand up to God and to despair at his own mission.[15]

Schleiermacher himself espoused this line of thinking and qualified the relevant passages in the Bible because he was of the opinion that Jesus's development must be thought of as free '"of anything that might be presented as conflict" (§93:4). Accordingly, all Gospel passages showing Jesus in his temptation and despair were deleted or re-interpreted'.[16] Yet this negation of Jesus's inner conflicts flatly contradicts the testimony of the Gospels, according to which Jesus certainly did struggle with his mission and God's will (see his struggle in Gethsemane alone; Matt. 26:36–46). One also wonders how Jesus is supposed to have saved us if he had no experience of such things as temptation and despair. That is why the early

---

14 Pneumatologists tend to argue in terms of Mary's virgin birth here, which was ultimately 'caused' by the descent of the Holy Spirit to Mary. See Alfons Nossel, 'Der Geist als Gegenwart Jesu Christi', in Walter Kasper (ed.), *Gegenwart des Geistes. Aspekte der Pneumatologie*, Freiburg 1979, 132–54, here 134–5.
15 For the debate about Essen's conception, see here the lucid explication in Magnus Lerch, 'Selbstmitteilung Gottes. Herausforderungen eines freiheitstheoretischen Offenbarungstheologie' (*ratio fidei*; 56), Regensburg 2015, 239–89.
16 Fischer, op. cit. 113.

church stipulated that Jesus could only save us in matters that he himself had endured.[17] Previously, Karl Rahner had branded heretical any form of conscious-ness theology that based Christology exclusively on Jesus's special trust in God and rejected any guarantees of a top-down Christology.[18] He did however admit that a legitimate form of consciousness Christology is possible because Christol-ogy does not have to reason ontically and materially, but it does have to argue ontologically in full knowledge of the union of being and consciousness.[19] We would like to add here that if Christology argues rationally and ontologically, it is capable of overcoming the aporias of the two-nature doctrine and any Christology based on ontic arguments.

Jürgen Werbick is talking here of the communication paradigm of modern Christology. Central to this paradigm is the idea of '*salvific* communication or the salvation of communication'.[20] In this interpretation, Jesus Christ appears as God's offer of a relationship and of communication with us human beings. He is God's yes to us: 'God's will to save humankind *occurs* in him.'[21] To quote Werbick: 'He is the *Gospel in person*, God's challenging word of acceptance, the realisation of His promise to humankind, inviting them to participate: I will be there for you.'[22]

Jesus is defined here on the one hand in communication theory terms as God's address to us. On the other hand, however, Werbick also says that he is God's agreement to communicate with us, further evidence of relational ontology. In this paradigm, God shows Himself to be 'so "self-empowered" and willing for a relationship that He has nothing to lose by being present in a finite human reality and being entirely Himself'.[23]

3.2 The modern paradigm shift in relational ontology and its impact on Christology

The term 'relational ontology' alludes to a paradigm shift in modern philosophy

---

17 We remind readers of the early church's axiom, cited earlier: *quod non assumptum est, non sanatum est*, see Irenaeus of Lyon (*Adversus haereses*, V 14:1–2), Tertullian (*De ressurectione carnis* 10), quoted here in Jürgen Werbick, 'Von Gott sprechen an der Grenze zum Verstummen' (*Religion – Geschichte – Gesellschaft*; 40), Münster 2004, 130.
18 See Karl Rahner, *Foundations of Christian Faith*, 279–90.
19 Ibid.
20 Jürgen Werbick, *Gott-menschlich. Elementare Christologie*, Freiburg 2016, 308.
21 Ibid. 242.
22 Ibid. 110.
23 Ibid. 265.

that has seen metaphysics replaced by transcendental philosophy.[24] What seems crucial to us is the realisation that ultimate validity is no longer aimed for on the basis of ontological, substance-theoretical statements, but from an anthropological perspective. Thus, it is no longer conceived in terms of substances or natures, but of relationships. Since God's reality is thought of as the relational reality of love, such relational thinking seems a suitable means of explaining God's existence to humankind.

From a relational ontological perspective, Christology is not about the incomprehensible claim that a creatural substance is one with the substance of God, but that Jesus's creatural nature is defined in its originating in, and striving towards, the divine nature. In this tension resides God's being. It is precisely because God is the relationship, and within Him there is room for even the greatest imaginable differences, that Jesus can reveal God's relational actuality through his distinct relatedness.[25] God's living word can become tangible reality within Him because this word contains and expresses God's commitment to the Other with Him.

The singularity of Jesus Christ would therefore not be defined, in this line of thinking, by statements about his two natures, but rather by statements about the singularity of the relationship from which he springs and which he mediates for us.[26] The distinctness from God that Jesus himself repeatedly stresses could then be understood as a distinctness that characterises Jesus absolutely as the recipient and as the one arising from and sent by the Father. In accordance with trinitarian thinking, this would be distinctness conceived entirely as relationship, so that Jesus would live the relationship and make it possible for us to experience the relationship that characterises God's relational actuality itself. Or, to quote Karl-Heinz Menke: 'For the historical self-differentiation of Jesus from the Father is the revelation of the intra-trinitarian self-differentiation of the eternal Son from the eternal Father.'[27]

So from this perspective, if one asks what constitutes Jesus's singularity compared with other humans, one should not expect any substance-ontological statements that might in themselves lead to a denial of Jesus's true humanity

---

24 On this, see the detailed discussion in Klaus von Stosch, *Offenbarung*, Paderborn 2010, 11–24.

25 See Menke, *Fleisch geworden aus Maria*, 125: 'The relationship that "the Other in God" (the Son) *is*, must be the constitutive feature of the creature in which God is incarnate.'

26 See Wolfhart Pannenberg, op. cit. 349–57.

27 Karl-Heinz Menke, 'Gott sühnt in seiner Menschwerdung die Sünde des Menschen', in Magnus Striet / Jan-Heiner Tück (eds.), *Erlösung auf Golgota? Der Opfertod Jesu im Streit der Interpretationen*, Freiburg 2012, 101–25, here 103.

or so to idealise his humanity that he can ultimately only be thought of as our saviour. Rather, the only objective can be to see Jesus's special relationship with the Father, and the manner in which he mediates this relationship and makes us able to experience it, as the starting point for what is traditionally called his *divine nature*. Menke therefore explicitly declares that 'Jesus's relationship with the Father [is] not the experience of a man begot by Joseph and born of Mary to God, but the beginning of the constitutive nature of his personhood'.[28] The unique or completely singular aspect of Jesus's existence must therefore be sought in the fact that this man was always shaped – constituted even – by the same relationship that is also the relationship between his self-declarations and his self-identity in the mystery of God.

In line with Jürgen Werbick, one could also say that Jesus allows his identity to be defined by 'God's existence and His dominion'[29] to such a degree that his self-identity can be defined as a 'missionary identity'.[30] Jesus wants to bear witness to God's love of humankind through his words and deeds. 'God's dedication to and absorption in His Logos, and the man Jesus of Nazareth's absorption in his witness-bearing [...] constitute the nature of his existence as a witness.'[31] Jesus thus proves himself to be the faithful witness of God and as a reliable hermeneutist of God;[32] he is 'God's salutary existence among men and for them'.[33]

Jesus, according to Werbick, derives his identity from being God's presence among humans. This is why Werbick speaks of Jesus as being God's coming among us: 'God comes to humans in His Christ, asks to be allowed to enter and, for His part, allows us to enter.'[34] 'Thus the finite, mortal human life of Jesus is the "motion" of God towards humans, which occurred and will occur forever in Jesus's coming into this world: God's coming becomes human.'[35]

If God Himself comes to humankind in Jesus, however, then something happens to Him in that encounter '*quo majus nil fieri potest* – than which simply nothing greater can occur'.[36] For what greater event could there be than meeting a God who has chosen humankind? Werbick sums it up thus: 'What occurred in him

---

28 Menke, *Jesus ist Gott der Sohn*, 444.
29 Werbick, op. cit. 444.
30 Ibid. 65.
31 Ibid. 67.
32 Ibid. 30.
33 Ibid. 68, n. 8.
34 Ibid. 90.
35 Ibid. 47.
36 Friedrich Wilhelm Joseph Schelling, *Philosophie der Offenbarung. Ausgewählte Werke*, vol. 2, Darmstadt 1972, 13 & 27.

was something than which nothing greater could occur: God's deepest, unequivo-cal, insurmountable, absolutely decided desire to be with humankind.'[37]

But how can we conceive of this advent of God to humankind? How can God's commitment to humankind become tangible reality in Jesus? How should we think of the singularity of Jesus's relationship with God, which we just mentioned following Karl-Heinz Menke? To answer this question, Menke and Werbick both refer to the effect of the Holy Spirit and to the effect of the entity within the godhead representing the permanent relationality of God. Werbick makes it clear that Jesus can be God's coming 'because God's eternal relational willingness and relational capacity makes it possible for God the Father to give human actuality to His eternal desire for relationships and communication – the eternal Logos – which lives out this desire for relationships in human fashion'.[38] It is thus God's good spirit that allows us to encounter God's word of acceptance in human form.

Following Walter Kasper and Hans Urs von Balthasar, Menke also refers in similar fashion to God's spiritual actuality as the mediating principle for the con-ceivability of incarnation. He therefore declares that 'the event of Christ is itself the fruit of the working of the spirit'.[39] Simply by virtue of having always been filled with the spirit of God, Jesus is able to live from his intimacy with God, which enables him to experience his self-differentiation from God entirely as a relationship coming from God and moving towards Him, and to open this rela-tional actuality up to the whole of humankind. Menke is therefore completely correct to say that pneumatic Christology depends entirely on the fact that Jesus's being the Logos did not arise over the course of his life from his increasing open-ness to the spiritual reality of God, but that it was a given from the very beginning of his existence.[40] According to this conception, from the very beginning of his existence Jesus is also the existence of God's commitment, because in becoming

---

37 Werbick, op. cit. 207.

38 Ibid. 280.

39 Karl-Heinz Menke, 'Das heterogene Phänomen der Geist-Christologien', in George Augustin / Klaus Krämer / Markus Schulze (eds.), *Mein Herr und mein Gott. Christus bekennen und verkünden*, Freiburg 2013, 220–57, here 251. Jürgen Werbick also offers a similarly comprehensive spiritual-Christological reasoning and stresses that 'God's presence occurs through his spirit as the culmination of humanity' (Werbick, *Gott-menschlich*, 275).

40 Menke, *Das heterogene Phänomen der Geist-Christologie*, 238: 'If, however, Jesus first *becomes* the Son through the spirit of the Father, then can his humanity – as critics of Moltmann's pneumatic Christology rightly ask – be any more than a creatural "outside" of a divine "inside" (of the Holy Spirit)?' Alongside Moltmann and various Anglican advocates of pneumatic Christology, Menke also denounces the pneumatological Christology of Leonardo Boff, who from Menke's point of view no longer sees the decisive event as the incarnation of God but as the inspiration of the community (ibid. 254).

a person he is already constituted by the spirit of God, which allows him to rely entirely on God's relationship without being lost within it.[41]

The main thing, therefore, is not to seek the singularity of Jesus in his nature or in his being, but in his relationship with God. Naturally, this relationship also shapes his consciousness and hence his being – from the very beginning. But the cause of this shaping is not a transformation of his substantive nature, but the type of relationship of which he has always been part.[42] Rahner articulates it thus: 'From the very beginning, Jesus the man is in a union of will with the Father that has completely dominated his entire reality from the very beginning, in an "obedience" from which he derives his entire human reality; he is quite simply the one who has constantly received from the Father and who has always entirely delivered himself up to the Father in all aspects of his existence; [...] he is the one whose "basic disposition" [...] is the radically fulfilled origination from God and assignation to God.'[43]

Jesus's singularity and divinity consists therefore not of any supernatural powers but of Jesus's knowing that he comes entirely from God and devotes himself entirely to God. This devotion to God is so entirely constitutive of his life that his will has no desires other than the Father's. His will is therefore so united with the will of the Father that I do indeed experience God's good will when I encounter Jesus, who represents this will for all people. This illustrates the objective of consciousness Christology. It is not a matter of speculating about the inner life of Jesus of Nazareth but rather about the testimony that makes it possible to experience God's love of humankind and mercy in him, through him and with

---

41 Menke also sees this as the decisive link to belief in the virginity of Mary. He declares: 'The spirit creates from the material disposition of Mary the man which he unites hypostatically (personally) with the pre-existing Son' (Menke, *Das heterogene Phänomen der Geist-Christologen*, 247; see also Menke, *Fleisch geworden aus Maria*, 127). However fundamentally correct Menke's view may be here, his repeated mention of the creation of the human Jesus 'from the material disposition of Mary' is extremely peculiar. If Jesus really was created only from her, then he would have to be a clone of Mary, and it would be impossible to explain how he came by his one Y chromosome.

42 As described above, Essen's approach too is to discuss the consciousness of Jesus to portray his divinity. However, he does not attribute the special consciousness of Jesus to his having been brought about by the spirit, but rather to an ontological specificity of Jesus, running the risk in the process of being unable to express the true humanity of Jesus appropriately: '[...] and if, *on the other hand*, Jesus was originally sure of his immediate, no longer mediated certainty through the love of God for the purpose of its self-presence in him, then Jesus's self-consciousness exceeds every known form of consciousness and self-consciousness because it is not within the anthropological possibilities of humankind' (Essen, *Die Freiheit Jesu*, 290).

43 Rahner, *Foundations of Christian Faith*, 279–90.

him. God looks at us in him and in doing so His word of acceptance becomes tangible reality.

Within the categories of relational ontology therefore, Jesus's singularity is that, with the help of the Holy Spirit, he has devoted the entire course of his life to letting his freedom be filled with the will of the Father, to live in accordance with it to communicate God's love. His specificity is demonstrated by the fact that he derives 'his personal identity from desiring God's will as his own and to be there so that this will may come about ... His humanity consists of being the living word of God'.[44] It is worth highlighting that Jesus can only be the living word of God and only devote his freedom to desiring God's will because from the very beginning of his earthly existence he was gripped in singular fashion by God's good spirit and is permanently encompassed by it. He therefore enjoys a unique and special intimacy with the will of the Father, brought about by the Holy Spirit, which makes him the living word of God, and thus the one God speaks in unaugmentable intensity through the man Jesus of Nazareth. From a Christian perspective, this self-declaration can be thus asserted because Christians see themselves as having been accepted by God in Jesus of Nazareth and recognise in him the actuality of the pledge of the divine living word.

However much understanding Muslims might have for this, they would continue to question the historical basis for these claims and why one may not speak of other humans as God's living word. We shall examine these questions further in the next section.

3.3 Testing against the historical Jesus

There can of course be no question of providing – effectively in retrospect – a biblical justification for the new conception of the theory of hypostatic union we have developed up to this point. Yet we would at least like to show how the Christology we have reformulated in the light of categories of modern consciousness philosophy stands up to the historical test of biblical testimony and the facts that can be gleaned from it. We put forward these suggestions primarily to demonstrate the historical plausibility of our reasoning, and to set out the fundamental notions of biblical testimony on which it is based. Only by seeing how the Christology we have outlined stands up to scrutiny will the expectations and questions with which the Christian author of this book intends to approach the Qur'an and the Muslim tradition become clear.

---

44 Werbick, *Von Gott sprechen an der Grenze des Verstummen*, 129.

Approaching the life of Jesus of Nazareth inductively from below will provide only clues about the dogmatic claims that have been made so far. Jesus's singularity cannot be explored neutrally from a historical distance; it can only be extrapolated from the believer's personal encounter with Jesus. Accordingly, the experience of the Resurrection, which illustrates the death-defying power of the love of God like no other experience, is not a neutral historical fact; its true meaning only becomes apparent when the witnesses are touched by this historical event. The foundations of the Christian faith are the historical encounters with Jesus of Nazareth, and this faith must not contradict the information generated by historical research.

At the same time, it is clear that it takes more than historical facts to move a person to belief; the reality of Jesus Christ cannot be adequately appreciated without faith. This is linked to the fact that this reality is a relationship that can only be adequately captured and comprehended if I devote myself unreservedly to it. Human love too can only be recognised and experienced in the act of loving. The statement of faith that God Himself, in His unconditional love of humankind, speaks to me and moves me with through Jesus Christ can thus be traced back to a historically attestable fact that should not contradict this meaning, for instance to the celebration of the Eucharist. At the same time, however, it cannot be inferred from such facts but only in the tangible reality of faith. The Austrian philosopher Ludwig Wittgenstein expressed this in the following terms:

> What inclines even me to believe in Christ's Resurrection? It is as though I
> play with the thought. – If he did not rise from the dead, then he decomposed
> in the grave like any other man. *He is dead and decomposed.* In that case
> he is a teacher like any other and can no longer *help*; and once more we
> are orphaned and alone. So we have to content ourselves with wisdom and
> speculation. We are in a sort of hell where we can do nothing but dream,
> roofed in, as it were, and cut off from heaven. But if I am to be **REALLY**
> saved, – what I need is *certainty* – not wisdom, dreams of speculation – and
> this certainty is faith. And faith is faith in what is needed by my *heart*, my
> *soul*, not my speculative intelligence. For it is my soul with its passions, as
> it were with its flesh and blood, that has to be saved, not my abstract mind.
> Perhaps we can say: Only *love* can believe the Resurrection. Or: It is *love* that
> believes the Resurrection. We might say: Redeeming love believes even in the
> Resurrection; holds fast even to the Resurrection.[45]

---

45 Ludwig Wittgenstein, *Culture and Value*, ed. G. H. von Wright, tr. Peter Winch, Chicago 1980, 33e.

One could say with Wittgenstein at this juncture that love breaks through the boundaries of our hell and refuses to accept the finality of death. In its fulfilment, love tears down all barriers and all borders and in its striving for permanence and definitiveness becomes faith in the resurrection. Only love is capable of recognising the lover as the one imparting unconditional love. As a result, it also recognises that the reality of the love for which Jesus lived became, through him, with him and in him, an enduring reality after his death.

If we now look for historical precedents for the singularity of Jesus of Nazareth, then it is immediately clear that this singularity cannot be derived from history; one can only name certain clues in the life story of Jesus to make the Christian statement plausible. These clues derive their force from the Church's testimony that Jesus Christ remains alive within it and can be experienced in the sacramental consummation of the Church in precisely those characteristics we know from his life on earth.

Modern dogmatics highlights two particular characteristics of Jesus for which the historical record provides plausible evidence and which are therefore central to the reconstruction of Christology.[46] One is Jesus's especially intimate relationship with his Abba in heaven. His life originates from an intimacy with God that makes him appear completely human, embodying the reality of God's commitment and making it tangible. The second characteristic is that his dealings with his fellow men appear to have been free from any fear and inclination to ostracise.

Jesus's particularly intimate contact with God is demonstrated by his addressing God as Abba (e.g. Mark 14:36) and particularly by the special authority with which he taught and acted. He clearly assumed that Satan's rule was definitively broken (Luke 10:18) and that the kingdom of God had come with him (Mark 1:14). His claim to have the power to forgive sins (e.g. Matt. 9:2–6) makes it clear that he believed that the forgiving presence of God became tangible in his actions.

On the basis of his special relationship with his Father in heaven, Jesus also seems to have found the strength to approach strangers naturally and attentively. As the finite human that he was and remained, he never excluded anyone because they were a stranger to him and scared him. He acted kindly towards women, healed the sick and the leprous with his touch and his proximity, and stood up

---

46 For a brief compilation of the main facts about the historical Jesus, see Rudolf Hoppe, 'Jesus – das Paradoxon Gottes. Überlegungen zu Botschaft und Wirken des Nazareners', in *Impulse* 60 (2001) 2–6; Helmut Merklein, 'Jesus, Künder des Reiches Gottes', in Walter Kern / Hermann J. Pottmeyer / Max Seckler (eds.), *Handbuch der Fundamentaltheologie. Vol. 2: Traktat Offenbarung*, Tübingen 2000, 115–39; and Angelika Strotmann, *Jesus von Nazaret (Grundwissen Theologie)*, Paderborn 2012.

for people on the margins of society. Instead of keeping a fearful distance from sinners and the unclean, he advocated the removal of all discriminating borders and barriers. He invited those maltreated by the community and those official doctrine excluded from God's love to his merry banquets in the villages of Galilee. All were welcome to celebrate with him.

In this respect, and from the perspective of the historically critical methodology, one may admit on the one hand that Jesus lived in consciousness of making God's beneficial closeness and mercy tangible to people. He felt that he had been sent by the Father and devoted his freedom to invoking his heavenly Father.[47] On the other hand, one may declare that it was precisely the relationship of coming from the Father and moving towards the Father that endowed Jesus with the self-assurance to impart the communion with God to other people and to recognise them in their otherness. It thus becomes clear that the innate goal of all statements about Jesus's singularity is to disclose the experience that there occurs in him a form of recognition of his own person that can only be adequately proved if Jesus is regarded as imparting God's salvific reality with full authority.

Therefore, if one notes that the fundamental characteristic of Jesus's identity is his special intimacy with the Father and, rooted in this relationship, his insight into and recognition of the spiritual fulfilment of other persons, then Jesus's freedom shows the same attributes that provide for the spiritual fulfilment of the inner-trinitarian Logos.[48] For according to traditional trinitarian theology, the

---

47 See, among others, Mark 1:15–16, 1:22 & 14:36; Matt. 7:21 & 12:50; Luke 10:22, 11:20 & 22:29.

48 We should point out at this juncture that it would be wrong to assume that the divine Logos and the person of Jesus Christ are identical, as the Christologist Georg Essen has implied. As we have already seen, Essen speaks of the unmediated immediacy of the relationship with the Father in the case of the inner-trinitarian Son but also understands the relationship between the historical person Jesus Christ and his Father as an unmediatedly immediate relationship with God (see Essen, *Die Freiheit Jesu*, 287–91). Starting from this assumption, he proceeds to his thesis of the 'identicalness of the person of the Son of God with the man Jesus' (ibid. 297). Essen does admit that Jesus can only express the love of his Father in human fashion (ibid. 311), but Magnus Lerch's criticism is able to demonstrate that Essen takes as his basis for the human freedom of Jesus the term 'real symbol', which assumes an actual 'numerical identicalness of the medium of revelation with the revealer' (Lerch, *Selbstmitteilung Gottes*, 310). In contrast to this, Lerch resorts to a necessary mention – for the category of self-revelation – of 'ontological inseparability of the medium from the subject and content of the message' (ibid.). This leads to the conclusion that the figure of the medium of revelation – Jesus Christ – 'is in differential union with the subject of the revelation' and that the medium, subject and content of the revelation correspond to one another but are nevertheless not identical (ibid. 196–7 & 393). On this, see also my own comments on the interpretation of the real symbol of Jesus Christ, in Klaus von Stosch, *Gott*

inner-trinitarian Logos has two main characteristics. First, it is the Begotten, i.e. it is completely absorbed in coming from the Father and moving towards the Father – so much so, in fact, that the Father speaks through it. Equally one can say that Jesus of Nazareth is absorbed in coming from the Father and moving towards the Father, and is therefore the one who allows his will to be entirely determined by the will of the Father and can be God's living word.

Second, it is the inner-trinitarian Logos that breathes the Spirit together with the Father. It is therefore bound to the Spirit through the Father and with the Father, and in God it enables the absorption of every otherness into the oneness of God. Jesus of Nazareth is also the one who allows all-encompassing, fear-free communion (and therefore union in difference) through his unique bond with the Father. So filled is he with the spirit of God that he can recognise and acknowledge his fellow humans as God meant them to be; he can, in a sense, see them through God's eyes and offer them His promise of life.

The singularity of Jesus is not to love all humans and to let them be as they are, but in the final analysis to perceive in love which aspects of the others' otherness may remain and which otherness requires firm contradiction in order to enable an all-encompassing recognition of otherness. One can therefore characterise his freedom as the capacity to honour others' otherness without fear through constant reference to, and intimacy with, the Father. This is a perceptive respect that is capable of seeing from a perspective of love which aspects of others' otherness can be honoured without self-contradiction in the universal intention of recognition and which aspects require firm contradiction.

Yet one can also trust that even when Jesus decisively rejects the concrete realisation of others' freedom (for example with the Cleansing of the Temple, John 2:13–22) it is in order, by his very refusal, to further others' freedom. For even if one makes ill use of one's freedom, the possibility for freedom remains intact on the basis of its essential structure to realise its otherness in a way that is once more compatible with the goal of universal recognition. Hence one can interpret Jesus's contestation of the fulfilment of others' freedom as a recognition of the others' unfulfilled possibilities, just as one can understand his recognition as liberating recognition which trusts others to advance along the path he took before them.

It is therefore not possible to record gnosiologically the goal of all-encompassing love embodied in the figure of Christ by simply testing whether this man, who declares the imminent coming of the kingdom of God with an unprecedented

---

– Macht – Geschichte. Versuch einer theodizeesensiblen Rede vom Handeln Gottes in der Welt, Freiburg 2006, 362.

claim to authority, genuinely acknowledges every human being. Love does not have to mean, in a positivist sense, that the other is acknowledged and left to be exactly the way he or she is. It is as hard for me to know whether a person really is a figure of God's unconditional love towards every other human as it is for me to know whether one person loves another. Love can only be reliably recognised in love; and so the love of God in Christ can only be recognised through the Holy Spirit of love and therefore in faith.

Nevertheless, there are a series of (fallible) criteria which may allow us to recognise this profession of love as being reasonable. I can gain utter (yet still only symbolically conveyed and therefore conditional and vulnerable) love only in an act of love that is addressed to me and reciprocated by me. Thus, it is only of myself that I can say with utter certainty that I have been truly recognised by a person and loved as I ought to be. If, however, I experience this recognition as unconditional and decisive in a way that is not justified or derived from any worldly factor, then that is perhaps a starting point for me to see in this love a reality pointing to something more than humans are able to offer one another, and which I can claim not only for myself but for the community of the faithful and ultimately for the whole of humankind.[49] The Church is sustained by the experience that this loving commitment becomes tangible reality for us all in Christ.

3.4 Multiple incarnations?

Of course, any form of true love can be a reason to trust in the unconditional nature of God's love as described above. Any person can become God's Logos for another and make God's good living word tangible. It is surely wrong to see God's self-commitment as being realised exclusively in Jesus Christ, and one can join Karl Rahner in seeing every human as an event of God's self-revelation.[50] This is precisely the advantage of a form of Christology that no longer argues for the special status of Jesus Christ in terms of substance but is based instead on anthropology and relational ontology. Matthew 25:31–46 makes it clear that any unconditional encounter between two people may represent an encounter with Christ.

Yet here we should also note an important distinction. The self-identification of God with the Logos 'does not occur with the same intention of self-revelation in

---

49 For transcendental-philosophical verification of this starting point, see Stosch, *Offenbarung*, 75–80.
50 See Rahner, op. cit. 116.

every needy person that befalls me as the trace of the passing of time'.[51] It is also a typical reaction of the just in Matthew 25 that they are not conscious of their encounter with the Logos. Yet even if an encounter with the needy is not recognised *per se* as God's self-revelation, it is nevertheless in effect an encounter with God in pauper's clothing. That is why there is no cause for concern about people before Jesus or outside Christianity's sphere of influence, because they can experience God's self-commitment in every human being (and not just in the Prophet).

The basis of this phraseology is, however, the realisation through faith that Jesus of Nazareth does indeed hold God's self-commitment for every human being, and therefore other experiences of unconditional love may also be accepted by him as God's self-commitment and may also be experienced as such independently of this Christian phraseology. From a Christian perspective, nothing speaks against the fact that other modes of givenness in revelation can form the basis of similar statements. On the contrary, many contemporary Christian theologians rejoice at how vividly the Jewish religious philosopher Emmanuel Levinas explains that it is truly the call of God that I encounter in the needy. It is now widely accepted among Christians that God's commitment to humankind can be experienced in the Torah and in God's bond with Israel.

Pluralists always ask at this stage whether other humans than Jesus of Nazareth might not be God's self-commitment in the same way so that they become universal grounds for the statement that God devotes His unconditional love to every human being. It does not strike me as particularly useful at this juncture to look, as Karl-Heinz Menke and Brian Hebblethwaite do, for reasons why the Logos can only be incarnated once.[52] Claiming such incapacity on God's behalf contradicts the concept of God's omnipotence and it is not part of Church doctrine. Instead, it seems more intelligent to me to point out, as Rahner does, that no other religion claims that one man is the form and living word of the love of God for all humankind.[53] Since Jesus Christ represents God's self-commitment to all humans, it is difficult from a purely pragmatic viewpoint to see why the event of

---

51 Jürgen Werbick, 'Ist die Trinitätstheologie die kirchlich normative Gestalt einer Theologie der Selbstoffenbarung Gottes?', in Magnus Striet (ed.), *Monotheismus Israels und christlicher Trinitätsglaube* (QD 210), Freiburg 2004, 70–92, here 88.
52 See Karl-Heinz Menke, *Das unterscheidend Christliche. Beiträge zur Bestimmung seiner Einzigkeit*, Regensburg 2015, 113–66. Brian Hebblethwaite, *The Incarnation. Collected Essays in Christology*, Cambridge 1987, especially 165–6.
53 From a Muslim point of view, Muhammad did proclaim the Word of God to all humans, but he never claimed to *be* this essential word of God for us humans, nor do Muslims interpret him as being so.

the incarnation of the Logos should be repeated. Therefore, without even stating the claim of the necessary uniqueness of the incarnation, we can say that it is completely rational and even essential that Christianity insist on the singularity of God's self-love in one universal mediator of salvation. And if, as Christians, we wish to stay within the mainstream of contemporary theology and attract many Christians into a dialogue with the Qur'an with us, it cannot be a good idea to ontologically downgrade our position and claim several incarnations.

Another issue is whether God can express His living word to us other than in human form; whether there is a different mode of givenness of the Logos than as God made flesh. On this particular point, the aforementioned state of the dialogue between Judaism and Christianity means that the Church must show its willingness to entertain this possibility. Georg Essen is sceptical on this topic, as he rightly insists that the mode of givenness of the revelation must match its content. When God reveals Himself as love, He can only do so as the living word of love. And what more tangible form is there for this living word than a human who, encompassed and pervaded by the good spirit of God, becomes that word?

There is no more appropriate and more intensive means of experiencing love than in another person. God's good will can only be made tangible if it is liberating and lovingly enfolds human beings.[54] On the other hand, we know from our experience of interpersonal relationships that the love of another person can be experienced in a variety of ways, although we would not be able to rank the various forms of this self-revelation here. It is therefore conceivable that God not only reveals the fullness of his love to us in human form, but also gives us His essential word in a love poem and is thus able to spark it into love. Is it not also the case that we can be so excited by a poem written for us that the poet's love becomes real to us? Can a poem not make the absent writer present and make us see life afresh in all its beauty? It seems to me, therefore, that it is conceivable for Christian theology that the God of Jesus Christ also reveals Himself in His beauty and love through an aesthetic language event, seeking to win over humans for God and God's good will. So if Muslims see the Qur'an as a similar Word of

---

54 See Jürgen Werbick, 'Vergöttlichung Jesu? Die koranischen Jesus-Deutungen als Herausforderung zu christlich-christologischer Selbstreflexion', in Stosch / Khorchide (eds.), Streit um Jesus, 255–69, here 265: 'There is no other way for people to be won over for the occurrence of the goodwill of God than for this to happen to them in a tangible way; it must occur to them so that this happening frees them from their self-inflicted bonds by which they allow the fateful and powerful actions of bad will run their course among humankind and contribute to them. God dedicates Himself entirely to the actions of His good will in life and in the mission of Jesus Christ.'

God, which makes the beauty of God aesthetically tangible and intends to spark us into love, then from the point of view of a Christian belief in incarnation, there is no reason, in principle, to deny the possibility of this mode of givenness of God's affection. Rather, it would be good to analyse soberly whether this interpretation is applicable to the Qur'an, and whether the content of the Qur'an is compatible with the attested Christian concept of God's pledging of Himself in the man Jesus of Nazareth – which is precisely the task to which this book aims to contribute.[55] For if the Qur'an's statements about Jesus directly and comprehensively contradict the Christian belief in Jesus as Christ, then it would be hard for Christians seriously to contemplate the possibility of interpreting the Qur'an as God's address to humankind. It is therefore time to study the Qur'an's statements about Jesus of Nazareth in detail and subsequently to compare them with what we have said so far.

---

55 In the meantime, see the extremely interesting observations of Mahmoud Ayoub, *A Muslim View of Christianity. Essays on Dialogue*, edited by Irfan A. Omar, New York 2007, 111–83.

4

A Holistic Reading of Surahs 19, 3 and 5 in the Context of a Diachronic Reading of the Qur'an's Verses about Jesus

The first Qur'anic statements about Jesus were written during the middle Meccan period.[1] The verses that emerged during this early phase are not predicated on any elaborate theological image of Jesus and avoid many of the common titles by which he is referred to. We shall repeatedly link the development of our image of Jesus to elements about Mary, especially in the context of Surah Maryam (Q 19), which we shall soon examine in detail. In addition, the proclaimer of the Qur'an does not seem, at this early stage, to differentiate between Islam and the other monotheistic religions as being different religious communities.[2] Christian

---

1 We assume for the purposes of our study that the Qur'anic surahs of the Meccan period can be classified formally and typologically and can be placed in some kind of chronological order on the basis of literary-critical criteria (see Nicolai Sinai, *Fortschreibung und Auslegung. Studien zur frühen Koraninterpretation*, Wiesbaden 2009, 59–71). Nöldeke and Weil's chronology of the Qur'anic surahs has heuristically proved itself as a good basis for exegetical analysis, and we shall follow their chronology in this study. However, for Mecca we shall use the further development of the chronology of the surahs, based on Nöldeke, that Angelika Neuwirth presented in her commentary as well as its literary-critical analysis. We shall occasionally engage in additional discussion when there are tensions with the classical Muslim dating efforts, especially during the Medina period.

2 We subscribe to Fred Donner's description of the Muslim community in Mecca as a 'believers' movement' or, in more detail, as 'strongly monotheistic, intensely pietistic, and ecumenical or confessionally open religious movement that enjoined people who were not already monotheists to recognise God's oneness and enjoined all monotheists to live in strict observance of the law that God had repeatedly revealed to mankind – whether in the form of the Torah, the Gospels, or the Qur'an' (Fred Donner, *Muhammad and the Believers. At*

traditions were welcomed at first, perhaps in the hope that this might facilitate the emergence of a unified monotheistic faith community.[3]

During this phase and even later, the proclaimer of the Qur'an observes the divisions within the Jewish (Q 43:65) and Christian groups (Q 19:37; 43:58; 21:93) and between Jews and Christians in Medina (Q 2:113; 2:139f). In our historical reconstruction of the situation on the Arabian Peninsula in the seventh century, we looked in detail at how deeply Christological controversies had split Christianity at this time (see Chapter 2). We also explained that the many battles between Persia and the Eastern Roman Empire had exacerbated the conflict between Jews and Christians. We draw the reader's attention for the last time to the mutual persecutions and assassinations that occurred during the kingdom of Himyar's shift from Jewish to Christian rule, and also to the persecution of the Jews by Emperor Heraclius. All these conflicts were aggravated during the emergence of the Qur'an by the fact that Heraclius was bent on punishing the Jews for supporting the Persians in Jerusalem.

It therefore stands to reason that the proclaimer of the Qur'an wished to oppose these factions and dissensions with a united movement in which everyone believed in one God. So, in the middle Meccan period, the Qur'an invited Muhammad's audience to form a single monotheistic community that accepted Jews and Christians on principle as the bearers of divine guidance, even if human weaknesses had split these groups.[4] The late Medinan Surah 42 (*al-Shura*) exhorts those who

---

the *Origins of Islam*, Cambridge 2010, 75). However, we do not know any whether Jewish and Christian groups were also present during the Meccan period. The fact that they were first mentioned by name in Medina and played a role in theological discourse there would seem to speak against a consciously interdenominational and ecumenical movement that also counted Christians and Jews among its ranks. Neither do we believe that the 'believers' movement was an eschatological movement mobilised by a belief that the end of the world was nigh. Our final criticism of Donner, who regards Islam as emerging as an independent religious community only during the Umayyad caliphate's imperial project (ibid. 194–5), is that its character was already changing during the Medinan period and so Islam emerged as a separate religious community while Muhammad was still alive. Our main reason for assuming this is that the Qur'an became increasingly critical about Jewish and Christian theologoumena during the Medinan period. It was nevertheless still the case that as it established itself, the religious community also accepted, with specific conditions, people of different religions.

3 See discussion of a single community in Q 21:92. Angelika Neuwirth sees in this appeal for unity a reminiscence of John 17:11, which appears to stand in curious contrast to the actual Christian divisions (see Neuwirth: *Imagining Mary – Disputing Jesus*, 411).

4 This is made clear in Q 23:52–53 for example, when Christians and Jews are criticised for allowing themselves to be divided by their individual scriptures despite being a single community. This surah sets out what the characteristics of this community ought to be: fear

hear the Qur'an to respect the commandments pronounced by Noah, Abraham, Moses and Jesus (Q 42:13).[5] Muhammad, it is said, should not argue with them because ultimately all will be united (Q 42:15) – the vision of unity is obviously the inspiration for this statement. Even during the Medinan period, it is noticeable in the Qur'an that God's will is clearly at work in the divisions and pluralism of Jews and Christians, although it does not delve into what God's purpose might be (Q 2:253). And the oft-quoted passage in Q 5:48 also emphasises that from the Qur'an's perspective, the range of different beliefs is part of the divine plan of salvation.

Hence the proclaimer of the Qur'an is not concerned by the variety and differences between the religions, but interestingly – still during the Medinan period – he is actually irritated by the salvific exclusivism of Judaism and Christianity and their corresponding missionary zeal (see Q 2:111; 2:113; 2:120).[6] It is clearly the Qur'an's enduring vision to present its own faith not as exclusive but as one element of the dialogue between religions.

In the middle Meccan period, as we have outlined, the proclaimer of the Qur'an strove to position his own religious beliefs within the biblical tradition. He therefore incorporated a small number of very specific statements about Jesus and Mary into his own conception, while formulating them in a new way to forge a consensus with Jews and Christians. Underpinning this is a vision of unity willing to support plurality and reconciliation, and this becomes even more significant in the late Medinan period. During this period, however, the proclaimer of the Qur'an increasingly intervenes in Christians' Christological debates to correct errant views and proposes a new and original codification of their basic ideas. These kinds of intervention are also implicit during the Meccan period.

---

of God (23:57), belief in the signs of the Lord (23:58), rejection of idolatry (23:59) and alms and yearing for the Lord's return (23:60). All these criteria are valid for all religions. There are none of the markers of Muslim identity that are used later in the Medinan period. It is also striking that the term 'Lord' is used repeatedly, seizing upon a name for God employed by Jews and Christians alike.

5 It is not clear exactly who Muhammad's opponents are in this surah. They are probably not Jews and Christians in particular, but simply the Arabs of Mecca; there is a reference to the fact that Muhammad is proclaiming the same faith as Christians and Jews.

6 On Qur'anic criticism of exclusivism, see Mouhanad Khorchide, 'Eine Frage der Lesart. Islamische Positionen zum religiösem Pluralismus', in *Herder Korrespondenz Spezialheft* 2 (2010) 17–20, here 19. In his explanation of Q 2:113, for example, al-Tabari already mentions reports of disputes between Jews and Christians on the issue of salvific exclusivism. Abu Ja'far Muhammad b. Jarir al-Tabari, *Jami' al-bayan 'an ta'wil al-Qur'an*, edited by Abdullah b. Abd al-Muhsin al-Turkiy, vol. 2, Cairo 2001/1422, 434–6.

4.1 Jesus in the Surah Maryam

As has already been mentioned, the first surah referring specifically to Jesus of Nazareth was proclaimed during the middle Meccan period. It is Surah 19 of the Qur'an – Surah Maryam. It combines the story of the birth of Jesus with that of John the Baptist, enshrining the relationship between the two figures and their parents as one of its central themes. In both cases – and later with Abraham and his father – the surah focuses on parent-child relationships. The account of the birth of John begins with a detailed portrait of the situation of Zachariah, which forms both the start of the surah and a narrative introduction to its topic. From a theological perspective, the very first verse of the story interprets it as a reminder of God's mercy (Q 19:2), and this simultaneously sets out the main theological theme of the entire surah – God's mercy.[7] It is interesting that God's mercy should feature so prominently of all places in a surah that has parent-child relationships as its theme and also depicts the birth of Jesus in such detail. This means that the relationship of parents to their children is being implicitly appraised in terms of mercy and extrapolated from that. Furthermore, the life of Jesus is also presented in these terms and interpreted accordingly.

Jesus is not mentioned once by name in the core of the Surah Maryam.[8] It appears to be primarily about Mary, and it is no accident that it is she who lends her name to Surah 19. And yet it also carries several important messages about Jesus that are highly significant for Christianity, although they do not coalesce into a separate doctrine.

4.1.1 Zachariah and John

Zachariah appears as a pious man who is utterly devoted to God and gives himself up to God's mercy. His three-day silence is interpreted as a sign of divine mercy with the intention of encouraging him to trust in God's promise (Q 19:10). This is noteworthy insofar as this same sign is presented in Luke's account as God's

---

7 See Neuwirth, *The Qur'an and Late Antiquity*, 366–7; Angelika Neuwirth, *Der Koran. Vol. 2/1: Frühmittelmekkanische Suren. Das neue Gottesvolk: 'Biblisierung' des altarabischen Weltbildes*, Berlin 2017, 605 & 641. Neuwirth rightly and repeatedly points out that the discovery of mercy as a name for God is a special legacy of Mary in the Qur'an, and that the combination of this name of God with a female figure is no coincidence given the similarity between the word for 'mercy' (*rahma*) and the word for 'womb' (*rahim*).
8 According to Angelika Neuwirth, the core of the surah consists of the following verses: 1–33, 41–57, 59–74 (see Neuwirth, *Der Koran. Vol 2/1: Frühmittelmekkanische Suren*, 599–604).

punishment for Zachariah's lack of trust and afflicts the latter for much longer than three days (see Luke 1:20). The biblical God seems unkind and cold-hearted in comparison here, because He is so hard on the poor, pious man, who has merely and understandably asked for a clue so that he may have confidence in the angel. He does indeed receive this sign in the Bible too, but the fact that he must remain mute until the birth of his son means that he is unable to pass on this sign and the fulfilment of his wish is an ordeal. Readers of the story might be inclined to conclude that it is better not to bother God with one's uncertainty and, above all, one ought not to ask God for signs but immediately believe, however unlikely God's message might sound. For the Bible, the greatest bliss lies in believing without seeing, as the initially doubting Thomas realises at the end of the Gospel of John (see John 20:29).

In the Qur'an, on the other hand, Zachariah's muteness is merely a sign designed to encourage him to trust. The God of the Qur'an is always willing to give signs. He is not as petty and spiky as the biblical God initially appears to be. For the Qur'an, the state of the intermittently mute Zachariah, so seemingly unpleasant, is from Zachariah's internal perspective an experience of God's pure mercy. His muteness is to him a sign of joy, and it helps him to make room for God's great goodness in his life and to prepare for becoming a father. Whereas the wise old priest Zachariah is severely embarrassed in the Bible when he comes out of the temple after his temple service and is incapable of uttering a single word (see Luke 1:22), the Qur'anic Zachariah, despite the announcement to the contrary, is first allowed to speak and praise God, i.e. complete his priestly duties (Q 19:11). While the biblical Zachariah is in a sense demoted by God, in the Qur'an God treats him with leniency and forbearance. He plays no further role in the rest of the surah, but elsewhere he is mentioned as Mary's guardian (Q 3:37) and included among the ranks of the prophets (Q 6:85). There is therefore a good argument for saying that Zachariah is rehabilitated here in comparison with the biblical account. It should not be forgotten, however, that Zachariah is also rehabilitated in the Bible after his son's birth and is also given a significant song of praise to proclaim, one that has become famous within the Church (see Luke 1:68–79). The Bible does not treat him as harshly as one might initially think, therefore, but uses his muteness as an expansive introductory device to prepare the ground for the birth of Jesus.

Verses 12–15 of Surah Maryam present the mission of John the Baptist, and John is honoured at length. His parents play no further part after his birth, although the Qur'an notes that he always showed them respect. Yet the focus of the narrative shifts to the new prophet who is accorded a far higher status than in the biblical tradition. Surah Maryam tells Jesus's story in parallel with John the

Baptist's, picking up on the Bible's linking of the two. At the same time, the surah circumscribes some of the passages in Luke's Gospel that emphasise Jesus's superiority to John. John too is depicted as a very special person who is endowed even as a boy with the gifts of wisdom, compassion and integrity. His deference to his parents is also stressed and peace encompasses his whole life, from the day of his birth until his death (Q 19:12–15). One should therefore beware of exaggerating Jesus's singularity. The proclaimer of the Qur'an is clearly not interested in the perfection of Jesus distinguishing him from other prophets, but in a specificity that describes what constitutes a prophetic existence more fully. John is not described as a servant of God, though, and he is capable of speech while still an infant. Moreover, the statements about John are written in the third person whereas Jesus speaks for himself, and with Jesus peace is mentioned with the definite article, whereas the indefinite article is used for John. Lastly, there are no statements about John's symbolic role, and so, despite all the Qur'an's rehabilitation of his person, he is presented as being of lesser significance than Jesus overall.[9]

In spite of this enduring hierarchy, it is important to realise that from the very beginning the Qur'an is raising the person of Jesus too high (to quasi-divine status). It nevertheless seems questionable to us whether this necessarily represents a devaluation of Jesus of Nazareth or of the Christian faith as a whole. It is probably a case here of differences being signalled without any immediate move to institute polemical demarcations.

4.1.2 Mary and her child

Following the story of the birth of John, the Qur'an describes the story of Jesus, son of Mary.[10] The focus of the preliminary story is now no longer on the father as it was with John, but on the mother after whom Surah 19 is named. The birth story opens with a detailed description of the scene of the angel's annunciation of Jesus's birth (Q 19:16–21). The scene has a similar composition to God's dialogue

---

9 Although one may dispute this judgement regarding Surah Maryam, it will become clear from the Qur'an's subsequent statements that notwithstanding all the parallels between the two figures, the Qur'an also sees Jesus as being more important than John the Baptist.
10 Referring to Jesus as the 'son of Mary' is not necessarily a rejection of the Christian term 'Son of God'. It may well be an honorific title for Jesus; at least that is how it seems to have been used in the earlier Syriac Infancy Gospel. On this see Geoffrey Parrinder, *Jesus in the Qur'an*, 1965, 28. It is very unusual in the Christian tradition otherwise, and its interpretation strikes us as useful as a counter-discourse. In defence of this interpretation see, for example, Anja Middelbeck-Varwick, *Cum aestimatione. Konturen einer christlichen Islamtheologie*, Münster 2017, 117.

with Zachariah, but this time the initiative comes from God. Whereas Zachariah begs God for help (Q 19:3–6) and the annunciation of the birth is an answer to his request (Q 19:17), the annunciation of Jesus's birth to Mary comes about without any request on her part. While Zachariah explicitly asks for a successor and heir (*walīy*, *wārith*, see Q 19:5–6), Mary simply withdraws from human company without any further explanation.[11] Her encounter with the spirit of God in human form (Q 19:17) causes her to seek out the Lord of Mercy. This is the first time in the surah that God's title of Lord of Mercy is functionally introduced. It becomes clear through the figure of Mary that God not only sends signs of mercy but is in His very nature the Lord of Mercy, and may therefore be proclaimed to as such.

The child that is announced to Mary is not meant as a mere sign either but described as merciful himself (see Q 19:21). Thus, the theme of mercy is amplified in the context of the birth stories even before Jesus is born – a development reflected in the biblical account when one recalls the song of praise for God's mercy with which Mary responds to the angel's annunciation (see Luke 1:46–55).

For starters, Jesus is introduced by God as 'a sign for all people', having been sent to demonstrate His mercy to them (Q 19:21). And so, with this very first reference to Jesus in the Qur'an, the unique nature of his mission becomes clear: he is not simply the conveyor of signs; he is God's sign in person[12] – a fact that will become significant when we reflect on the description of Jesus as the word of God. Here, however, it is not Jesus himself speaking, but God or the angel speaking about him prior to his birth to give Mary courage. The resulting theological notion of Jesus as a sign of God remains central to Meccan discussions of Jesus

---

11 Luxenberg interprets this verse as meaning that it is allegations that she is bearing a child out of wedlock that leads Mary to withdraw to an isolated spot. However, this interpretation contradicts the chronology provided in the Arabic text at Q 19:16–17. The reason his attempted interpretation is invalid in our opinion is, as so often, the reinterpretation of an Arabic word for which Aramaic roots are claimed (see Christoph Luxenberg, *Die syro-aramäisch Lesart des Koran*, Köthen 2004, 149–50). He finds the same theme of legitimacy in Mary's confinement in Q 19:24 purely by reinterpreting the Arabic word to seek its alleged Aramaic origin – an operation that strikes us as philologically and theologically untenable. For criticism of Luxenberg, see the philologically illuminating article by Sidney Griffith, 'Syriacisms in the "Arabic Qur'an": Who were "those who said Allah is the third of three" according to al-Ma'ida 73?', in Meir M. Bar-Asher and others (eds.), *A Word Fitly Spoken. Studies in Medieval Exegesis of the Hebrew Bible and the Qur'an*, Jerusalem 2007, 83–110, especially 90–8.

12 See also the al-Tabari's Qur'an commentary on Q 19:21, *der diese Bedeutung Jesu als Zeichen Gottes unterstreicht. Abū Ǧaʿfar Muammad b. Ǧarīr al-Ṭabarī, Ǧāmiʿ al-bayān ʿan ta'wīl al-Qur'ān*, edited by Abdullah b. Abd al-Muhsin al-Turkiy, vol. 15, Cairo 2001/1422, 488–9.

and is cited several times (see Q 23:50; 21:91), although only ever with reference to Mary. At the same time, it is clear that Jesus's and Mary's roles as signs are intended not only for Israel but for all people, indeed for all worlds (Q 21:91). In the Medinan period, the word 'sign' is applied in much the same fashion as the Gospel of John speaks of Jesus's miracles (see Q 3:49f) but no longer to Jesus in person.[13] It is also used repeatedly in the Qur'anic enunciation to describe verses of the Qur'an (see, for example, Q 2:252; 3:58 and perhaps also 5:75).[14]

Calling Jesus a manifestation of God's mercy (Q 19:21) links him to the usual names for God in a total of seven surahs from the middle Meccan period.[15] This mercy is soon afterwards shown to and through Mary in surprising fashion. Jesus (or perhaps God Himself or an angel)[16] encourages her, directs her attention to a stream beneath her and shows her how to pluck some dates. Like the angel in the

---

13 We shall discuss the use of the word 'sign' in Q 5:114 later. Nevertheless, it should be noted at this stage that this term seems to have been originally adopted from the Aramaic (see Parrinder, *Jesus in the Qur'an*, 51).

14 This terminology highlights an analogy between the function of Jesus and the verses (and all other *'āyāt!*) of the Qur'an that strikes us as significant for Christian-Muslim dialogue because it gives both sides hermeneutic opportunities for mutual understanding. Just as it can be helpful for Christians to see and understand the Qur'an in analogy to Jesus, Muslims can be encouraged to understand the man Jesus as a functional equivalent of the verses of the Qur'an; both are signs from God.

15 See Neuwirth, *The Qur'an and Late Antiquity*, 290.

16 It is not very clear linguistically whether Jesus really speaks in verse 24 or if it is in fact God Himself or an angel. Given, however, that both personal suffixes in verse 22 refer to Jesus, there is a very good case for regarding Jesus as the speaker here. Since Jesus is also able to speak in verse 30 as an infant and Mary points to Jesus in verse 29 to protect her from people's allegations that she is a harlot, there is a lot of contextual evidence pointing to the fact that Jesus really is the speaker. In any case, that is the easiest explanation for Mary's surprising notion that an infant might speak in her defence. It could, of course, also be God's inspiration that gave her this idea. But in the Qur'an at least there is no report of such inspiration, and it therefore seems, applying Ockham's razor, that the aforementioned explanation is preferable. Muslims exegetes have also speculated as to who the speaker might be – Jesus or the angel. They mention two ways of reading the words *'fanādāhā min taḥtihā'* (he called her from under her [the angel]) or *'man taḥtahā'* (he called who was under her [Jesus]). For al-Qurtubi, for example, this refers to the angel Gabriel (see Abu 'Abdallah Muammad b. Amad al-Ansari al-Qurtubi, *al-Jami' li aham al-Quran*, edited by Hamid Amad al-Tahir, vol. 13, Cairo 2009, 433–4). Al-Tabari, on the other hand, first mentions several accounts saying that it is Gabriel who speaks to Mary here (see al-Tabari, *al-Jami' al-bayan*, 501f), but then names other accounts that invoke Jesus as the speaker before ultimately advocating the latter position (see ibid. 503–5). It therefore seems to us that the logical conclusion is that Jesus could already speak before his birth, even if we will limit our use of this version in our theological interpretation, since it was controversial even in the Muslim tradition and is not unequivocal from a philological point of view.

desert to the prophet Elijah (1 Kings 19:5–7), He urges her to revive her spirits by eating and drinking (see Q 19:24–26). Muslim commentaries on this passage point out that the trunk of the palm tree under which she was sitting had dried out[17] and so its newfound capacity to provide fresh fruits (Q 19:25) might prefigure Jesus's subsequent power to awake the dead, allowing him to breathe life into clay birds and resuscitate the dead (see Q 3:49 and 5:110 respectively). Taking these three scenes together, it is clear that the saving power Jesus shows in the Qur'an is extended to all God's creatures.[18]

After the annunciation of the birth, the Qur'an proceeds to portray the birth of Jesus, describing in detail Mary's contractions and the pain they cause her (Q 19:23). Interestingly, Mary's contractions are not mentioned once in the Bible or in the Christian tradition (see for example Luke 2:6f),[19] and so the idea took root within Christianity that Mary gave birth without pain. The background to this notion was that Mary was without sin and was therefore not affected by God's curse on Eve (Gen 3:16). It became an accepted convention that she was a virgin before, during and after Jesus's birth, and her virginity during the birth could be taken to mean that she gave birth without pain. Here the Qur'an rightly reminds Christians too that Mary was fully human and therefore suffered pain during childbirth.

The Qur'an goes even further. Mary not only has to suffer pain during delivery; she is under even greater threat after giving birth because the child's illegitimate conception engenders accusations and she is compared to a whore (Q 19:27f). Mary has no option but to point to Jesus so that he can now defend her (see Q 19:29), given that he has already spoken words of encouragement to Mary – according to a philologically plausible reading – while in her womb. In this, her behaviour is very similar to Mary's at the beginning of the Gospel of John, when she also points to Jesus with great confidence (see John 2:4–5). This gesture was extremely important in Oriental iconography, so we may assume that it was familiar in the milieu of the Qur'an. However, Jesus is already an adult in the relevant section of the Gospel of John and the matter at hand is not Mary's own need but the lack of wine at a wedding party. The Qur'an, on the other hand, discusses Mary's personal problems and describes how God comes to her aid. To relieve her hardship in the desert, God refreshes her with a stream and fresh fruit (Q

---

17 See al-Tabari, *al-Jami' al-bayan*, vol. 15, 510–11.
18 If one wishes to see it as such, this is a reminder of the cosmic dimension of Jesus Christ's salvific power – a point that is of lasting significance considering Western Christology's fixation on redemption from the power of sin.
19 Interestingly, the ideal of holy women being free of pain can be verified in the Talmud (see Sota 12a), which means that the Qur'an revises tradition on this fascinating subject.

19:24–25). When she is distressed and under pressure from people who refuse to believe that she was a virgin when she gave birth, God helps her by empowering the infant Jesus to speak out in her defence.

4.1.3 Jesus's self-image

Compared with John's characterisation, it is striking that Jesus himself speaks and presents himself as the servant of God, who is completely encompassed by God's blessing. Jesus is speaking here (Q 19:30–33) not only to his mother but to all people.[20] His reason for intervening is to articulate God's mercy and to intercede on his mother's behalf.[21] Contrary to a few verses earlier, there is no doubt that it is Jesus speaking here. How are we to interpret this speech by an infant?[22]

Within the Muslim exegetical tradition, the granting of this power to Jesus is often understood as symbolising that God appointed Jesus a prophet at an early age. This demonstrates that being a prophet is not a distinction that can be earned, but a choice made by God (see also Q 22:75). Yet the recipient of this choice must necessarily have certain qualities if it is to bear fruit. Hence al-Zamakhshari points to commentaries interpreting the talking baby as a sign that 'God granted Jesus prophetic status (nubuwwa) while he was still a child',[23] and that 'God had already endowed the child with absolute reason at such a young age'.[24] One ought

---

20 Muslim exegetes all agree that it is Jesus speaking here (Q 19:30–33).

21 See Karl-Josef Kuschel, *Die Bibel im Koran. Grundlagen für das interreligiöse Gespräch*, Ostfildern 2017, 557.

22 According to Parrinder, *Jesus in the Qur'an*, 78, the motif of the speaking infant Jesus only occurs at the beginning of the Arabic Infant Gospel and does not feature anywhere else in apocryphal literature. Since the most recent research has called the date of this text into question, however, it is quite possible that the Qur'an is the first text of late antiquity to include this motif about Jesus. Yet even if the motif did predate the Qur'an, one still wonders why the Qur'an picks up on it. The relevant literature often harks back to Homer, but this seems fairly bold to us, as we can see no evidence that Homer was of any relevance to seventh-century discourse on the Arabian Peninsula. In any case, no one can seriously claim that Homer was more relevant to discourse on the Arabian Peninsula than he was to that of the Roman Empire. In the light of these interesting parallels, it is all the more remarkable that it is in the Arab context that we find the first example of the infant Jesus speaking.

23 Hüseyin Ilker Çinar, 'Maria und Jesus im Islam. Darstellung anhand des Korans und der islamischen kanonischen Tradition unter Berücksichtigung der islamischen Exegeten' (*Arabisch-Islamische Welt in Tradition und Moderne*; 6), Wiesbaden 2007, 56.

24 Ibid. 77. In his exegesis of verse 30, Razi sets out in detail how one can logically and rationally support the theory that Jesus was made a prophet while still a small child; see Fakhr al-Din al-Razi, *al-Tafsir al-kabir aw mafati al-ghaib*, edited by Hani al-Haj, vol. 21, Cairo 2002, 213–14.

nevertheless to consider that the ability described by the Arab word *'aql* is located in the heart, and so Jesus's gift of reason should not be taken to mean that he had a super-brain or a supernatural intellectual power. Here, though, it can only imply a capacity for emotional insight, which the Qur'an obviously believes that a child can have – a remarkable sign of trust from the Qur'an, which invites us to take a fresh look at the capacities and talents of infants and children.

So Jesus's prophetic status is immediately accompanied by an omen distinguishing him from other prophets. This omen is bestowed on him in the cradle and must therefore include characteristics that can be attributed to a human being from birth. This ties in neatly with the Sufi tradition which declares Jesus to be 'the only one of all the prophets [...] the incarnation of [...] love',[25] and regards him as the 'epiphany of divine beauty'.[26] Jesus thus emerges as God's image, making God's love and mercy tangible for humans. We should therefore probably interpret his speech as an infant in metaphorical terms as relating to the eschatological irruption of the beauty of God into people's lives – which is what parents actually experience on their first encounter with their children.

Rather than spending any more time on general considerations of why the Qur'an gives the infant Jesus a voice, we shall now turn to the content of Jesus's self-image. This begins with Jesus referring to himself as a servant of God (Q 19:30).[27] Both Christian and Muslim exegesis long considered the description of Jesus as a servant of God to be a dilution of his singularity.[28] What this view overlooks is that the phrase used so prominently by Jesus here picks up on one of the oldest early Christian creedal statements.[29] It quotes the central title of Ebed (in Arabic: *'abd*) JHWH from Isa. 52:13–53:12 and the other servant songs, and is already in evidence in the Epistle to the Philippians (Phil 2:5–11). Jesus's self-description here is remarkable because modern exegesis accepts that the historical

---

25 Navid Kermani, *Wonder Beyond Belief: On Christianity*, tr. Tony Crawford, London 2017, 44.

26 Ibid. 91.

27 The statement that Jesus is the servant of God remains important in later elucidations of Christology in the middle Meccan period (Q 43:59; 21:26). The naming of Jesus as the servant of God is still found in Medinan Christology, but it is mentioned only one more time, in a context that we will come to examine later (see Q 4:172).

28 In the Muslim tradition, we refer to the commentaries of al-Razi, al-Qurtubi and Ibn Kathir which interpret Jesus's description of himself as the servant of God as an anti-Christian apologetics against the claim that Jesus should be regarded as the Son of God. See for example al- Razi, *al-Tafsir al-kabir*, vol. 21, 210; al-Qurtubi, *al-Jami' li ahkam al-Qur'an*, vol. 13, 446; Abu l-Fida' Isma'il Ibn Kathir al-Qurashi al-Dimashqi, *Tafsir al-Qur'an al-'azim*, edited by Muhammad Bayyumi, vol. 5, Cairo 2008, 192ff.

29 See Schedl, *Muhammad and Jesus*, 565; Parrinder, *Jesus in the Qur'an*, 36.

Jesus used these same servant songs to interpret his destiny,[30] and so this self-assessment can be easily put in its historical context and to any theologically well-versed reader, Jesus's words constitute a striking statement about his destiny. No other Qur'anic figure presents themselves in such terms, although God does often speak of His servants and many humans are designated His servants. However, this is a unique occurrence of someone describing himself as God's servant. Here we have an example of a Christological title being appropriated and put in a new context, probably for overtly critical purposes.[31]

What is noteworthy is that neither here nor at any other point in the Qur'an is there any mention of the obvious idea, derived from Second Isaiah, that this title is associated with Jesus's atonement for humankind's sins. Overall, the Qur'an provides no material to support the emerging association with the death of Jesus. This is obviously a significant gap in the Qur'an, which often indicates new theological priorities by what it omits. Just as it completely avoids the image of Christ suffering on the cross, of significant importance for the Gospels,[32] so the Qur'an rejects any representation of the salvific power of ritual sacrifice.[33] The title of 'servant of God' is thus re-appropriated and re-embedded in its wider biblical context (see Gen. 34:5 and Josh. 1:13 in relation to Moses; Job 1:8 in relation to Job; Ps. 113:1 and Ezra 5:11 in relation to Israel, to name but a few). Nevertheless, its pointed use with regard to Jesus places a peculiar emphasis on his person, raising Christological implications.

After Jesus's description of himself as the servant of God, his self-presentation continues with the statement that God has gifted him the scriptures or teaching. The Arab word employed here is '*kitāb*', which is used in the Qur'an not merely in the sense of 'scripture' but also to signify 'teaching', rendering the statement more open to interpretation than is generally acknowledged. The Muslim tradition normally interprets this passage as meaning that Jesus, as other messengers before him, was given a scripture – the equivalent of a book. Yet '*kitāb*', as Tabataba'i

---

30 See Helmut Merklein, 'Studien zu Jesus und Paulus II' (*Wissenschaftliche Untersuchungen zum Neuen Testament*; 105), Tübingen 1998, 188.

31 Comparing Jesus's self-conception with his self-image in the Arab Infancy Gospel, it is also possible to conclude that the Qur'an is consciously correcting what it regards as an erroneous form of Christology. Since it is not known exactly when this Infancy Gospel was written, the converse might equally be true: that the Gospel is distancing itself from the Qur'an. However that may be, it is virtually impossible, given the state of contemporary sources, to reconstruct whether the Qur'an is already striking a polemical pose towards Christianity in its Meccan surahs.

32 See Neuwirth, *The Qur'an and Late Antiquity*, 343.

33 Ibid. 341–2 with a reference to Q 22:36–37.

makes clear in his exegesis,[34] does not necessarily mean a book; the statement
may also refer to the teaching of Jesus, and could therefore simply mean that God
entrusted His message to Jesus.[35] Jesus would then be the one who is familiar with
the will of God and lives his life according to it. One might perhaps even go so far
as to see Jesus himself as God's message.[36] It is not clear what exactly we are supposed to make of this passage, because the Qur'an has not yet developed a more
precise Jesuology at this stage of its proclamation and simply categorises Jesus
roughly as a prophet. It is nonetheless striking at first sight that Jesus is described
in Q 19 as a prophet, whereas previously – from a diachronic perspective – he
had only been talked about as a messenger, a warner and a servant of God (see Q
19:30). We shall explore this striking observation in more detail in Chapter 5 when
we turn to Qur'anic prophetology.

What is important to the proclaimer of the Quran at this juncture is to embed
Jesus's prophetic mission in anthropological terms. Jesus is presented as someone
who from the very beginning does everything a pious and exemplary human being
does: he is blessed[37] – in everything he does;[38] he prays, he gives alms,[39] honours
his mother, is not domineering (Q 19:31–32),[40] and peace is with him throughout
his life, from the day he was born until the day he dies (Q 19:33).[41] It is precisely
this perspective spanning Jesus's entire life that reinforces the impression that the

---

34 In his exegesis, Tabataba'i cites two verses in which he understands *kitāb* to mean
'teaching' (or *revelation*, *Sharia* and *lifestyle*). On Q 42:17 see Seyyed Muhammad Hussein
Tabataba'i, *Tafsir al-mizan*, vol. 18, Tehran 1987, 59, and on Q 57:25 ibid. vol. 19, 353.
35 Equally, the gospel given to Jesus in Q 57:27 and Q 5:46 may be the gospel as lived and
taught.
36 This is reflected in the thinking of Hajj Muhammad Legenhausen, 'Jesus as Kalimat
Allah, the Word of God', in Mohammad Ali Shomali (ed.), *Word of God*, London 2009,
129–56.
37 According to al-Tabari, this can mean 'that Jesus's blessing consists of encouraging good
and preventing evil' (Çinar, *Maria und Jesus im Islam*, 54), indeed that Jesus is by God's
blessing the teacher of good (*mu'allim al-khair*).
38 Or: wherever he was (*wa-ja'alanī nabiyya[n]*) (Q 19:30).
39 It is not quite clear whether *zakāt* can really be translated here as 'alms', as it is later in
the Medinan verses. In terms of its root, it can also be understood as '(inner) purification'.
This observation does not however, to our minds, change the fact that Jesus is being
presented as exemplary here.
40 At any rate, Jesus is given all of these things as his mission and nothing in the Qur'an
plausibly suggests that Jesus did not fulfil this mission.
41 It is noteworthy that in verse 33 the Qur'an mentions both the day Jesus dies and the day
he is raised to life again. It therefore straightforwardly assumes that these two events of such
significance for Christianity actually happened. On the discussion as to whether Jesus really
died on the cross, see Klaus von Stosch, 'Jesus im Koran. Ansatzpunkte und Stolpersteine
einer koranischen Christologie', in Stosch / Muna Tatari (eds.), *Handeln Gottes – Antwort*

Qur'an is concerned less with a specific phase of his life or message, only with his life and teachings as a whole.

4.1.4 An anti-Christological intervention in Q 19:34–40?

It appears that the peaceful and unpolemical view of Jesus and Mary expressed in the core verses of Surah Maryam soon required clarifications to be made to the pagan Arabs[42] that the Qur'an did not consider it legitimate to view Jesus as the Son of God or to assume that God could have children. This is clearly the goal of the insert in Surah Maryam directly after Jesus's aforementioned self-description (Q 19:34–40 and then 88–94). This insert, which must also have been introduced during the middle Meccan period, appears in the context of Surah al-Zukhruf (43), another surah dating from the middle Meccan period, to have modified Surah Maryam.[43] However, Surah al-Zukhruf can scarcely have been addressed to Christians, because no one but pagan Arabs worshipped the daughters of God (see Q

---

des Menschen (Beiträge zur Komparativen Theologie; 11), Paderborn 2014, 109–33, here 127–32, as well as our remarks below.

42 The historical context provided in Chapter 2 should have made it clear that Christianity was widespread on the Arabian Peninsula by the seventh century, and that one can assume that the Arabs in Mecca were also influenced by Christian (and Jewish) ideas. They must also have been versed in the Bible, and therefore the appeal to biblical figures is not yet, in our opinion, a sufficient clue that it is Jews and Christians who are being addressed; it merely shows how deeply rooted biblical discourse was on the Arabian Peninsula in late antiquity. By referring to the Arabs as pagans, we are seeking to emphasise that they seem to have incorporated the Christian stimuli from their environment into their own polytheistic milieu, which is why they could easily add Jesus to the daughters of God as part of their polytheistic belief system.

43 On the formal reasons for this thesis, see Neuwirth, Imagining Mary – Disputing Jesus, 401; Neuwirth, Der Koran Vol. 2/1 Frühmittelmekkanische Suren, 600, 619–21. More specifically, Angelika Neuwirth assumes in her reconstruction that Surahs 19 and 43 each influenced the revisions made to the other. According to this analysis, the insertion in Surah 19 was triggered by Surah 43. There, it is Muhammad's people who ask him to what extent Jesus is not another godhead (verse 57f). This accusation and Jesus's explanation (verses 62–65) have a clear situative context in Surah 43, which is why this section is an integral part of the surah. However, the insertion in Surah 19 is abrupt, and there has until now not been no explicit speculation about the nature and essence of Jesus. It is therefore more likely on the basis of the discussion and pagan questioning in Surah 43 that Surah 19 was also revised again (see Neuwirth, The Qur'an and Late Antiquity, 300–5). On the subject of the separateness of our insertion in Q 43, the same results as those of Neuwirth can be found in Frank van der Velden, 'Die Felsendominschrift als Ende einer christologischen Konvergenztextökumene', in Oriens Christianus. Hefte für die Kunde des christlichen Orients 95 (2011) 213–46, here 234–5.

43:16),[44] and also Christians are not generally known to make angels female (see Q 43:19).[45] One can therefore assume that these other mid-Meccan texts – presumably prompted by the misunderstandings of pagan Arabs rather than, as yet, by the dispute with Christians or Jews – are refining their statements regarding Jesus.

The pagan Arabs seem to have understood the statements as signalling that the Jesus of Q 43 could be viewed as the biological son of God. Jesus would in that case be the *walad* of God, something that Q 19:35 categorically dismisses. This rejection is probably not aimed at Christians[46] because no Christian would ever describe Jesus as the *walad* of God.[47] Arab Christians are instead to regard him as the *ibn* of God, as people must have known at the time the Qur'an was written.[48] Q 19:88 (and also 43:81) are therefore, as al-Razi mentions in his Qur'an commentary,[49] not levelled at Christians but at pagan Arabs who believe that God had a *walad*.[50]

---

44 Muslim exegetes also see the pagan Arabs as the target audience of this criticism (see, for example, al-Tabari's Qur'an commentary on Q 43:16: al-Tabari, *al-Jami' al-bayan*, vol. 20, 560–2.

45 The question of whether God can have daughters is not a secondary question but the main theme of Surah 43, proving that the dispute being playing out here is definitely for the benefit of pagans. See Q 43:15–22 and the related elucidations in Neuwirth, *Imagining Mary – Disputing Jesus*, 405.

46 Traditional Muslim exegesis has famously applied this criticism to Christians. However, it fails to distinguish between the words *walad* and *ibn*, and so we subscribe to Neuwirth and Ayoub's exegesis, which we shall now examine in more detail.

47 Van der Velden, *Die Felsendominschrift*, 233, sees Q 19:35 as a clear hardening of the position of Q 17:111, which we shall discuss next, because it uses the phrase *min waladin* instead of *waladan*, and so God has nothing resembling a son. Even if van der Velden is correct that the Qur'an opts for a harsher formulation here than in Q 17:111, his observation does not alter the fact that both Qur'anic passages were probably addressed to pagan Arabs, as we shall see. This is not to dispute the fact that Q 19:35 was interpreted in anti-Christian fashion very shortly after the emergence of the Qur'an and may well have been used in this sense in the inscription on the Dome of the Rock.

48 See Ayoub, *A Muslim View of Christianity*, 125. *Walad* means offspring, without any defined gender. That is also why Syriac Christians talk of Jesus as the *ibn* of God. Sidney Griffith, to whom we are grateful for this tip, also points out that Q 6:101 makes it clear that the Qur'an associates the idea of a *walad* with the pagan notion that God had a spouse, and that is obviously unacceptable to Christians (see Griffith, *The Melkites and the Muslims*, 419). Q 72:3 points in the same direction.

49 See al-Razi's commentary on Q 19:88, al-Razi, *al-Tafsir al-kabir*, vol. 21, 254–5.

50 Incidentally, this use of language persists throughout the rest of the Qur'an. Each time he talks of God's *walad*, it would seem that the proclaimer of the Qur'an has pagan Arabs in his sights (see Q 2:116; 6:101; 10:68; 17:111; 18:4; 21:26; 23:91; 25:2; 39:4; 43:81; 72:3). The sole exception may be the statement in Q 4:171, and we shall therefore study that particular case in more detail below. Conversely, this observation does not imply that Christians are

It cannot of course be completely ruled out that the Qur'an's attacks on poly-theists is also implicitly directed at Christians. After all, mention of a *walad* of God might be a dramatic polemical escalation, designed to demonstrate to Christians the foolhardiness of their beliefs. Yet such a rhetorical flourish would surely be more effective if it were to employ Christian terminology rather than vocabulary that Christianity consciously avoids. We think that it is more likely here that the Qur'an is criticising pagan Meccans who have included Jesus in their pantheon of gods while still insisting that their own goddesses are superior to him.[51]

One obvious non-Christian context springs to mind when the proclaimer of the Qur'an protests in other surahs of the middle Meccan period at the idea that God might have children.[52] Q 17:111, for example, fears that talk of a child of God would mean that God had to share His power and 'is not so weak as to need a pro-tector'. But the Christian idea of God's self-revelation is intended to exclude any notion that God acts out of necessity or loses power through incarnation,[53] and so the mid-Meccan surahs are primarily to be read as a critique of pagan theories[54] – if, that is, we do not wish to accuse the Christians of the time of being completely

---

always meant when there is talk of God's children as *ibn* or *abnā'* (for a counter-example of a statement from the late Meccan period that is clearly tailored to pagan Arabs, see Q 37:149; for the reasoning as to why only pagan Arabs can be meant here, see Neuwirth, *Der Koran. Vol. 2/1: Frühmittelkoranische Suren*, 201–2).

51 See Neuwirth, *Imagining Mary – Disputing Jesus*, 406, regarding Q 43:57–59. By means of linguistic and stylistic arguments, Neuwirth tries to show that Q 43:57–65 served as a template for the polemical insertion in Q 19:34–40, proving the anti-pagan purpose of this insertion too from her point of view (see ibid. 407–8). Nevertheless, she also thinks that one cannot rule out the interpretation that this is implicit criticism of monophysite forms of Christology.

52 Q 21:30 reads in any case as if God were addressing polytheists. The long passage about Abraham in the same surah is also critical of idols. Q 21:34–35 alone criticises an idea that might be attributed to Christians and polytheists alike. On the other hand, it is clearly polytheists who are criticised in Q 17:40 for imputing children to God. They are also described here as people who do not believe in the afterlife (Q 17:45). Interestingly, it is in this context that God says that He has conferred special distinction on some prophets (Q 17:55). In any case, the surah's addressees are consistently pagan Arabs who do not believe in life after death.

53 See Klaus von Stosch, *Einführung in die Systematische Theologie*, Paderborn 2014, 49–51.

54 This opinion is also mirrored in many classical commentaries. Al-Razi, for instance, assumes for his exegesis of Q 19:88 that this passage is based on a discussion with Arabs who worship the daughters of God as angels (see al-Razi, *al-Tafsir al-kabir*, vol. 21, 254–5). And in his exegesis of Q 17:111 / Q 43:81, he also seems to assume that the interlocutors in the relevant surahs are pagan.

ignorant of Christianity. In the late Meccan Surah Yunus, too, the proclaimer of
the Qur'an is obviously taking on polytheists when he explains how powerless
their idols are next to God (Q 10:34f). Thus the child of God referenced in Q 10:68
should not be understood in the Christian sense either.

Let us now take a further, closer look at the apparent anti-Christian insert
in Surah Maryam. After the remark that God cannot have a child (Q 19:35),
Q 19:36 follows Q 43:64 in declaring that God is the Lord of Jesus and of all
people, i.e. it rejects the notion of Jesus's divinity. This is presumably aimed at
a mythological interpretation of Jesus, which regards Jesus as a *walad* of God or
deifies him in some way. For Q 19:35 clearly emphasises God's omnipotence by
saying that God can call life into being through His word alone – a thought that
is profoundly embedded in the monotheistic tradition, and which no Christian
would contradict.

It is therefore likely that the aim here is to pull the rug from under any pagan
appropriation of the Qur'anic statements about Jesus in Surah Maryam. Yet we
cannot fully exclude that there is an anti-Christian agenda behind this insertion.
When it says that God can do anything He wishes and therefore makes possible
everything that Jesus does (Q 19:35), then this is equally true for Christians. Yet
a monotheletist Christology can obscure this truth because the mortal Jesus can
have no will dedicated to God and this might give rise to the impression that
Jesus can unfurl his power without reference to the Father. The argument that this
is aimed at Christian groups is supported by the fact that the proclaimer of the
Qur'an turns his back on the disputes that have obviously arisen around Jesus (Q
19:34–37). Instead of getting caught up in Christological debates, the proclaimer
of the Qur'an appeals to his listeners to take his own theocentric and eschatological focus seriously and to make them the centre of their own faith. The birth
stories give way directly to a passionate eschatological message (Q 19:37–40)
which adopts a core idea of Jesus's redemptive optimism. It says in the Qur'an
that the 'matter will be decided' and we are presented as the heirs to the earth (Q
19:39–40). This is reminiscent of the optimism of the historical Jesus that Satan's
powers have been defeated and that the kingdom of God has come and is irrevers-
ible (see Jesus's vision of the fall of Satan in Luke 10:18).

In view of the eschatological certainty of the matter, the proclaimer of the
Qur'an appeals for faith (Q 19:37–40). It takes until Q 19:88–92 for him to repeat
how terrible it is to suggest that God has a child. And Q 19:93–95 stresses that
all people will come one by one on the day of Resurrection and therefore God
alone can sit in judgement, not Jesus. However, Jesus is a clear sign of the hour
of judgement – 'This gives knowledge of the Hour: do not doubt it. Follow me

for this is the right path' (Q 43:61) – which would appear to recognise a special eschatological role for Jesus in the Qur'an.[55]

While the interventions in Surah Maryam can be interpreted in a number of different ways, Surah al-Zukhruf should be taken as a more serious attack on Christians. Like Surah Maryam, this surah does not aim its criticism solely at the adoration of Jesus. Q 43:59, for instance, stresses that Jesus is 'an example for the children of Israel'. This is justified later when the surah notes that Jesus has received 'clear signs' (Q 43:63) regarding Israel and can therefore demands that people obey him (Q 43:63). This command is primarily addressed to the children of Israel, however, and so this passage can also be seen as an attempt by the proclaimer of the Qur'an to invite the Jews to recognise Jesus's singularity, bringing an end to the terrible squabbling between Jews and Christians and laying the foundations for fraternal bonds between the communities of the one God (see the introduction of this chapter).

The role of the Holy Spirit in Jesus's birth is only alluded to, not highlighted, in the surahs of the middle Meccan period. When it is said that God breathes His spirit into Mary (Q 21:91), then this is in complete accordance with the breath of God's spirit creating the first human being.[56]

The middle Meccan period contains many positive statements about Jesus that are remarkable to Christian ears as well, even if the main title of Jesus and attributions to him are still absent. Jesus is introduced as a sign from God expressing God's mercy.[57] In addition, Jesus appears as the servant of God and an exemplary person, as the one who has been apprised of God's will and owes his life to Him and is therefore a prophet, meaning that it is possible that the scripture that was given to him is present in his teaching. Jesus provides clear signs and calls for obedience, yet subordinates himself radically to God and refuses any attempts to

---

55 However, the grammatical reference is not clear here. It is possible that it is not Jesus who is designated, but that the verse itself is the sign of the Hour. Nevertheless, the aforementioned idea also corresponds to popular beliefs and various accounts, all of which regard Jesus as a recurring figure of the end of days. That is why Angelika Neuwirth chooses in her as yet unpublished commentary on Surah 43 to relate this verse to the parousia of Jesus, and writes that he represents the apocalyptic folklore of his time.

56 See, for example, the mid-Meccan verses 15:29 and 38:72, along with the late-Meccan Q 32:9. What is striking is that the same term 'breathing in' is used in the context of the bird miracle (see Q 3:49; 5:110), and so Jesus here takes on a god-like role and one can understand how he was regarded as the spirit of God in the Medinan period.

57 It even seems to us that the infant Jesus is, in a sense, an incarnation of God's mercy. At the very least, we are surprised that an infant speaks and therefore see the infant's very existence and his charisma as the reason people are convinced.

deify him. A Christian source could have said exactly the same things about Jesus, and this would also raise several interesting points for a modern reconstruction of Christological thought.

At the same time, the proclaimer of the Qur'an is remarkably disinterested in looking beyond Jesus's noticeable singularity to contemplate his nature. It is obviously all too clear to him that this matter could very easily cause disputes, which is why he chooses not to speculate. Accordingly, the proclaimer of the Qur'an begins in the middle of the Meccan period to reject Christological exaggerations, preparing the way for him to gradually incorporate his statement about Jesus into his own prophetology (see Chapter 5). We shall see in the next section that the first signs of this are already evident in Surah Maryam.

4.1.5 Further themes in Surah Maryam

Verses 41–58 verify the good tidings of God's mercy previously announced in the birth stories. Isaac and Jacob had already been granted God's mercy (Q 19:50). Moses too was shown God's mercy, although this actually concerned his brother Aaron (Q 19:53). This makes it clear that mercy is understood first and foremost in the Qur'an as a social relationship and is revealed in this context. There is also mention of Ishmael, who earns God's goodwill (Q 19:55), and Idris, who is raised up by God (Q 19:57). It becomes apparent that the affection God shows to John and Jesus, He has demonstrated to humankind for generations. The first on the list is Abraham, whose family conflict is depicted, projecting the theme of parent-child relationships onto the past. Abraham's rift with his father, which was recorded in earlier rabbinic accounts, offers an informative contrast to Jesus's relationship with his mother. Whereas Jesus can defend his mother because she is just, Abraham has to attack his father for worshipping idols (Q 19:41–48). For Abraham too, God is the Lord of Mercy and named as such. But God is also a demanding God who will not tolerate that Abraham's father is Satan's companion. Abraham therefore intervenes on his father's behalf and begs for forgiveness. But Abraham's father threatens to stone Abraham. Whereas Mary has complete trust in her son, Abraham's father – who is still nameless at this point – turns against the prophets.[58] God's reaction is not described here (see Q 9:113f, though) because the sole focus of this passage of the surah is on the prophets. However, Abraham's behaviour embodies the fourth commandment of the Decalogue. He continues to intervene on his father's behalf and shows him deference even when the latter

---

58 His name is given as *Azar* in Q 6:74.

turns against him and away from the faith. This explains why both John (verse 14) and Jesus (verse 32) were said to be full of reverence for their parents.

Incidentally, this passage marks the starting point of a Qur'anic prophetology because, alongside general statements, it also discusses each individual prophet's specific characteristics. While Abraham is portrayed as the great intercessor for his people (as he is in the Bible), the proclaimer of the Qur'an emphasises the noble reputation of Isaac and Jacob (Q 19:50). The most visible hallmark of Moses's prophetic status is the private communion to which God summoned him to the mountaintop (Q 19:52). Ishmael 'commanded his household to pray and give alms' (Q 19:55) and is therefore honoured as a man of faith who will later become the ancestor of the Muslims. Finally, Idris is presented as a man who is raised to a high position, which is why the Muslim tradition assumed at an early stage that this is a description of Enoch's ascension.[59] Although these verses do not yet represent an elaborate prophetology, these examples do show that each prophet has a special vocation, mission and charisma that distinguish them from other prophets. At the same time, they are all included in a lineage and their profound similarities are summarised in a formula (Q 19:58) – a similarity based on the fact that they have all received proof of God's mercy or choosing, mirrored by the fact that they all respond to the Lord of Mercy with prostration, prayer and profound emotion. It is the same devotion to the merciful God that was already noticeable in Jesus's idea of himself as the servant of God. It thus becomes clear that the special qualities of Jesus described in the Qur'an do not mark Jesus out from the prophetic line but qualify him for it, in the same way that each of the other prophets qualifies and is accepted due to certain individual characteristics.

Further eschatological embedding of prophetology in the form of a divine sermon (Q 19:58–73) that features an interesting insertion about the descent of the angels (64f) is followed by another editorial insertion designed, like verses 34–40, to define the surah's theological message in more detail (Q 19:74–98). Like the entire final section of the surah, it considers how humans accept or reject God's guidance. The most notable aspect for our own discussion is the exclusion of those who believe that the Lord of Mercy accepted a son (Q 19:88–92). To counter this belief, it is stressed that all people come before God as servants (Q 19:93) and are judged by God (Q 19:95). This judgement will demonstrate God's love for those who believe and do righteous deeds (Q 19:96). The fact that no specifically Muslim markers of identity are used in this passage, as they were for Ishmael, clarifies that this surah proclaims God's mercy for all people who believe in Him

---

59 See Yoram Erder, 'Idris', in *Encyclopaedia of the Qur'an* 2 (2002) 284–6, here 484.

and live out this belief. Jews and Christians are thus included, via their prophets, in the surah's hopeful promise.

At the same time, it is emphasised that the Qur'an bears good tidings for all God-fearing people of its time, for God's mercy is now expressed to them in their own language. God is warning a stubborn people (Q 19:97). The first and permanently elected people should understand that they will only remain chosen if they dedicate themselves to God and trust in His mercy; if they do not, soon not even a whisper will be heard from them (Q 19:98). The choosing of the Muslims is therefore not to be seen as the replacement of the Jews as the people of the covenant, but rather as a sign from God that He is capable of bringing ever more people to Him. God wishes only to demonstrate His good will not only to humans but to the world as a whole, but His willingness to cooperate and His mercy can be no substitute for humans' joyful acceptance of His actions, and so God is free to seek out new partners if people close their hearts to Him.

Surah Maryam's overwhelmingly joyous and encouraging message is echoed by the manner of its recitation, which is bright, genial and buoyant, inviting all people with heart and reason to be moved by God's mercy. The welcoming character and friendly tone of the surah towards Christians is reflected in the fact that it has – as has already been mentioned – been dated to the Meccan period by the Islamic exegetical tradition. According to Muslim exegesis, it was given to the Muslims in the year 615 before their first Hijrah on the road to Abyssinia where they sought refuge from its Christian king. Accounts report that this king, the Negus, was also greatly enthused by Surah Maryam,[60] and so Christians to this day should feel free to read this surah as also being addressed to them, and hear God's voice speaking through it.

4.1.6 Prophetological consolidation in the late Meccan and early Medinan periods

The verses of the Qur'an from the late Meccan and early Medinan periods contain their own prophetology, which incorporates Jesus into the line of the prophets (Q 6:83–88) and qualifies his role while also painting a sharper picture of his singularity. The Qur'an repeatedly stresses, with the aim of relativising his impact, that we should not make any distinctions between the prophets (Q 2:136; 3:84).[61] On

---

60 See Alfred Guillaume, *The Life of Muhammad, A translation of Ibn Isḥāq's Sīrat rasūl Allāh*, Karachi 1967, 152.
61 It does, however, depend on one's reading here, insofar as the only thing that this can

the other hand, two special characteristics of Jesus are proclaimed at the very start of the Medinan verses: God gave him 'clear signs' and 'strengthened him with the Holy Spirit' (Q 2:87; 2:253). It is explicitly stated that this specificity justifies Jesus's elevated rank (Q 2:253) and place in Qur'anic prophetology. Evidence within the text of the Qur'an also makes it clear that Jesus's strengthening with *rūḥ al-qudus*, the Holy Spirit, is a statement about his singularity, repeated once later (Q 5:110), and the Qur'an makes no other mention of a person being fortified with the Holy Spirit.[62]

Jesus's second characteristic named in Q 2:253 is the assurance that he received a communication or a message that precludes any doubt – the *bayyina*, meaning something clear, well reasoned and obvious. In the Muslim tradition, these *bayyina* are generally understood as Jesus's miracles. The clear signs cannot, however, be classified as a specificity of Jesus per se, because they were also applicable to other prophets such as Moses (see, for example, Q 3:184; 5:32; 9:70; 14:9; 40:22). They are also more of a general hallmark of any prophet in the Qur'an, because they provide clarity by testifying to God's word and making it intelligible to humankind,

---

mean is that no ontological value distinctions may be made about the messengers, even though the prophets are indeed distinct in their various gifts and tasks, and God does in fact explain this. According to this interpretation, humans are not allowed to make distinctions according to their own rules of interpretation, but it remains legitimate to appraise the divine clues in a prophetology that defines the specific qualities of each prophet. If one considers the closer context in the second surah, for instance, it becomes clear that the reasoning behind the criticism of hierarchical prophetologies is that Jews and Christians use them to outdo one another. The aim of the proclaimer of the Qur'an is therefore to head off such claims to superiority rather than rule out different perceptions of the prophets.

62 According to the fourth interpretation given by al-Razi, *ar-rūḥ* is what was breathed into Jesus and *qudus* is God himself (Çinar, *Maria und Jesus im Islam*, 124). The interpretation al-Razi comments on is therefore an example that the Islamic tradition does not categorically identify the Holy Spirit with the archangel Gabriel, but is extremely alive to the fact that here we are dealing with the breath and spirit of God Himself, which first enables the virgin conception of Jesus, even if al-Razi ultimately prefers the interpretation that the Holy Spirit should be equated with Gabriel. Al-Zamakhshari demonstrates that prominent exegetes from the Islamic tradition can come to different conclusions. In his commentary on Q 2:87 – the first mention of the Holy Spirit, if one reads the Qur'an in the order of the surahs – he mentions the interpretation of the Holy Spirit as a divine holy spirit without citing the angel Gabriel once. Al-Zamakhshari thereby comes out clearly against the tradition of the angel. In his commentary on Q 5:110, he interprets the Holy Spirit with the holy/pure words of Jesus, but then mentions in passing: 'and it is said that this refers to the angel Gabriel', although he appears not to favour this orthodox opinion. See Mahmud Ibn 'Umar al-Zamakhshari, *al-Kashshaf 'an Haqa'iq al-tanzil wa-'uyun al-aqawil fi wujuh al-ta'wil*, edited by Ahmad b. Muhammad b. al-Munaiyir, vol. 1, Cairo 2012, 172–4, 705–7.

as if they were giving a clear speech.[63] Yet the Qur'an mentions again and again that the effect of these clear signs is not always as successful as one would expect. They were repeatedly met with disbelief and suspicion, provoking allegations that these miracles might actually be magic (see Q 61:6; 5:110). Perhaps the Holy Spirit was responsible for the clarity of the signs given to Jesus, and so their persuasive power and the clarity of their message (see this same word root in Q 55:4) could only unfold if they were viewed with the help of the spirit,[64] or if the spirit prevented people from hiding the full and obvious truth. For Jesus too, the clarity of the signs would be promoted by his strengthening through the Holy Spirit. This would lend the miracles and the signs themselves a different quality than those of the Old Testament prophets, because here and now they would be evidence of a special, spirit-induced affinity with God and of His authorisation.

Such thoughts remain speculative, however, especially as a diachronic reconstruction shows that the proclaimer of the Qur'an only began to nuance his declarations about Jesus later. It is the second great surah about Jesus, Al 'Imran, that provides these nuances. This observation dovetails nicely with the historical analysis above, which suggests that Medina was far more influenced by Christian groupings than Mecca was. Accordingly, the second surah, al-Baqara, repeatedly addresses Christian groupings directly. Yet the dispute with the Jews and with pagan Arabs continues to play an important role, and therefore the criticism – for example, suggestions that God accepted a *walad* – is easier to understand as referring to pagan Arabs and not yet to Christians.[65] Indeed, Christianity only crops up again as a major theme in the third surah, Al 'Imran.

---

63 See the reference to communication in Q 55:4, which can also be traced back to the same root as bayyina, namely *bāna*.

64 This would fit well with the bread of life sermon in the Gospel of John. In John 6:30 too, it is a matter of the disciples asking for (clear) signs, whose presentation by Jesus they then fail to grasp (John 6:35–36). The author of John's Gospel tries to point out that the gift of the 'bread of life' can only be comprehended with the help of the Spirit (John 6:63). This is precisely what distinguishes Jesus from the Old Testament prophets, who are seriously downgraded in chapter 5 of John's Gospel when their acts are compared with Jesus's (see John 6:49).

65 According to this reconstruction, Q 2:116 would therefore be directed at pagan Arabs. Q 2 contains a lengthy section addressing Jews in particular but also Christians, people of the scripture, believers, etc. The blocs with clearly identified addressees contain passages in which the *mushrikūn* (verse 96) are also addressed. In verse 105 they are named along with a group of People of the Book. The statement in verses 116–117 is not ascribed to any particular group by name (otherwise the statements in Q 2 are clearly addressed to the respective group), but the statement itself allows us to identify 116–117 as being aimed at the pagans.

4.2 Surah Al 'Imran

Jesus was incorporated in his own right into Muslim prophetology back in the pre-
and early Medinan periods, but it was obviously some time before he next appears
as a central theme of the Qur'an. He does so in a surprising fashion in Surah Al
'Imran (Q 3), on which Angelika Neuwirth has written a recent detailed commentary. Her analysis is that it pits the private law of the house of 'Imran against that
of the house of Abraham as part of an anti-Jewish polemic. 'Imran (Amram) is
Aaron's father, and the Qur'an uses it to refer to Mary's mother as Amram's wife
(*imra'atu 'imrāna*, see Q 3:45). It places the old priestly dynasty alongside that of
Moses on the one hand, but also traces a genuinely Christian matrilineal dynasty
back from Mary with specifically female traits.[66] This explicitly pluralistic conception is embedded in a notion of the ambiguity of certain verses of scripture
which was very common in the early days of Islam (see Q 3:7), and so Neuwirth
suggests that the principal theme of this surah, prompted by Christology, is the
ambiguity of the scripture.[67] The tone of the surah's address to Christians does
indeed strike us as a further invitation to join the community of the meek with
an offer that they will be recognised – this may be due to the ambiguity of the
writing – in their otherness.

In any case, it is noteworthy that Jesus's disciples are described as *muslimūn* (Q
3:52), as are the Christians who accept monotheism as a common tenet (Q 3:64).
It is interesting that Jesus's disciples also describe themselves as helpers ('*anṣār*)
of God – a term that the proclaimer of the Qur'an also uses for Muhammad's
helpers in Medina (see, for example, Q 9:100–17); this is further evidence of the
Christian-friendly tone of Surah Al 'Imran. The end of the surah's discussion of
Jesus is also conciliatory, calling for unity between all *muslimūn* in a manner that
was likely to make Christians feel included (Q 3:84). One may therefore conclude
that Surah Al 'Imran contains a range of references that seek to forge a constructive link to Christianity and in particular to Jesus Christ.

The core of Surah Al 'Imran probably dates back to the early Medinan period.
Its central verses include the prologue in verses 1–32 and a narrative core of verses

---

66 On Surah Al 'Imran's emphasis on feminine traits, see Angelika Neuwirth, 'Mary and
Jesus: Counterbalancing the Biblical Patriarchs. A Re-reading of *sūrat Maryam* in *sūrat Āl
'Imrān* (Q 3:1–62)', in *Parole de l'Orient* 30 (2005) 231–60.
67 See Angelika Neuwirth, *Koranforschung – eine politische Philologie? Bible, Koran und
Islamentstehung im Spiegel spätantiker Textpolitik und moderner Philologie*, Berlin 2014,
87–8. It is not only the verses of the Qur'an that are ambiguous, but all signs of God by
which He nevertheless tries to offer us reliable guidance.

31–62.[68] Both of these passages refer to discussions with people of the scripture (*ahl al-kitāb*).

There then follows a section (verses 63–99) containing a direct message for the people of the scripture.[69] It is dominated by a religio-political discourse criticising Jews and Christians for their sense of privilege, accusing them, among other things, of falsifying scripture (verse 80). From verse 100 to the end of the surah, the conversation turns to the faithful, although the historical context from verse 121 on shows the community's growing self-confidence due to the battle of Uhud, which Muslim records situate around 625.[70] The surah concludes, from verse 190 onwards, with an apparently inclusive prayer for all the faithful, i.e. for all monotheists with criticism of certain groups.

4.2.1 Prologue (verses 1–32)

The surah's prologue reflects a debate with predominantly Jewish scholars – but maybe Christian interlocutors too – about the ambiguity of scripture. The background to this was a process of clarification within the Muslim community about how to deal with ambiguous verses.

At the very beginning of the surah, after repeating the profession of shared monotheistic faith (Q 3:2), there is a description of the sending down of the scripture containing the truth to Muhammad. There is a simultaneous declaration that this scripture confirms the guidance previously provided in the Torah and the Gospels (Q 3:3–4). The use of the scholarly terms *'injīl* and *taurāh* already shows the context of the conversation with Jews and Christians. The proclaimer of the Qur'an accommodates these religions by recognising their scriptures as revealed scripture. Conversely, it also claims the same status for the revelations of Muhammad as for the time-honoured scriptures of the more ancient religions. God is portrayed in His omnipotence, omniscience and care for humankind (Q 3:4–6) and then comes the aforementioned and decisive verse about the ambiguity of scripture, which explicitly states that scripture contains both unambiguous and ambiguous verses (Q 3:7). What is philologically controversial here is whether this verse should be read to mean that believers and those with firm knowledge know the meaning of the ambiguous verses. It seems a more plausible interpretation to

---

68 See Neuwirth, *Mary and Jesus: Counterbalancing the Biblical Patriarchs*, 233.
69 See Mathias Zahniser, 'The Word of God and the Apostleship of 'Īsā: A Narrative Analysis of Āl'Imrān', in *Journal of Semitic Studies* 37 (1991) 77–112, here 84.
70 See 'Ali ibn Ahmad al-Wahidi, *Asbab nuzul al-Qur'an*, edited by Kamal Basyuni Zajlul, Beirut 1991/1411, 124–6.

us, theologically speaking, that God alone knows the meaning of the ambiguous scripture and that the faithful must permanently wrestle with this ambivalence. The ambiguous verses also belong, in this reading, to God's address to people and He must therefore always work hard at them.[71] Since this interpretation is not wholly compelling from a philological point of view, we do not wish to lose sight of the alternative reading of this passage – according to which the Qur'anic verses are not permanently ambiguous but can be deciphered by scientific study – as another option. In any case, the proclaimer of the Qur'an makes it clear in this passage that only people 'with confusion in their hearts' can be lured from the righteous path by the ambiguous verses of the Qur'an.

Instead of cleansing the scripture and making it unambiguous, the proclaimer of the Qur'an therefore encourages us first and foremost to enter into contact with God so that He can take hold of our hearts and prevent us from deviating (Q 3:8). At the same time, he warns us not to use the ambiguous nature of certain verses to cast doubt on the clarity of the scripture in its entirety. The fact that God in His mercy stands by humans and keeps His promises, although the possibilities of His forgiving presence end when a person turns away from God (Q 3:8–10), must be accepted as a fundamental message of Holy Scripture that brooks no ambivalence. Anyone who doubts this clear fundamental statement will, in the eyes of the Qur'an, share the fate of the ancient Egyptians and end up in hell (Q 3:11–12). This is followed by eschatological imagery and pronouncements (Q 3:14–17) and an insistent appeal for a profession of monotheistic faith (Q 3:18).

It is in this context that we find the much-cited and oft-discussed phrase that true religion, in God's eyes, is *Islam*, although this does not as yet mean an established religion but rather – in accordance with the literal sense of the Arabic word – 'devotion to the one God'.[72] This is made explicit by the fact that, as has been explained above, the surah refers to Abraham (Q 3:67), Jesus and his disciples as Muslims (*muslimūn*) at various points. The proclaimer of the Qur'an warns all monotheists against hatred and envy of each other (Q 3:19) and urges them to devote themselves entirely to God (Q 3:20). Rather than thinking that their own reassuring thoughts about God will save them from hell (Q 3:24), people must dedicate themselves absolutely to God (Q 3:28). Finally, the prologue culminates in a promise of reciprocal love between God and humankind, in which humans

---

71 This interpretation also suggests itself from an intertextual perspective. The two words *mutashābih* and *muḥkam* are the Arab terms for the Aristotelian categories *amphibolos* und *pithanos*, and it is therefore extremely likely that this kind of distinction was so prevalent in the debates of late antiquity that it was also used by the proclaimer of the Qur'an.
72 See Mohammed Arkoun, op. cit. 565–71, here 569–70.

will experience God's willingness to forgive them (Q 3:31f). It is striking that the prologue of the second surah in the Qur'an to focus on Jesus of Nazareth describes the relationship between God and humans in terms of love. It is still humans who have to take the lead and love God first, but if one takes this verse together with the later statement in Q 5:54, which is also developed in the context of a debate about Jesus, one may see the Qur'an as an assurance that God in His love makes the first step towards us.

This highlights the core of the Christian message about God without acknowledging the person of Jesus, but it is indirectly linked to him because the descriptions drive the prophetology and Jesuology that is about to be developed in precisely this way. The Qur'an alludes to this by saying that God encourages His servants to love, adopting Jesus's description of himself in Q 19:30. This is not intended to signal Jesus's special nature but rather his profound humanity, which invites all people to devote themselves to the one God, who will respond to them with love and mercy.

It is nevertheless revealing how intensely the proclaimer of the Qur'an warns again of the threat of divisions in the faith (Q 3:19–23) and insists that God retains power over everything (Q 3:26–27). The proclaimer of the Qur'an obviously has Christian and Jewish quarrels in mind and their attempts to place obstacles between God and the faithful. The verses of Holy Scripture can be misunderstood in the same way, and they are therefore very explicitly linked to God and His love of humankind. Nor is scripture of any value if it does not lead to a living relationship with God. Only if people stick to God in their heart of hearts will they be able to endure the ambiguity of the scriptures and stay loyal to God, even in disputes. Love therefore comes into sight as a way of tolerating ambiguity, and believers need this so that they can be a blessing to one another.

4.2.2 Narrative core (verses 33–62)

Verse 33 marks the beginning of the narrative development of the story of Jesus's birth, and this adopts similar motifs and themes to Surah Maryam. Whereas the stories of Mary and Zachariah were only loosely linked in that surah, in Surah Al 'Imran they are embedded in a biographical and spiritual relationship,[73] and

---

73 In Surah 19 Zachariah's wish to have a successor or heir (walīy/wārith) is formally fulfilled by the birth of John and is – like Jesus's birth – symbolic proof of God's mercy. Its theme is not developed further, though, since John does not continue Zachariah's temple duties and therefore does not accomplish his desired role. In Surah 3, however, the biographies of Mary and Zachariah overlap – as they do in the Protevangelium of James

the surah thus becomes an account of the election of the house of 'Imran, which explains its title. Angelika Neuwirth pointed out some time ago that the house of 'Imran is a symbol for Christians in this surah; it is placed alongside the house of Abraham and is therefore equal in standing to the Jews (Q 3:33). Neuwirth also recognised the surah's emphasis on Jesus's female genealogy.[74] 'Imran is named as the spiritual patriarch of this house, but he does not once appear as an active character in the story. It is his wife who is active and promises to dedicate her child to God (Q 3:35). Although the child is a girl – Mary, the mother of Jesus – her mother keeps her promise and lets her grow up in the temple, and so Mary is presented as having a special bond with God. At the same time, the text rejects the identification of Mary with the Church. Mary is no longer the temple itself, but she stays in it.[75] The Christian allegories that form the backdrop to this story have no role in the Qur'an.[76]

Zachariah is entrusted with taking care of her in the temple and this seals the bond between John's and Jesus's lines. In the same way that Zachariah is supposed to look after Mary, one might understand John as the one who is to watch out for Jesus. However, Mary does not need any care because God endows her with everything she needs in the temple (Q 3:37). Men are mere accessories in the genealogy of Jesus. Neither does Jesus require a male protector, living instead in his proximity to God and sustained by Him.

It is only after the lines have been intertwined in this way that Surah Al 'Imran begins the actual birth story of John the Baptist, which of course opened Surah Maryam. This time, though, the divine response – conveyed by angels – is more detailed and describes John as a prophet and one of the righteous (Q 3:39). However, the surah refrains from providing any more details about John's character and breaks off its description of events after repeating the interpretation of Zachariah's silence as a sign. This means that the subject matter focuses on God as the one who cares mercifully for humankind. However, the narrative involves fewer flourishes, and God is also portrayed less frequently in anthropomorphic terms; instead, it is His functions and titles that are precisely mentioned.

This tendency continues in the story of Jesus's birth. Mary's suffering does not

---

– for Zachariah takes charge of her (Q 3:37). Mary is thus associated with Zachariah's priestly line, founded by Aaron. That is why the mother of Mary can be called Amram's wife, because she belongs to the *spiritual* family of the house of Amram.

74 See Angelika Neuwirth, *Mary and Jesus*, 231–60.

75 See Angelika Neuwirth, *Die koranische Verzauberung der Welt und ihre Entzauberung in der Geschichte*, Freiburg 2017, 197–8.

76 See Neuwirth, *Der Koran. Vol 2/1: Frühmittelmekkanische Suren*, 648–9.

receive a mention, but her election is attested to with powerful words reminiscent of the Ave Maria (Q 3:42). But this is also woven into the cadence of customary Islamic prayers, preventing her from being singled out in worship (Q 3:43). Surah Maryam is more open to interpretation in this regard and is therefore more susceptible to misunderstandings by pagan Arabs and Christians, which is why the third surah now defines the status of Mary in more specific terms. At the same time, though, the image of Mary as the archetypal believer, so crucial to Christianity, is plausible for these passages too. Mary has been chosen and purified by God, and her attitudes to prayer are a model for the whole community of the faithful.

What is particularly interesting here is the rejection of the apocryphal character of the Christian testimonies that influenced the Qur'an. Whereas the Proto-Gospel of James, which the Qur'an relies on to a considerable degree for its Maryology, repeatedly emphasises the apocryphal and hence esoteric nature of its views, the proclaimer of the Qur'an aims to reveal the previously hidden content of the stories. His desire is not to reveal an esoteric cult for the elite, but God's benevolence towards all people.

The birth of Jesus is portrayed in starkly reduced terms too. There is now no more than a quick allusion to his speaking as an infant (Q 3:46). Instead, the proclaimer of the Qur'an argues in favour of precise theological recognition for his claim, but systematically avoids any of the titles for Christ that have caused schisms and disputes within Christianity.

The backdrop to these theological refinements is probably increased debate with Christian groupings in Medina. According to Muslim accounts, it was the visit of a delegation of Christians from Najran that prompted the Qur'an to elucidate the role of Jesus once more in Surah Al 'Imran.[77] If Jesus is not the Son of God, what is he? That is the question posed by Christians, and Surah Al 'Imran attempts to answer it.[78] This involves the use of a host of titles for Jesus which

---

77 See al-Wahidi, *Asbab nuzul al-Qur'an*, 99–100. According to traditional accounts, however, this meeting ended in deadlock, i.e. the Christians in Muhammad's time obviously did not consider that the proclaimer of the Qur'an had made sufficient concessions.

78 It robs the passage of its theological dignity if one claims, as van der Velden does, that Q 3:45–59 is a Syriac-Christian ecumenical convergence text. See Frank van der Velden, 'Konvergenztexte syrischer und arabischer Christologie. Stufen der Textentwicklung von Sure 3,33–64', in *Oriens Christianus. Hefte für die Kunde des christlichen Orients* 91 (2007) 164–203. What does emerge from this interpretation, however, is the proclaimer of the Qur'an's willingness to respond to the needs and thoughts of his Christian listeners. Rather than seeing this step through the lens of literary criticism, it seems more rewarding and exegetically more convincing in terms of relations between Islam and Christianity to see this as a deliberate compromise by the Qur'an for Christian groupings.

are then repeated in other places and engage with crucial categories of traditional Christology. Surah Al 'Imran clearly employs extremely risky terminology, making concessions to Christians in order to win back Jesus Christ for world history and integrate him into Islam's own conception of the history of salvation. The surah appears to want to liberate Jesus Christ from a Christian monopoly and make him available for Arab interpretation. This is clear from the very first mention of Jesus in Q 3:45. Here, Jesus is announced by the angels as the word of God, and for the first time the name of Christ and thus the title of Messiah is mentioned.[79]

Whereas Islamic scholars generally interpret the use of the word Christ as a simple adoption of the common name for Jesus, casting doubt on any deeper theological significance,[80] classical Muslim exegesis repeatedly attempted to uncover the deeper theological meaning of the title of Messiah. According to Ibn 'Abbas, though, the description of Jesus as *al-masīḥ* means that 'Jesus anointed the sick with his hand to heal them'.[81] Al-Tabari says that God gave Jesus this name 'because he cleansed people of their sins' and 'was himself cleansed of sins and impurities'.[82] According to al-Razi, the term is a description of Jesus because he never touched a sick person (with the plague) without healing them, because he touched both viziers and sinners, and because he put his hand on orphans' heads for God. He was also anointed with pure and blessed oil and, having been touched by Gabriel's wing at birth, was protected from the touch of the devil.[83] Even though we do not wish to go as far here as Navid Kermani, who is of the opinion that the Messiah 'is a singular, indeed, a godlike person',[84] exegetic endeavours make it clear that the use of the title of Messiah is by no means clear and is open to a range of theological interpretations. These may enable Christians to see the title of Christ, which has been reduced almost to a simple name, with fresh eyes. The idea that being touched by Christ and his being touched are so highly charged

---

79 We do not view the fact that angels speak here as a sign that Qur'an is distancing itself from this statement. Angels are repeatedly entrusted with the task of proclaiming divine messages in the Qur'an without there being any noticeable intent to distance itself from them.

80 This scepticism is backed up by the fact that Messiah is explicitly used as a name for Jesus in Q 3:45.

81 Çinar, op. cit. 41.

82 Ibid. 133.

83 al-Razi argues that *masīḥ* is also a title which has been added to his name in order to accentuate his singularity and high rank (see al-Razi, *al-Tafsir al-kabir*, vol. 8, 55).

84 Kermani, *Wonder Beyond Belief*, 90. Kermani bases his view on the fact that the Messiah is the only one of the prophets who is '*rūḥullāh*: "the spirit of God"' (ibid.).

strikes us as extremely interesting. The proclaimer of the Qur'an does not himself offer any interpretation, but the way he integrates this first mention of the title of the Messiah into the text suggests that it comes with positive associations.

The following section of the surah states that Jesus will be brought near to God in this world and the next.[85] This lasting closeness of Jesus to God is, as an adverbial description of place, reminiscent of the Christian belief that Jesus sits at God's right hand. Being near to God, Jesus is one of those who will go ahead into the Gardens of Bliss (see Q 56:10–12) and drink from the spring (see Q 83:28). Interestingly, the category of 'those brought near' crops up repeatedly in the Qur'an, but it is never otherwise associated with a specific prophet.[86] It therefore appears that Jesus has the special honour of being brought near to God, is close to God from the very beginning of his life and therefore proclaims His words from infancy (Q 3:46) and cannot be destroyed by death (Q 4:158).[87]

The obvious next step from Jesus's special intimacy and proximity to God is to explore why he is called the *Word of God*. This term is not applied to any other prophet in the Qur'an either, and it is even repeated and reinforced again later. In Q 4:171 the closeness between God's Holy Spirit and Jesus is asserted in such strong terms that Jesus is even referred to as 'God's Word' and 'a spirit from God'. Without going any further into the anti-trinitarian thrust of this verse, it is interesting that the particular closeness, attributed to Jesus as early as the early Medinan period due to his being filled with the spirit,[88] is now escalated to such a degree that Jesus is not only strengthened by the spirit but identified with the spirit and viewed in an eschatological closeness to God that allows him (and only him) to

---

85 Literally, the verse says merely that Jesus will be held in honour in this world and the next, and will be one of those brought near to God. Our argument that Jesus is 'one of those brought near to God in this world and the next' is not imperative, but it does seem to stand to reason from the text.

86 It is said in Q 19:52 that God brings Moses close to Him, employing the same word root as in 'those brought near'. Here, however, it refers to a special distinction of Moses being invited to a private communion. Jesus is obviously enveloped in this special intimacy with God at every moment of his life, whereas Moses is only briefly granted the same treatment after a special intervention by God.

87 This last statement is of course, from a Muslim point of view, not restricted to Jesus but is also true of Muhammad, for instance. Nor is it meant as an exclusive statement by Christians, even if we are trying here to examine the belief in Jesus's Resurrection, which in Christian eyes obviously became manifest reality in Jesus.

88 See Q 2:87–253. This idea is already found with reference to Mary in other Meccan verses (Q 19:17 and 21:91), and there are also late-Medinan references to Jesus's strengthening (Q 5:110) or Mary's (Q 66:12). Q 4:171 obviously has a special status in this regard, and we must reflect on this in more depth.

be called the Word of God.[89] The entire weight of the image of Jesus in the statement in Q 3:45 obviously lies in the idea that Jesus is the Word of God, while we should not exaggerate the importance of his new designation as Christ.[90] Whatever one's particular view of the interpretation developed by the Islamic tradition, it is noteworthy that the proclaimer of the Qur'an does not shrink from using the highest Christian title of all for Jesus.

The earlier Qur'an commentators in particular saw the description of Jesus as the Word of God as a reference to the special circumstances of the creation of Jesus, which once more distinguished him from the rest of humankind.[91] Some are even of the opinion that this title seeks to clarify that Jesus is 'the incarnation of the glad tidings of God's mercy', bringing them very close to the essence of Christian interpretation.[92] 'Razi [...] for example also understands Jesus's word and his being the Spirit in the sense that as a person he is the incarnation of God's mercy.'[93] Most recently in this tradition, Muhammad Legenhausen has put forward arguments in support of the idea that Jesus in his personhood should be understood as the voice and word of God.[94]

---

89 Despite this special emphasis on the role of Jesus, it is absolutely clear to the proclaimer of the Qur'an that not only Jesus but also Muhammad leads his life in a particular closeness to God (see Q 53:9). Jesus's singularity should therefore be seen not in his special closeness to God but rather in the conviction that this closeness is gifted to him at birth so that he is divine even as an unborn child (Q 3:35) and can therefore act as God's message to us.

90 The parallel construction for the name of John the Baptist in Q 19:7 does not suggest that 'name' itself might be a theological title, even though one might naturally understand God's names in this sense.

91 See Ayoub, *A Muslim View of Christianity*, 129: 'While earlier commentators saw a special creation in Jesus as "the Word of God", more recent ones have consistently attempted to play down any distinction between Jesus and the rest of humankind.'

92 Friedmann Eissler, 'Jesus und Maria im Islam', in Christfried Böttrich / Beate Ego / Friedmann Eissler, *Jesus und Maria im Judentum. Christentum und Islam*, Göttingen 2009, 120–205, here 177; see Josef Imbach, *Wem gehört Jesus? Seine Bedeutung für Juden, Christen und Moslems*, Munich 1989, 93.

93 Bauschke, op. cit. 115. See also Razi's commentary on Q 4:171 (Al-Razi, *al-Tafsir al-kabir*, vol. 11, 117–8). In a similar vein, al-Qurtubi also mentions a similar interpretation of the description of Jesus as the Spirit in the sense of God's mercy incarnate (al-Qurtubi, *al-Jami' li-ahkam al-Qur'an*, vol. 7, 230–2).

94 See Legenhausen, 'Jesus as Kalimat Allah', 129–56; Legenhausen, 'Appreciating Muslim and Christian Christologies', in Klaus von Stosch / Mouhanad Khorchide (eds.), *Streit um Jesus. Muslimische und christliche Annäherungen*, Paderborn 2016, 59–80, here 69: 'Since love of God, virtue and supererogation are characteristics that the Qur'an ascribes to God's most favoured servants, it is clear that the Qur'an would include Jesus among those for whom the veils of separation have been rent asunder. If God becomes the tongue by which Jesus speaks, can this not be a way of understanding how Jesus is a word of God?'

It is nevertheless clear that the proclaimer of the Qur'an emphatically assumes that *he* is the Word of God. From the Qur'an's point of view, so to speak, Jesus Christ's position in the Christian tradition is therefore already occupied, indeed by its proclaimer and his oral recitation, in which God's word comes into existence.[95] Accordingly, the Qur'an is repeatedly described as the *Word of God* in more pointed linguistic form than Jesus is,[96] which nevertheless does not change the fact that Jesus is the only person in the Qur'an who is seen as the Word of God – an observation that Muslims too can use as special recognition of Jesus.

Over the course of the remaining surahs, the miracle of the virgin birth and some of Jesus's miracles are listed and, as in John's Gospel, acknowledged as signs. At the same time, though, their significance is downplayed. In a thoroughly modern fashion, they are not recognised as evidence but explicitly seen as convincing only believers (Q 3:49). Jesus is also referred to as a confirmation of the Torah (see also Q 61:6 and 5:46), although this would appear simultaneously to rescind some of the Torah's instructions.[97] The proclaimer of the Qur'an is obviously looking to chart a middle path between the position of the Sermon on the Mount where Jesus says that he did not change the Torah one iota (Matt. 5:17–8) and Paul's idea that Jesus has brought an end to the way of the Torah for Gentile Christians who believe in Christ (Rom. 10:4) – a half-way position that was common among Arab Christians of the time and is backed up by wide-ranging biblical evidence. Jesus emerges therefore as a reformer of the law rather than its opponent.

Another intriguing statement in the surah is that God will summon Jesus to Him and raise him to heaven (Q 3:55) – which in Christian hermeneutics is an allusion to resurrection and ascension[98] – and that He will stand by Jesus's disciples,

---

95 See in this context Neuwirth, *The Qur'an and Late Antiquity*, 92–5; Klaus von Stosch, 'Der muslimische Offenbarungsanspruch als Herausforderung komparativer Theologie. Christlich-theologische Untersuchungen zur innerislamischen Debatte um Ungeschaffenheit und Präexistenz des Korans', in *ZKTh* 129 (2007) 53–74.

96 Whereas the Qur'an repeatedly refers to itself as *kalām Allah* – in Q 9:6 and Q 48:15, for example – Jesus is called only *kalimat Allah*. In the wording of the Qur'an, however, the delineation of the two is not entirely clear, and there are parallel passages in which these words seem to be interchangeable (see Q 48:15 and 6:34) so that here we hesitate to accept the classical Muslim qualification of Jesus being called *kalimat Allah*. On this problem, see also Daniel Madigan, 'God's Word to the World: Jesus and the Qur'an. Incarnation and Recitation', in Terence Mebrigan / Frederic Glorieux (eds.), *Godhead Here in Hiding. Incarnation and the History of Human Suffering*, Leuven 2012, 143–58, here 145, n. 3.

97 The verse is not completely clear and may simply signal that Jesus allowed the Jews to do things that they had previously forbidden themselves to do.

98 Traditional Muslim exegesis views this simply as a protective act of God. To us, however, the text seems open to interpretation.

and those who succeed him, against the disbelievers until the end of time (Q 3:55). Indeed, God even appears to promise that the Church will be superior to the powers that aim to destroy it, at least if one accepts that the Church is no more than the community of the disciples and that its superiority must at least mean that unbelievers will not be able destroy it (see again Q 3:55). When the proclaimer of the Qur'an follows up on the story of Christ's Resurrection by emphasising that Jesus is Adam's equal in terms of his creation (see Q 3:59) and explains that he, like Adam and unlike anyone else, came into being through the immediate power of God's creative word, we find it hard to see this as a downgrading of Jesus. Yet this does show that Jesus was completely human, a view that the Qur'an subsequently underscores several times. It is nevertheless still clear how special Jesus's life was, from the moment of his conception until his resurrection and ascension. For that reason, we feel that the overall tone of Surah Al 'Imran does not yet pursue a polemical purpose, and it does adopt various titles for Jesus in prominent fashion. The surah is underpinned by a desire for monotheistic common sense to prevail that has devotion to the one God at its core while still permitting a variety of paths to Him; it teaches tolerance of ambiguity as part of a shared monotheistic faith. A tendency to criticise Christians is clearly directed at one specific group (Q 3:69) and not applied more widely.

Whereas in Surah Maryam it was still the case that the Spirit of God came to Mary in the form of an angel and encouraged her through his word (Q 19:17–19) while playing no part in Jesus's conception, the Medinan verse Q 66:12 speaks of God breathing His spirit into her private parts.[99] This is a striking phrase, which is mentioned nowhere else and obviously alludes to the virgin birth. It shows that a whole range of other Medinan verses back up the position of Surah Al 'Imran.

The Qur'an does indeed mention that God, in order to create Adam, breathed His spirit into the clay from which man was made (see Q 38:72) and obviously also sees this act of breathing as requiring the angels to prostrate themselves before God (see Q 15:29). Yet, however important the breath of the spirit into Adam, the breathing of the spirit into Mary's private parts is very different from the gift of the spirit involved in the creation of every human being, representing the special honour of humanity. It is the symbol of the virgin birth. It is therefore a pro-Christian clarification of the idea of the virgin birth and thus very reminiscent of the Christian profession of Jesus's conception by the Holy Spirit, although it does not on its own confirm it.

Regarding verse 48 of the third surah, it is worth considering in addition to

---

99 See a less specific formulation from the middle Meccan period in Q 21:91.

what we have already discussed that the scripture used to teach Jesus refers back terminologically to the 'Scripture [...] with the Truth' in verse 3, which God also sends to Muhammad. This means that both drink from the same source, and yet there is room for this word to take various forms in the Book of Wisdom, the Torah and the Gospel, which are by no means devalued in comparison with the original scripture. All the individual Holy Scriptures are clearly derived from the *kitāb*, the essence of all God's messages on which all religions draw. However, that does not mean that the existing historical scriptures have been somehow falsified and that Christians and Jews cannot rely on them. They do remain at the mercy of their ambiguity, which can only not cause problems if humans allow God to take hold of their hearts and if they do not deviate from Him.

The narrative core of the surah concludes once more with the monotheistic profession of faith (Q 3:62), which continually reminds the reader of the shared belief of the monotheistic religions at crucial junctures.

4.2.3 Religio-political arguments (verses 63–99)

In this section of the surah, the argument with Jews and Christians escalates further, and the Muslim position becomes increasingly precise. Put in a historical context, this debate is an invitation to Jews and Christians to side with the Muslims in their disputes with the Meccans and not to allow themselves to be prevented from showing solidarity with the Muslims by groupings that distort God's word.

First of all, Jewish and Christian groupings are criticised for thinking that they are entitled to claim a privileged position for themselves. The Qur'an rejects any kind of hierarchy of religious groups, just as it refuses exaggerated veneration of religious leaders, for we should not take others beside God for lords (Q 3:64). Believers should therefore distance themselves from any temporal power interests that religion uses to legitimise secular control over people.

The Qur'an also criticises the divisions between Jews and Christians, which are overwhelmingly related to the debate over which of the two groups is closer to God and which has the privilege of enjoying God's covenant or being His chosen people. The proclaimer of the Qur'an is disgusted by their dispute (Q 3:65) and puts forward a compromise solution.

Since Christians and Jews refer to their scriptures to back up these exaggerated and, from the Qur'an's point of view, unjustified claims, the Qur'an directly attacks the authority of these scriptures. The proclaimer of the Qur'an explicitly accuses a specific Jewish or Christian grouping of falsifying scripture (Q 3:78), denying their scriptural quotations any divine truth. The lie is not intrinsic to the scripture itself but lies in its deliberate falsification by the named grouping. The fact that it is still unclear to this day which group is being targeted here[100] means that the Qur'an's warning remains topical and is aimed at anyone who wishes to appropriate the scripture and twist it to suit their particular interests.

Other groupings openly betray the claims of their own scripture. They hide the truth (Q 3:71), knowingly spread lies about God and refuse to return borrowed money (Q 3:75). The important thing here is that the criticism is explicitly aimed only at specific groupings rather than at the two religions as a whole (Q 3:69.72.75.78.100). So any verses that directly address the people of the book without this form of explicit qualification ought to be interpreted as having specific groups in mind.[101] On the contrary, the Qur'an explicitly emphasises that God loves those who fear Him and live good lives without castigating any specific religion (Q 3:76).

Thus the proclaimer of the Qur'an does not challenge the notion that Jews and Christians are addressed by God in the Torah and the Gospels and that this address is permanent and also offers them a permanent path to God (Q 3:81). If, however, they seek to extrapolate from this that they are in sole possession of God's truth, he attacks them and rejects those claims. He also warns against conferring divine authority on any person, prophet or angel and accepting them as lords. The true theological path is to study the revealed scripture and think for oneself (Q 3:79–80).

As a result, the Qur'an also attacks any hierarchy of the prophets (Q 3:84) and insists that every religion must lead to devotion to the one God (Q 3:85). Even though Jews and Christians are honoured as eyewitnesses of God's affection (Q 3:99), the Qur'an criticises them if they do not believe and turn away from God (Q 3:98.94). Instead, they are invited into the community of those devoted to God.

---

100 Tabari lists several accounts inferring that the *ahl al-kitāb* here are the Jews, and does not therefore perceive the same openness to interpretation that we suggest (see al-Tabari, *Jami' al-bayan*, vol. 5, 522). However, the context of the verse leaves the specific attribution open and we do not see enough Qur'anic evidence to subscribe to here.

101 This is particularly true of verses Q 3:70–71, which contain criticism of a general nature. However, the restriction of the polemical statement to specific groups immediately before and after this make it clear that this criticism is destined for specific groups of Jews and Christians. It is also asserted in surahs that emerged around the same time that the respective criticism of Christians and Jews is levelled only at certain groups among them, although one does get the impression that most representatives of these religions are deserving of criticism (see Q 57:26–27).

4.2.4 Self-assurance of the Muslim community (verses 100–200)

The first twenty verses of the surah initially contemplate how the battle of Uhud
came about (c. 625). Afterwards, from verse 121 onwards, there is analysis of
the battle, at which the Muslims suffered a significant defeat in their dispute with
the Meccans, and so they are in urgent need of reassurance.[102] This explains why
the surah repeatedly offers words of consolation and attempts to encourage the
Muslims. We therefore read that God is aware of what the believers do and what
is in their hearts (Q 3:153–154) and has kept His promise (Q 3:152); God is portrayed as a protector (Q 3:150) who is willing to forgive (Q 3:129) and as forbear-
ing (Q 3:155). God's mercy is repeatedly celebrated (Q 3:159). This is followed
at the end of the surah by a common prayer by all monotheists (Q 3:190–198) and
a call for all believers to unite (Q 3:199–200).

Given our thematic focus, we have no intention of analysing this part of the
surah any further. Our only objective is to point out a few interesting details. What
is noteworthy is that the one community or *umma* the text invokes (see Q 3:104)
could most certainly include Jews. The surah would then reflect the fundamental
idea of the relevant treaty of Medina. It also becomes clear that the Qur'an's
attacks on internal disputes contains a significant political dimension, because the
aim must now be to close ranks to face the challenge of Uhud. It is explicitly stated
that there are also believers among the People of the Book who live out their faith
transparently and convincingly (Q 3:113–115). From the Qur'an's point of view,
these people are a minority (Q 3:110), but their existence is noted and they are
viewed as potential allies of the Prophet.

We need to add one further minor detail. When verse 145 says that no one
may die without God's permission, this asserts that from a theological perspective Jesus's death on the cross was not the work of the Jews or the Romans, but
an act of God. The Qur'an must therefore correct the Jews' perception that they
killed Jesus. Moreover, regarding the martyrs of the battle of Uhud, it states that
those of us who are killed in God's way should not be thought dead (Q 3:169).
This statement too must apply to Jesus, and he should therefore not be considered dead if he laid down his life believing in God. We should assume instead
that his Crucifixion does not change the fact that he has been saved and is with
God forever. Both verses seem to us to presuppose Jesus's Crucifixion, and it is
therefore necessary to subject the Qur'an's alleged denial of Jesus's Crucifixion to

---

102 See the many accounts of revelation occurrences about the verses after verse 121, e.g.
'Ali ibn Ahmad al-Wahidi, *Asbab nuzul al-Qur'an*, edited by Kamal Basyuni Zajlul, Beirut
1991/1411, 124–35.

much closer scrutiny, especially as the relevant verse was also proclaimed during the Medinan period.

4.2.5 Jesus crucified?

Although Surah Al 'Imran is still clearly positive in its attitude to Christianity, in the later verses of the Qur'an this enduring esteem of certain aspects of Christianity becomes increasingly mingled with rhetorical attacks on specific Christian sects.[103] Q 4:156–159 is often and unfairly seen as an anti-Christian polemic in this respect. We, however, still see esteem as the dominant tone here, as it is in Surah 3, and we identify no signs of polemical rhetoric here. One might even see the verses as a confirmation of the Christian resurrection story. That is because the Qur'an counters the Jews' claim that they killed Jesus with an insistence that Jesus lives and is saved by God because God has raised him (see Q 4:158). The proclaimer of the Qur'an quite clearly does not deny his death, and presupposes it in other places.[104] He simply underlines that Jesus has not definitively succumbed to his enemies' hatred. Jesus lives on, just like the martyrs whom God has also saved, although no one denies that their earthly bodies are dead (Q 3:169). Another informative verse in this respect is Q 8:17, in which God makes it clear to Muhammad that it was not the Muslims but He Himself who killed their foes. Thus God appears repeatedly as the true agent of history, and so it was not the Jews who killed Jesus but God Himself. Also, it is not his death that is the true message and reality about Jesus, but the fact that God has raised him up to Himself (see Q 4:157–158). His final death has thus not yet occurred and might only come about when all Christians and Jews believe (Q 4:159) – a prospect that seems unlikely for this story.

Anyway, let us now examine the wording of the much-discussed verses in 4:157–158. In M.A.S. Abdel Haleem's translation they read:

> And [the Jews] said, 'We have killed the Messiah, Jesus, son of Mary, the Messenger of God.' They did not kill him, nor did they crucify him, though it was made to appear like that to them; those that disagreed about him are full of doubt, with no knowledge to follow, only supposition: they certainly did not kill him – God raised him up to Himself.

---

103 See the corresponding perspective in Neuwirth, *Imagining Mary – Disputing Jesus*, 413.
104 Jesus says in Surah Maryam that he will die (Q 19:33/*'amūtu*), and God says of Jesus in Surah Al 'Imran that He will take him back (Q 3:55/*tawaffā*). The words 'You took my soul' also feature in Q 5:117.

In the Islamic tradition, these verses are usually interpreted by *substitution theory*. The part of the verse that Abdel Haleem translates as 'it was made to appear like that to them' is thus understood as meaning 'he (another) was made similar to him (Jesus)'. The trouble with this translation is that there is a plural in the Arabic text, i.e. *shubbiha lahum* and not *shubbiha lahu,* and the text does not mention anyone else;[105] the literature therefore has long since pointed out that it is impossible to infer the substitution theory from the Arabic wording.[106] This translation also causes theological problems because it presupposes that God killed an innocent person in Jesus's stead. Even if one were to assume that this person was a criminal or even volunteered – the Muslim tradition often assumes that God predestined Judas for this role or that some other disciple volunteered for this task[107] – this course of events would still be offensive because God's intervention punishes someone for an act they did not commit. It is Jesus who insisted at the trial that he was the Messiah, causing the Roman judicial system to rule that he be executed. Thus Jesus should surely be responsible for his acts, and it is strange that God would involve an innocent person. The swap could not have passed unseen without God's intervention, anyway, because the women beneath the cross, and especially Jesus's mother, would certainly have noticed this substitution unless God confounded them. Al-Razi asks completely justifiably at this juncture why God should have confused people to such an extent that they did not notice the exchange.[108] If God really did intend only to show that His prophets enjoyed special protection and that He therefore shielded Jesus from Crucifixion, it is incomprehensible that God would only acknowledge this nearly 600 years after the event, leaving the poor Christians to cope with this catastrophic and traumatic occurrence alone for centuries. One should not expect a merciful God to afflict the mother of a condemned man so malevolently with blindness that she thinks her son dead when he is actually with God. What is more, there are other passages in the Qur'an that take it for granted that Jesus did die,[109] contradicting

---

105 See Bauschke, *Jesus – Stein des Anstoßes*, 164.

106 See Parrinder, *Jesus in the Qur'an*, 112.

107 See Bauschke, op. cit. 165–6.

108 Ibid. 168.

109 The infant Jesus says himself in the Qur'an: 'Peace was on me the day I was born, and will be on me the day I die and the day I am raised to life again' (19:33), and one can therefore assume that Jesus knows of his own death. The other passages in the Qur'an mention the passing of Jesus (*tawaffā*), and it is controversial as to whether that means that Jesus of Nazareth really died. Yet *tawaffā* strikes us as simply a more pious wording of the verb 'to die' and casts no doubt on Jesus's actual death. This question is, however, contentious within Islam, in particular due to the traditional belief in Jesus's return.

the notion that someone else was killed in Jesus's stead. The substitution makes absolutely no theological sense, and it is also philologically questionable.[110]

If one rejects the substitution theory on these grounds, then one alternative is the docetism theory, which received backing among Ishmaelites and Gnostic interpreters of the Qur'an, but has few advocates among classical Muslim commentators. It supposes that God's intervention led to Jesus's external, human shell alone being crucified and killed, whereas 'his divine being remained untouched'.[111] In a similar vein, Claus Schedl notes that the Jews were able to crucify the body of the Messiah, but not the Spirit-Messiah, as he had been saved and raised by God.[112] This interpretation is undermined by its latent dualism and its opposition to the pleasures of the body. Mahmoud Ayoub therefore stresses that Islam does not recognise any form of docetism.[113]

If one rejects a docetic solution or a phantom theory,[114] one can still adopt some of the interpretation presented earlier and try to avoid its associated dualism. Kenneth Cragg and Hans Zirker have done interesting preliminary work in this regard. Cragg bases his interpretation on the observation that the cross is a topic in the Qur'an as well. The proclaimer of the Qur'an accepts quite openly that Jesus is to be crucified and that Jesus confronts this death by torture.[115] It is therefore impossible to claim that the proclaimer of the Qur'an tries to suppress any memory of the cross, and one may therefore ask with complete impartiality whether his argument is driving at something else entirely.

---

110 The fact that it nevertheless featured prominently in the Islamic commentary tradition might have something to do with the fact that such substitution theories abounded in early Christian heresies and potentially influenced the Muslim commentary tradition. 'With reference to Irenaeus, Basilides (died 160) is said to have taught that not Jesus but Simon of Cyrene [...] was crucified in Jesus's stead' (see Bauschke, op. cit. 175; Imbach op. cit. 97). But this is ultimately pure speculation.

111 Bauschke, op. cit. 170.

112 'The Jews' error was more that "they did not recognise Jesus as the coming of the Messiah. They were able to crucify the body of the Messiah, i.e. the mortal Jesus, but they could no longer attain the Spirit-Messiah with nails because Allah had raised him to Himself (see Surah 3:55)".' (Imbach, op. cit. 98; with reference to Schedl, *Muhammad und Jesus*, 469–70.)

113 Ayoub, *A Muslim View of Christianity*, 160: 'Islam, however, does not admit of docetism in any form.'

114 The phantom theory comes from Ibn Arabi and supposes that 'neither Jesus nor the substitute was crucified, but a phantom God had created expressly for this purpose' (Bauschke, op. cit., 171). However, this involves some of the same difficulties associated with the substitution theory we mentioned earlier, especially the issue of why God did not clear up the confusion at an earlier date.

115 See Kenneth Cragg, *Jesus and the Muslim: An Exploration*, London 1985, 168.

Maybe, Cragg suspects, his aim is simply to clarify that it was not the Jews who killed Jesus, but God Himself or the Romans.[116] The context of the Qur'an passage about the Crucifixion is indeed a conversation between God and the Jews claiming that they killed Jesus of Nazareth – a claim that the proclaimer of the Qur'an did not make up, incidentally, but that did indeed play a role in Jewish anti-Christian polemics, as a statement in the Talmud proves.[117] The sole point that God contests is that the Jews killed and crucified Jesus, not that he was killed and crucified. So it is possible to understand this passage as a clear signal that God is always the active agent and will not allow His grip on events to be usurped.[118] The Jews are in the wrong because they claim for themselves an act that was ordained by God.

This same interpretation may be applied to the other places in the Qur'an that mention the deaths of martyrs and can also be placed in a historical context. As the Surah al-Nisa' was presumably revealed at a time when Muhammad found himself caught up in conflict with the Jewish clans in Medina,[119] it could be that these clans signaled to him that they would deal with him as they had dealt with Jesus.[120] Muhammad might then have answered that they would never have the power to kill a prophet and that God was the real agent in the death of Jesus, i.e.

---

116 Kenneth Cragg, op. cit., 170.

117 See BT Sanhedrin 43a. Peter Schäfer, *Jesus im Talmud*, 148, explains how unusual this Jewish self-accusation is, and that it is based on the fact that the rabbinic point of view considered that Jesus had faced a legitimate trial. It is therefore doubtful whether one may truly apply the self-awareness that is expressed here to the Jews in Medina too.

118 In the same vein, see the interpretation of Parrinder, op. cit. 119, who rightly refers to the parallels with the understanding in John (see John 19:11).

119 It is not really possible to reconstruct when exactly this verse originated during the conflict with the Jews. In a critical analysis of the tradition, it is generally very hard to situate the details provided by the Muslim tradition about the conflict with the Jews in the Hijaz. On this subject, see for example the results of Schöller's study of the material handed down about the conflict with the Jews in Marco Schöller, *Exegetisches Denken und Prophetenbiographie*, Wiesbaden 1998. For further studies on these transmission issues, see William Montgomery Watt, 'The Condemnation of the Jews of Banū Qurayẓah', in *The Muslim World* 42 (1952) 160–71; Meir Jacob Kister, 'The Massacre of the Banū Qurayẓa. A Re-examination of a Tradition', in *Jerusalem Studies in Arabic and Islam* 8 (1986) 61–96; Michael Lecker, 'Did Muḥammad Conclude Treaties with the Jewish Tribes Naḍīr, Qurayẓa and Qaynuqāʿ?', in *Israel Oriental Studies* 17 (1997) 29–36. That is why we shall concentrate on the theological discourse in the Qur'an itself, which clearly refers to Jewish interlocutors, and try to fit this, whenever possible, into the overall scheme of our book.

120 We named above the place in the Talmud that one might quote as a historical reference here. However, the aforementioned argument by Schöller suggests that the Jews in the said passage in the Talmud were arguing on the basis of Jewish law. We are unable to presuppose this basis of argumentation for their conflict with Muhammad, and so the reader should consider this debate as just one possible explanation.

that Jesus would never have died on the cross if it had not been part of God's design. Muhammad's argument may have been that since God obviously had no such plans for Muhammad, the Jews would not be able to kill him. The well-known Qur'an scholar Nasr Hamed Abu Zaid came to a similar exegesis, commenting on Q 4:157:

> If we take account of the Qur'anic context of the statement 'They did not kill him, nor did they crucify him', then we note that the Qur'an is responding to the Jews here, not to the Christians ... In the historical context of this surah, the Jews threatened that they would kill the Prophet as they had killed Jesus. Yet the Qur'an calms the Prophet by assuring him that they neither killed Jesus, nor crucified him. The entire Qur'anic description has nothing to do with Christianity but with a dispute between the Prophet and the Jews.[121]

Another interpretation that seems more unlikely to us, although it cannot be completely excluded, is that God is trying to make it clear here that it was the Romans, rather than the Jews, who executed Jesus. We do now know, in fact, that the Gospels played down the guilt of the Romans in the execution of Jesus for tactical, proselytising reasons and it is definitely possible that the Romans were actually the ones pulling the strings in his murder. After all, there is no doubt that the Crucifixion was a form of punishment that could only be carried out by the Romans, and the Gospels' efforts to assign the primary blame to the Jews come across as somewhat artificial. God's pro-Jewish intervention would then, in a sense, protect the Jews in a climate of rampant anti-Jewish sentiment, and at the same time show that torture and death were not the final fate of Jesus of Nazareth, but that God raised him to Himself, i.e. he was resurrected.

However, this pro-Jewish interpretation is not at all enshrined in the Islamic tradition, and there is no supporting evidence for it anywhere else in the Qur'an. If God had intended His intervention to protect the Jews from Christian pogroms, then God would surely have ensured that the Muslims at least understood His message earlier than the twenty-first century. If this interpretation is only emerging now and devised as a response to the Holocaust, then one suspects that it is a result of wishful thinking rather than of precise philological analysis.

---

121 This is a direct quotation from an interview with Nasr Hamed Abu Zaid in the Egyptian newspaper *Al-Badil* on 08.02.2008, see Muhammad Faraj, 'A Conversation between Muhammad Faraj and Nasr Hamed Abu Zaid', in *Al-Badil* (2008); https://rowaqnasrabuzaid.wordpress.com/2008/04/12/ (14.02.2018).

The profession of God's might and power to shape history is, on the other hand, consistent with many other statements in the Qur'an. For that reason, one can pursue this line of interpretation and perhaps even conclude, as Hans Zirker does, that the Qur'an's description of the circumstances of Jesus's Crucifixion allow for the interpretation that Jesus, with God's aid, proved that he was stronger (than death) through his (actual) death on the cross.[122] Zirker comes up with the surprising interpretation that Surah 4:156–159 can be understood as a confirmation of the Christian belief in the Resurrection.[123] To quote Zirker:

> Jesus's opponents wanted to destroy him through the Crucifixion; they thought that they would be able to annihilate the Messenger of God. They appeared to have succeeded too, but they were mistaken. Death had not triumphed over Jesus; God raised him to Himself. [...] Paraphrased thus, the text [of the Qur'an] becomes part of the Easter proclamation.[124]

What is decisive in whether such an interpretation of the Qur'anic text is admissible is the aforementioned question of whether *shubbiha* refers to 'him' or 'it', i.e. if it was not an obvious, real crucifixion or if it was not really Jesus who was crucified. If, like Kenneth Cragg and many other exegetes, we assume that 'it', i.e. *the Crucifixion*, is the intended meaning,[125] then substitution theory can be excluded as an interpretive category, and it will be intriguing to see how the docetism theory develops. Cragg also highlights a variety of interpretations in this respect, all of which tend to suggest that this does not cast doubt on the real historical occurrence of the Crucifixion.[126] If one accepts this interpretation, then

---

122 See Hans Zirker, *Islam. Theologische und gesellschaftliche Herausforderungen*, Düsseldorf 1993, 135–42.

123 See ibid. 136, with reference to John 3:14; 12:34; Acts 2:33 and Phil. 2:9. Zirker considers his interpretation to be legitimate within the context of the Qur'an, but he holds out little hope that faithful Muslims will follow his mediation proposal because it is too close to the Christian creed. The new dialogue framework of comparative theology does, however, give us some grounds for hope that the interpretation he has developed may also be recognised as a possible interpretation by Muslims. The Muslim author of this book, in any case, sees no reason why this interpretive offer should be ruled out as impossible.

124 See ibid. 141. Zirker does admit immediately after this interpretation that it runs the risk of understanding the Muslim faith better than Muslims themselves do. One will therefore have to wait and see whether this kind of interpretation is accepted on the Muslim side. Mahmoud Ayoub has in any case already done important work in this direction.

125 See Cragg, op. cit. 172.

126 See ibid. 136. In a similar vein is the study by Todd Lawson, *The Crucifixion and the Qur'an. A Study in the History of Muslim Thought*, Oxford 2009, 95, 143, as, for example,

the Qur'an – according to Cragg's analysis – would not even need to reject the link between the cross and salvation, but merely the exclusive nature of this link.[127] What the Qur'an ultimately rejects – and this is also the view of Mahmoud Ayoub – is merely humans' power to destroy the Word of God.[128] By rejecting this, the proclaimer of the Qur'an knows he is in agreement with Christians, and so the Qur'anic perspective on Jesus of Nazareth testifies to a profound power that also carries a meaningful message for Christians.

Christians will surely be permanently irritated by the fact that the Qur'an can develop its Jesuology without making any reference to the cross. Yet before using that as an argument, one should consider that the cross has far less significance in Eastern Christianity than it does in the West. It is no coincidence that the Church of the Holy Sepulchre in Jerusalem has always been known as the Church of the Resurrection in the Eastern tradition.[129] The cross was obviously of only marginal importance for the Christian theology of the Eastern Churches, and so the proclaimer of the Qur'an does not necessarily have any critical intention towards Christianity by not engaging with the subject.

4.3 Surah al-Ma'ida

The fifth surah has the initially prosaic-sounding title of 'The Table' (*al-mā'ida*) and large sections of it can be read as the final surah of the Qur'an – that is in any case the opinion of Theodor Nöldeke and others, who in this agree with the Muslim tradition.[130] Some Muslim scholars view Surah 9 as the last surah, while other voices classify Surah al-Ma'ida as the final one.[131] The late date of the more recent parts of Surah 5 at least can be determined, among other things, by the fact that Muhammad is holding a form of final sermon here, highlighting that his proclamation has more or less reached its conclusion. Q 5:3 reads: 'Today I have perfected your religion for you, completed my blessing upon you, and chosen as your religion *Islam*.' Of course that does not mean that the whole of Surah 5

Tobias Specker, 'Das Kreuz – der trennende theologische Skandal', in *ThPQ* 161 (2013) 243–52, here 246, makes clear.

127 Cragg, op. cit. 183.

128 See Ayoub, op. cit. 176.

129 We are grateful to Angelika Neuwirth for this information.

130 See Theodor Nöldeke, *Geschichte des Qorāns. Erster Teil, Über den Ursprung des Qorāns*, Leipzig 1909, 227–34.

131 See Jalal al-Din al-Suyuti, *al-Itqan fi 'ulum al-Qur'an*, edited by 'Isam Faris al-Harastani, vol. 1, Beirut 1998/1419, 92–4.

should be classified in relation to this final sermon. Surahs 5 and 9 are two of the longer surahs, and they also appear to have expanded over a relatively long period. Yet in view of the Christologically relevant verses of these two surahs, it is highly likely that some of the considerations in Surah 5 originated chronologically after Surah 9, as we shall now explain more fully.

4.3.1 Structure and themes of the surah

The surah may be roughly divided into four main blocks. The framework is defined by a list of legal guidelines for the faithful in the context of Muhammad's farewell to them (Q 5:1–11) at the beginning and, at the end, by statements about Jesus, first stressing his singularity and lastly describing the organisation of the Eucharist (Q 5:109–120). The two longer middle sections contain, on the one hand, legal guidelines for the faithful (Q 5:87–108) and on the other a very detailed address to Jews and Christians (Q 5:12–86), with only small insertions in which the addressees are Muslims. The theme is the breaking of a bond with God (verses 12 and 14), breaches of religious laws and a call to respect them (42–50). Another topic is the breach of an alliance with Jews and Christians (51–58). The overall message is that the People of the Book are urged to comply with the laws in their scriptures (68–70) and not to exaggerate their beliefs (72–77) – for example, not to overdo the proper veneration of Jesus to the point where he becomes an idol. The block concludes with a clear honouring of Christ (82–86).

Alongside the title containing the highly meaningful allusion – for Christians – to the table of the Eucharist, the surah has another descriptive title: *al-'Uqud* (the agreements).[132] This name is actually a far more apt expression of the central theme of the surah, as it repeatedly discusses God's bond with people, agreements, alliances, laws and their observance. The surah therefore begins with an appeal to the faithful to observe the agreements (*al-'uqūd*). This theme then runs through the entire text: the faithful should observe the guidelines of the Qur'an. Christians and Jews should have obeyed their bond with God, the laws of the Torah and the knowledge of the Gospels; the Jews should have taken their alliance with the Muslims seriously. The establishment of the Eucharist by Jesus is – consistent with the message suggested by the introductory words – similar to the conclusion of a pact: God warns those who become unbelievers afterwards.

One central topic of the Surah al-Ma'ida, right at the beginning and then again

---

132 See *Der Koran. Arabisch-Deutsch*, Introduction and commentary by Adel Theodor Khoury, vol. 6, Gütersloh 1995, 25.

and again, are cultic relations such as guidelines for rituals and meals. It is striking that verse 6 of the surah, for example, sets out more precise rules for washing
before ritual prayers. The text obviously wishes to consolidate the ritual corner-
stones of Muslims' liturgical practice before the imminent end of Muhammad's
life. Conscious of the fact that the Prophet will soon no longer be around to serve
as an example, the aim of the surah is to ensure that, even in the Prophet's absence,
his liturgical practice will continue and the ritual markers of identity will galva-
nise the integrity of the Muslim community. This is particularly interesting from
a Christian point of view because it is the Surah al-Ma'ida that clearly notes the
establishment of the final supper by Jesus of Nazareth.

The allusion to the Eucharist is found in Q 5:110–115 after a summary repetition of many of the Qur'an's positive statements about Jesus.[133] These are supplemented by some notable elements such as an observation that Jesus raised the
dead to life,[134] and that God preserved him (during his time as an itinerant preacher
in Galilee?) from the children of Israel (Q 5:110). Our view, however, is that the
main message here is to confirm Jesus's establishment of the Eucharist.

The discussion of the Eucharist arises because people's misconstrual of Jesus's
displays of power as magic challenges his disciples' faith, and they therefore seek
solid reasons for professing their faith. They ask Jesus for God to send them a
table (with food) from heaven (Q 5:112). Jesus first of all commands them to
believe without any such sign (see John 20:29). Yet when they confess their lack
of faith and insecurity to him, begging for this sign to provide them with certainty
in their beliefs, and also assure him that in the future they will testify to their faith
at the table (Q 5:113), Jesus fulfils their wish and asks God to send down the table,
'a feast from heaven so that we can have a festival – the first and last of us – and
a sign from You' (Q 5:114).

Although one gets the impression until verse 113 that all of this is a description

---

133 See Matthias Radscheit, 'Table', in *Encyclopaedia of the Qur'an* 5 (2006) 188–91,
here 189; Karl-Josef Kuschel, *Festmahl am Himmelstisch. Wie Mahl feiern Juden,
Christen und Muslime verbindet*, Ostfildern 2013, 121–47. Kuschel's account provides a
particularly detailed and impressive analysis of the possible interpretations of this passage.
Unfortunately, his conclusion, with which we disagree, is that the scene of the table (which
we shall now discuss) is the eschatological banquet at the end of days (see ibid. 146).
134 Jürg H. Buchegger, *Das Wort vom Kreuz in der christlich-muslimischen Begegnung.
Leben und Werk von Johan Bouman*, Basel 2013, 156, emphasises 'that there is no
grammatical difference between the activities of Jesus and of Allah in their waking of the
dead'. He nevertheless continues to espouse the opinion that he must hold on to the fact that
'the Qur'an does not [manage] to make the link between the miracles and Jesus's mission'
(ibid. 157).

of a miraculous feast for the disciples alone, this verse, in our opinion, makes it abundantly clear that there is a cultic or ritual dimension to this.[135] Whether or not the semantics of the word 'table' point to the Eucharist,[136] the Arabic word for 'festival' or 'feast' (*'īd*) – a Qur'anic hapax legomenon – refers to the ritual feasts that had flourished under Islam. This term originally meant 'promise' or 'testimony' and only developed the meaning of 'feast' over time.[137] Yet even the original meaning is very, perhaps even more, appropriate for the Eucharist. The quotation 'until the end of time', like the previously elucidated testimony of disciples about the table, makes it clear that this is not a one-off sign but something that happens again and again. It would indeed be barely intelligible why a single miraculous feast should rescue the disciples from their wavering beliefs when shortly before the text refers to Jesus's awakening of the dead to life – an act the disciples would presumably consider to be more spectacular than a miraculous feast. The special significance of the waking of the dead is once more underscored by the fact that the same surah makes clear that he who saves someone from death saves humanity as a whole (Q 5:32). It represents salvation for all, an action that may not be overshadowed by the simple collective meal.

In our opinion, the best interpretation of the sending down of the table is as an allusion to the Eucharist, since this is the central event for the Church from which it derives trust in its faith. It is *the* sign that constantly renews the Christian faith over the ages, and it is the lynchpin of the enduring legitimacy of Christian testimony. It is noteworthy that the proclaimer of the Qur'an obviously accepts this testimony and even urges the disciples to take it seriously. That is because God not only fulfils the disciples' wish put to him by Jesus in verse 115 but also enrols them in a special responsibility founded on the Eucharist. Anyone who ignores the gift of the Eucharist and continues in unbelief, anyone who, with

---

135 This was already familiar in the Muslim tradition and so it can be no coincidence that this miracle took place on a Sunday according to several traditional exegetes, and established a Christian feast. See, for example, the corresponding indications in al-Zamakhshari (Çinar, *Maria und Jesus im Islam*, 167). Similar statements can be found in al-Tabari (vgl. al-Tabari, *Jami' al-bayan*, vol. 9, 123 ff.) and al-Razi (vgl. al-Razi, *al-Tafsir al-kabir*, vol. 12, 139).
136 According to A. Jeffery, the word used here – and found nowhere else in the Qur'an – may have come from the Ethiopian language as a special name for the table of the Eucharist (see Parrinder, op. cit. 88).
137 We are grateful for this information to Ahmad Pakatchi, who substantiates it with a reference to the first Arabic lexicographers Ibn 'Arabi (767–845) and his pupil Ta'lab (815–904), but also due to the word's Semitic roots. Dirk Hartwig also argues for translating it as 'testimony' in his forthcoming article for the Corpus Coranicum project, see TUK_1377 soon.

open eyes, refuses communion with Christ in the Lord's Supper will receive the harshest imaginable punishment. This statement fits perfectly with the Christian self-conception of there being nothing worse than for a person to turn away from God's word of acceptance when it is offered in binding and intelligible fashion and when he or she has previously been accepted into the community of Jesus's disciples. We would of course express this less bluntly nowadays, but the text is completely in line with Christian beliefs in late antiquity and even the Middle Ages and is also open to modern interpretations.

The culmination of the Muslim religion at the end of Muhammad's life and his liturgical legacy to his community are placed in the context of Jesus's own legacy – an explicit endorsement of Christian liturgical practice. Muhammad thereby subscribes to the Christian tradition in positive, productive and autonomous fashion. This surah, named after the table of the Eucharist, therefore lays out a far more peaceful attitude to Christianity than people have hitherto believed. In the next section we would like to focus on a few polemical passages that demonstrate that the Qur'an is no longer so emphatic about its common ground with Christians, since it also cites clear differences and categorically distances itself from specific Christian groupings.

4.3.2 Criticism of any deification of human beings

A first central criticism in the surah escalates the accusation already articulated in Q 3:64 that some Jews and Christians tend towards instituting themselves as lords, and expounds on this point. It now says that Jews and Christians describe themselves as the 'Sons of God' and His lovers (Q 5:18). This reproach is so similar to an accusation in Q 9:30–31 that there is a good argument that it picks up historically on the same controversial situation. Let us therefore look at the relevant passage from the ninth surah.

Interestingly, it is not only Christians who are accused of worshipping Christ as the Son of God; the Jews are admonished for doing the same with Ezra (see Q 9:30). This scene feels slightly surreal in that we do not know of any Jews who worship Ezra as the Son of God, and there is no evidence in religious history of any such groups. Traditional Muslim exegetes are clearly somewhat uneasy about this insinuation, and they speculate that there must have been a corresponding Jewish grouping, while simultaneously admitting that contemporary Judaism no longer holds any such views.[138] But perhaps the thrust of the verse is a completely

---

138 Al-Zamakhshari, for example, explains that only the Jews who lived in Medina

different one. The concrete accusation of worshipping 'Uzair (or Ezra, with whom traditional exegesis equates 'Uzair) could, according to Patricia Crone, building on Paul Casanova's argument, be traced back to an incorrect reading of the name Azael. This may be based on the fallen angels of the Ethiopian Book of Enoch, who are also called the sons of God. Despite insufficient evidence for Casanova's theory and the fact that it leaves certain questions unresolved, Crone suggests that the most likely explanation is that Q 9:30 refers to the Jewish veneration of an angel-like intermediary.[139]

Yet reading Q 9:30 in its Qur'anic context throws up a far simpler explanation suggestion. The Jews are accused not only of viewing Ezra as the Son of God but also of worshipping their scribes in the same way. Christians too are admonished for having taken their scholars and monks or bishops, like Christ, for 'lords instead of God alone' (see Q 9:31). At first glance, one is tempted to respond that Christians do not worship bishops and monks like God. It turns out on closer inspection, however, that the situation at the time of the emergence of the Qur'an was somewhat different. As prominent an author as Pseudo-Dionysius the Areopagite expressed the idea that their anointment made bishops similar to gods.[140] Monks also enjoyed the greatest reverence in the Oriental Church and often had even greater authority than bishops. Holger Zellentin notes how strongly the Qur'an criticises this veneration, and so Q 9:30–31 appears to attack these same people.[141] Regardless of whether bishops or monks are the target here, this interpretation, or something like it, is backed up by the evidence that mention of the sons of God in Q 9:30–31 was already interpreted as an expression of Christian arrogance in classical Muslim exegesis.[142]

---

genuinely regarded 'Uzair as the Son of God (Çinar, *Maria und Jesus im Islam*, 146 with reference to Q 9:30). 'Al-Razi goes on to explain that this view was probably widespread among Jews at the time, but has since become insignificant' (ibid. 148).

139 See Patricia Crone, 'The Book of Watchers in the Qur'ān', in Haggai-Ben Shammai / Shaul Shaked / Sarah Stroumsa (eds.), *Exchange and Transmission Across Cultural Boundaries. Philosophy, Mysticism and Science in the Mediterranean World*, Jerusalem 2013, 16–51, here 41–51. Karl-Josef Kuschel highlights evidence in the Talmud that Ezra really did enjoy religious veneration by Jews (Kuschel, *Die Bibel im Koran*, 204). However, neither he nor his principal witness Heinrich Speyer can name one piece of evidence that proves that Ezra was actually worshipped by Jews as the Son of God.

140 See Pseudo-Dionysius the Areopagite, *De ecclesiastica hierarchia*, V, 2.1., quoted in Peter Neuner, *Ekklesiologie I. Von den Anfängen zum Mittelalter* (*Texte zur Theologie. Dogmatik*; 5.1), Graz 1994, 63–4.

141 See Zellentin, *The Qur'an's Legal Culture*, 221, 225. We are dubious as to whether it is really bishops and not monks who are the target here. This is, however, less central to his argument than he thinks, due to the considerable veneration of monks.

142 See Mun'im Sirry, *Scriptural Polemics. The Qur'an and Other Religions*, Oxford 2014, 141.

That such hubris might indeed be the target here is supported by a Qur'anic accusation from around the same time that Christians and Jews called one another God's sons and protégés (Q 5:18). Just as in Q 9:30, the word 'son' is represented in Arabic by *ibn* or *abnā'* – a metaphorical denomination – leading to Christ, Ezra, angels or contemporary authorities being endowed with divine power in both religions, from which people inferred a special relationship between God and their own community. Traditional Islamic exegetes pointed out long ago that the occasion of revelation in Q 5:18 consisted of Jewish leaders rejecting Muhammad's threats of judgement with the suggestion that they have nothing to fear as sons of God – a piece of contextual information that could also credibly apply to Q 9:31, as Mun'im Sirry explains.[143]

Whatever one's view of this historical reconstruction, it seems plausible to us that the Qur'an attacks in Q 9:30–31 abusive practices that exist in both religions. One must indeed acknowledge that there have been, and still are, clerical traditions and cults of the saints that unquestionably feed the Qur'an's suspicions,[144] just as there may have been phases in Jewish history when Ezra and the associated return to the Promised Land gained a superhistorical significance. Faced with such extreme situations, the voice of the Qur'an steps in to warn against such blindness (Q 9:30).

Here there is no blanket criticism of Christian or Jewish beliefs, but an objection to exaggerated intensifications of these forms of belief. One particular reproach levelled specifically at Christianity in this context is that it occasionally confuses God with Christ. To quote: 'Those who say, "God is the Messiah, the son of Mary" are defying the truth' (Q 5.17.72). These verses are followed by a riposte that lays bare the positions the Qur'an observes in the groups it is criticising. In the first case, it clarifies that God alone is powerful and He can therefore also destroy Christ and Mary. On the other hand, Christians and Jews appear to think that they are safe from judgement because they believe that they enjoy an especially privileged relationship with God. They misconstrue the fact that they have been chosen to devote their lives to God as a privilege that shields them from God's judgement and therefore removes them from His control (see again Q 5:18). From the Qur'an's point of view, every person including Jesus, Ezra, the scribes and the bishops is subject to the rule of God, who alone has all the power.

---

143 Ibid. 140.
144 See the very concrete criticism in Q 9:34 of the scribes and monks or bishops, which are reminiscent of Jesus's statements about the Scribes and the Pharisees, and which was probably the result of painful experience.

In the second case, Christ himself answers, saying, "'Children of Israel, worship God, my Lord and your Lord." If anyone associates others with God, God will forbid him from the Garden, and Hell will be his home' (Q 5:72). In its invitation to devote one's life to God, Christ's message is clearly regarded as being consistent with the Qur'an's message, whereas the proclaimer of the Qur'an focuses on those Christians who degrade God into an idol and reduce Him to Christ. Incidentally, the Qur'an's formulation in Q 5:17.72 is also dubious from a Christian perspective, as of course God cannot be reduced to one of the persons of the Trinity. In particular, one would barely find a single Christian who would sincerely reverse the order of the usual Christian profession of faith and say that God is Christ.[145]

In our historical considerations in Chapter 2, however, we saw that some in Emperor Justinian's entourage made theological arguments during the Theopaschite Controversy that Christ can not only be called God, but equally God Christ.[146] Tellingly, this was the precise theological context in which Justinian made the title of Jesus Christ as *one of the Trinity* binding for the whole empire.[147] Sidney Griffith drew attention to the fact that the Qur'anic defence against Christ as *'thālithu thalāthatin'* in Q 5:73 adopts a Syriac honourific title for Jesus, who is always described there as One of Three.[148] This honourific title was also common in Byzantine Christianity, and it is employed here with a critical purpose. The formulation, as in Q 5:72, turns the usual Christian expression around and picks up on theological considerations we see voiced only in the Theopaschite Controversy. The background to these theological thoughts is an idea that still occasionally features in Christological debate, namely the idea that there is nothing we can say about God that is not said through Jesus Christ,[149] and so one has the impression that God is restricted to Christ. This downgrades God to an idol that has lost its power by becoming something finite.

Reducing God to an idol is indeed an enduring, inherent risk of any Christology, and the proclaimer of the Qur'an rightly condemns it. In view of Surah

---

145 This, in any case, is the argument of Griffith, *Al-Naṣārā in the Qur'ān*, 311, who diagnoses in this a Qur'anic counter-discourse designed to demonstrate to Christians what it is that they are doing when they deify Christ. We are, however, not sure how effective this rhetorical escalation is if it invents a new formula that nobody would use.
146 See again Uthemann, *Kaiser Justinian*, 20.
147 Ibid, 34–5.
148 See Griffith, *Al-Naṣārā in the Qur'ān*, 317; for a more detailed discussion, see Griffith, *Syriacisms in the 'Arabic Qur'an': Who were 'those who said Allāh is the third of three' according to al-Mā'ida 73?*, 100–8.
149 See Menke, *Jesus ist Gott der Sohn*, 27, 78, 444, 506, 518.

al-Ma'ida's energetic proclamations of esteem for Christians (see Q 5:82 alone) and the recognition of the enduring legitimacy of the Christian path of salvation (Q 5:48), it can be assumed that the Qur'an's criticism is not intended as a general criticism but as a denunciation of a specific Christological exaggeration.[150] Insofar as the historical traces of this escalation point to Byzantium, there is a plausible suspicion of a vein of anti-Byzantine sentiment running through these passages that would date from the late Medinan period – a possible interpretation that we shall examine more closely now.

This accusation is justified from a theological perspective in Q 5:116, when the Qur'an specifically has Jesus say that God knows everything about Jesus but, conversely, Jesus himself does not have divine knowledge. It is true that the Christian tradition has taken its lead from passages such as John 10:30 and John 16:15, as well as statements in the Synoptic Gospels about Jesus's prescience, in its repeated attempts to project divine omniscience onto Jesus. Yet at the very latest it was historically critical exegesis that made it clear to Christian theologians that this was not a viable path. It also systematically and totally contradicts the kenotic idea, which must influence Christology and whose consequences for Jesus's humanity the Qur'an also repeatedly points out.

The proclaimer of the Qur'an has obviously had dealings with Jews who venerate their scribes and Ezra to such a degree that they begin to take the place of God. In precisely this vein, the Qur'an attacks Christians who put their clerics or monks and Jesus in God's rightful position. In criticising these forms of human deification, the proclaimer of the Qur'an insists that all power is with God alone and all humans are subordinated to him.

Q 5:75 provides an additional and particular illustration of the great store the proclaimer of the Qur'an sets by the integrity of Jesus's mortality. In this instance, the Qur'an relates its criticism of the deification of Jesus to the seemingly trivial statement that Mary and Jesus ate food like other ordinary mortals. The interesting thing is that this self-evident observation is also what Muslim exegetical tradition repeatedly employs as an argument against the Christian faith.[151] This intervention,

---

150 There are certainly signs within the Muslim exegetic tradition of an awareness that the proclaimer of the Qur'an is not targeting Christianity as a whole in Q 5:17 but a specific Christological sect. See Sirry, *Scriptural Polemics*, 146: 'Qāsimī cites Rāzī's observation, however, he notes that the verse may in fact refer to a group (*qawm*) of Christians who said that the reality of God is the Messiah and no other.'

151 See, for example, Çinar, *Maria und Jesus im Islam*, 155: 'Regarding the sentence "Both ate food" (Q 5:75) he [al-Tabari] adds that Jesus and his mother were ordinary mortals who needed food and water. This is clear proof that they could not be divine and not the

which seems almost scurrilous from a modern perspective, and its prominent reception become immediately comprehensible when one recalls the intensive wrangling within contemporary Christianity over whether Jesus was free of any form of corruptibility. Regardless of how widespread the Julianism we analysed in Chapter 2 really was, one may assume that related debates cast doubts over the integrity of Jesus's mortality and the authentically human nature of his eating habits for a long time afterwards. It is eminently comprehensible and, from a Christian point of view, of lasting helpfulness that the Qur'an reminds us of the integrity of Jesus's humanity. Christians must therefore agree that however free from original sin – and as a result from the consequences of the Fall – they were, Jesus and Mary nevertheless ate normally and thus fully shared the weaknesses of human nature. How else is a Christian to hold on to the soteriologically significant idea that through Jesus Christ God allows Himself to be touched by human cares and needs?

4.3.3 A break with Christianity?

The rest of Surah al-Ma'ida discusses a conception of God that not only places Jesus and Mary at God's side but also replaces God with a belief in them, to the extent that faith in God seems lost. Verse 116 says: 'Take me and my mother as two gods alongside God?'[152] This passage is often understood as if the proclaimer of the Qur'an saw Mary and Jesus as persons of the Trinity, but the text only takes aim at the veneration of Mary and Jesus as idols. There are naturally other parts of the Qur'an that testify to a critical dispute with tritheist ideas within Christianity (in particular Q 4:171–172). Yet one should not impute an erroneous conception of the Trinity to the proclaimer of the Qur'an. When the Qur'an stresses, for example – in an apparently doxological passage – the Christ Jesus is not only God's word but also His spirit (see Q 4:171), then it is surely no coincidence that he uses the precise terminology that Christians employ for trinitarianism. The Qur'an therefore connects word and spirit – the two historically tangible elements of the Trinity – to Jesus, thus preemptively pulling the rug from under any speculation regarding social trinitarianism.[153] The next sentence makes it clear that this

---

Creator Himself.' Al-Razi also thinks that this is intended as an implicit accusation against Christians, because they allegedly say that Jesus and Mary ate only with their human part and not with their divine part (al-Razi, *al-Tafsir al-kabir*, vol. 12, 65).

152 The Arabic words *min dūni* do not actually mean 'alongside' as they are often translated, but 'without/excluding'.

153 For an introduction to the strengths and weaknesses of social trinitarianism, see Stosch, *Trinität*, 112–36.

profession is designed to stifle the notion that God can be counted in any way and that, from a pragmatic point of view, humans would be advised not to embroil themselves in trinitarian speculation (Q 4:171).

Incidentally, this is the only passage in which Christians are warned not to attribute a *walad* to God. The proclaimer of the Qur'an appears to be giving the following warning: if Christians go so far in their trinitarianism (flying in the face of their own tradition!) to claim that there are three denumerable entities in God, then they are speaking like the pagan Arabs who ascribe children to God in the biological sense and don't understand that God requires neither advocates nor intermediaries. So if Christians start to develop asocial trinitarianism, they can no longer be recognised as monotheists and make themselves the equals of the polytheists (*mushrikūn*) from whom they are otherwise clearly distinguished in the Qur'an.

So there is obviously a debate in the Qur'an about the internal threat of trinitarianism. However, Q 5:116 does not take aim at social trinitarianism but instead at the deification of humans, which has reached a point where belief in God will disappear entirely. The Qur'an's criticism is therefore obviously about a form of Christianity that has lost all faith in God.[154] This is backed up by the fact that the criticism in Q 9:29 is levelled at a form of Christianity that no longer qualifies as monotheism. It does not strike us as very useful here to look for sects who view themselves in this atheistic manner. This is instead a criticism of a threat that lurks within Christianity to this day. The proclaimer of the Qur'an dissociates himself from any Christians who consider God's being made man to mean that individual humans are dispensed from all criticism, blurring the boundary between God and humans. When Christians idolise humans, they act like humans who have lost all commitment to God. Reading such passages in isolation, one might get the impression that Muhammad consummated the definitive break with Christianity towards the end of his life. This reading is backed up by the extremely harsh verse 5:51, which appears to suggest that Muslims should not cultivate friendly relations with Jews or Christians.

The term that is used here, *auliyā'*, refers less in the Qur'an to 'friendships'

---

154 In any case, this interpretation seems obvious if one reads Q 5:116 in the context of the passages in Q 9:29–31 that originated around the same time. So it makes no sense to us that Frank van der Welden, 'Kotexte im Konvergenzstrang – die Deutung textkritischer Varianten und christlicher Bezugstexte für die Redaktion von Sure 61 und Sure 5,110–119', in *Oriens Christianus. Hefte für die Kunde des christlichen Orients* 92 (2008) 130–173, here 170, sees East Syriac arguments against the Theopaschites here and thus a transposition of an intra-Christian controversy.

than to 'alliances' and 'patronage'. But *walīy* can also be a 'guardian', 'protector' or 'helper'. To translate it as 'friend' is therefore misleading.[155] It suggests that one should not bind the (contractual) loyalty of one's own tribe or one's own person to those who actually mock one's own religion and are hypocrites. It is, however, clear from verse 57 that the verse is only aimed at those Jews and Christians 'who ridicule and make fun of [their religion]'. One must therefore read these verses very carefully in context, which consists here, on the one hand, of the aforementioned forms of criticism of Christology and trinitarianism, which indeed also imply an estrangement from traditional forms of Christianity; yet there are also some very positive statements about Christianity here. If one reads on from the polemic passages attacking any curtailing of Jesus's humanity by Christians, it becomes clear by Q 5:82 at the latest that the Qur'an does not tar all Christians with the same brush. Here the Qur'an sharply criticises the Jews and 'those who associate other deities with God', and then it says: 'You are sure to find that the closest in affection towards the believers are those who say, "We are Christians."' In the next verse, it justifies this praise by stating that priests and monks are not given to arrogance and that they react to Muhammad with emotion and empathy (Q 5:83).[156] Evidently, the Qur'an is of the opinion that there are Christians who do not make idols and who therefore do not associate with other gods. It is completely possible to have friendly relations and agreement across religious boundaries with these Christians.

It is interesting that the aforementioned Christians are also allowed to express themselves in the Qur'an. They claim in their defence that they believe in God (Q 5:84) and are thus not affected by the accusation expressed in Q 5:116, especially as they have been promised eschatological rewards (Q 5:85). In other places in the surah, the People of the Book[157] are promised forgiveness (see Q 5:65–66), and there is also an explicit reference to Jews and Christians who believe in God and the Last Day and need have no fear of God (see Q 5:69).

---

155 See also the use of the term in Q 7:155, where it would be impossible to translate it as 'friend'. In Q 9:52 too it obviously means God as a protector.

156 There is hard evidence of the high esteem in which monks were held on the Arabian Peninsula even in the pre-Islamic period. See Irfan Shahid, *Byzantium and the Arabs in the Sixth Century*, vol. 2/1, Washington, DC 2002, 166–7. When van der Velden takes Q 5:83 as his basis for assuming that there were meetings between Muslim and Christian dignitaries with liturgical elements, we think this goes beyond what one can decently extrapolate from the verse's wording. See Van der Velden, *Konvergenztexte syrischer und arabischer Christologie*, 186.

157 We shall need to examine in its own right why Christians are repeatedly classified as People of the Book or People of the Scripture. It is possible that the Syriac Christians referred to themselves in these terms.

During the same period, therefore, the Qur'an pronounces devastating criticism at church officials (Q 9:29–31) as well as voicing its highest esteem (Q 5:83–84). Since Q 9:29 can be seen historically as the start of mobilisation for a battle against a Byzantine army (*ghazwa Tabuk*, the Battle of Tabuk in 630[158]), the hierarchy's clear criticism seems to be directed at the veneration of bishops and monks in the imperial Byzantine church. Equally, from a theological point of view, we showed earlier that the arguments against the Christians here adopt arguments recorded in imperial edicts. It is also possible to apply the Qur'an's criticism to the Syriac Christians, who also showed great reverence towards monks and worshipped Christ as 'one of Three'.

Whichever Christian groupings may be alluded to here, we should warn readers generally against jumping to the conclusion that the proclaimer of the Qur'an actually means all Jews and Christians whenever he speaks of *the* Jews and *the* Christians. Qur'anic Arabic clearly does not use 'the Jews' or 'the Christians' as a universal qualifier, and it is therefore always conceivable that the reference is only to specific groups within these religions. Political associations are potentially foremost in the Qur'an's mind regarding 'the Jews', on the simple basis of the presumed betrayal by Jewish clans, who, according to traditional accounts, stabbed Muhammad in the back at the decisive battle against the Meccans.[159]

An observation that applies to the whole surah is that the Qur'an does not turn against Jews and Christians in general, but identifies concrete problems in certain groups within these religions. The Qur'an draws explicit attention to quarrels within Judaism and Christianity stemming from their having broken the convenant with God (Q 5:13–14). Verse 15, in a bout of overtly anti-Gnostic rhetoric, admonishes them for having hidden parts of the scripture and viewing it as an esoteric, secret teaching. The accusation is not intended to cast aspersions on all Christians and discredit the Bible *per se*, but to distinguish the spirits. Overall, the interreligious community of the table, to which the surah issued an invitation at the very beginning (Q 5:5), remains a prospect. At the end of the surah there is also the promise that humans, even when punished by God, never lose their dignity as servants of God (Q 5:118), and so sin will never entirely separate them from God.

The proclaimer of the Qur'an is therefore entirely willing to endorse some of the central starting points of Christology. Yet in the same breath it emits warnings

---

158 See Mujahid b. Jabr, *Tafsir*, edited by Muhammad 'Abdassalam Abul Nail, 1989/1410, 367; Guillaume, *The Life of Muhammad*, 602–9; Kuschel, *Die Bibel im Koran*, 202–3.
159 See Reza Aslan, *No god but God. The Origins, Evolution and Future of Islam*, New York 2005, here 87–92.

about the false path taken by Christian theology, and we see these as being of fundamental importance. The Qur'an confirms Jesus's miracles but issues a reminder that Jesus can only perform them with God's help, and that through them and through all his acts he wishes to deflect attention away from himself and towards God.[160] The Qur'anic Jesus conveys this same intention, and he can therefore summon Christians to obey. As the Qur'an makes clear: by listening to Jesus and entrusting ourselves to him, we can learn with him to look away from him and put God at the centre of our lives. Yet this path is always a path of faith, subject to challenges. Amid these challenges God bestows the Eucharist upon His Christian community, which was given through Jesus but at the same time emphasises that God is the true agent of this act. The allusion in Q 5:114 to the words of institution cannot be accidental; it is clear that it rejects the tradition of Jesus's words of institution, which downplay the epiclesis. It is always God who bestows and acts, even during the Crucifixion. Of course, this does not mean that the Qur'an denies human actions, simply that it shifts the emphasis away from inflated religious mortals who think they control everything themselves – and are therefore always in conflict – towards the perspective of humans as servants of God for whom Jesus sets an outstanding example.[161] It is perhaps possible with the Qur'an – at least within the hermeneutics of a Christian reading – to record that Jesus's singularity resides in the fact that he is so filled with the spirit of God that he becomes the Word of God for us, illustrating through his life and his teachings what it means to be a servant of God and, for that precise reason, what it means to be an exemplary human being.

---

160 The Qur'an contributes to this intention via a selective reception of the reported miracles and expunges all natural miracles – which are indeed historically controversial nowadays – while positively adopting the stories of healing. See Parrinder, *Jesus in the Qur'an*, 84. One exception is the miracle of the birds, which is reported several times in the Qur'an. Although the only Christian account of this miracle is in the Apocrypha, we can assume that this legend of Syriac origin was read throughout the Orient at the time of the proclamation of the Qur'an and was interpreted as a theological indication of Jesus's creative power. See van der Welden, *Konvergenztexte syrischer und arabischer Christologie*, 184, n. 51. The proclaimer of the Qur'an does not recoil from granting a positive reception to a text that is so important for Christian popular religion, but as in all the accounts of miracles, he makes it clear that here too God was the real agent.

161 Strikingly, the Qur'an not once criticises Jesus, even though it seems to take a criticial view of even Muhammad himself (see Q 80:1–2). There is no doubt whatsoever from the perspective of the Qur'an that Muhammad should be honoured as a fine example (see Q 33:21) and so if it is to be acceptable to Muslims, its emphasis on the singularity of Jesus must never detract from esteem for Muhammad.

5

Jesus's Position in Qur'anic Prophetology

In our detailed analysis of the Jesus verses in the Qur'an, we have seen that the proclaimer of the Qur'an describes Jesus not as the *Son of God* or as *God made man* but as a *prophet* and a *messenger*. The proclaimer of the Qur'an does however accommodate Christian sensibilities by also calling Jesus the *Word of God* and the *Messiah*. Far more prominent, and more significant for the proclaimer of the Qur'an's own shaping of how Jesus should be understood, is the description of Jesus as a prophet. We have not subjected this major title to closer analysis in previous chapters because its central importance to the Qur'an as a whole merits particular attention in its own right. One can only fully comprehend the naming of Jesus as a prophet and a messenger if one analyses precisely how prophetology is portrayed in the Qur'an as a whole. We would therefore like to focus in the following section on the phenomenon of prophetology in the Qur'an,[1] before seeking to define the relationship between prophetology and Christology.

Our understanding of prophecy and prophets (Greek: προφήτης) has been greatly influenced by the Hebrew Bible, and so there are significant challenges inherent in transposing this phenomenon to other religious traditions.[2] The main danger is a failure to recognise developments within the biblical tradition that

---

1 Although we have deliberately confined ourselves in this book to Qur'anic prophetology, this should in no way call into question the manifold importance of prophetology for Islamic theology in other respects. We cannot even begin to go into the great diversity of the Islamic tradition in this regard, and will purposely focus on the Qur'anic prophetology alone. Our reasons for adopting this approach are firstly the exegesis of the Jesus verses and, secondly, the fact that too little attention is often paid to the foundations of Qur'anic theology.
2 See Wassilios Klein, 'Propheten/Prophetie', in *Theologische Realenzyklopädie* 27 (1997) 474–5.

have led to changes in our understanding of prophecy and expanded and complicated our perception of prophets.[3] For the sake of religio-historical and comparative observations, we must content ourselves for now with a minimal religious and
phenomenological definition as a starting point:

> The verb to prophesy, from the Greek *prophemi* (*pro* = 'for' or 'forth' + *phemi*
> = 'to say', i. e. 'to say beforehand' or 'to foretell'), refers to a wide range of
> activities that defy any single categorisation but which include divination,
> visions, auditions, and oracles. These activities are associated with men and
> women who possess distinctive personal characteristics, speak or write in a
> special idiom, and act in a specific social setting. The prophet straddles the
> boundary between humanity and the divine. Through inspiration or ecstasy,
> she or he experiences a call from beyond and, as a result, feels compelled to
> proclaim an instruction, exhortation, warning, or prediction to members of
> her or his community. Thus understood prophecy may be said to include four
> components: a transcendental source, a message, a human transmitter, and an
> audience.[4]

As will become clear from the following study, these last four components of
prophecy are prerequisites for the proclamation of the Qur'an by Muhammad.
The mid-Meccan surahs in particular identify themselves in their introductory
and concluding sections as a reading (*qur'ān*) and a message from a transcendent
scripture, and Muhammad is charged with conveying this to an audience.

Our initially phenomenological approach to prophecy in the Qur'an[5] is designed
to safeguard us against having false and anachronistic expectations of the proclamation of the Qur'an and understanding it primarily as an erratic text. Naturally,
there are questions such as why the literary prophets in the Qur'an are not named
by their names,[6] and why people are described as prophets who do not fall into

---

3 Ibid. 499–510.
4 David S. Powers, 'The Finality of Prophecy', in Adam J. Silverstein / Guy G. Stroumsa
(eds.), *The Oxford Handbook of the Abrahamic Religions*, Oxford 2015, 254–71, here 254.
5 For a synchronic reconstruction of Qur'anic prophetology, see Uri Rubin, 'Prophets
and Prophethood', in *Encyclopaedia of the Qur'an* 4 (2004) 289–307; Bobzin provides an
excellent overview of the semantic conceptual field of prophets' titles in the Qur'an and how
they have evolved: Hartmut Bobzin, 'The "Seal of the Prophets": Towards an Understanding
of Muhammad's Prophethood', in Neuwirth / Sinai / Marx (eds.), *The Qur'an in Context*,
565–83.
6 See A. J. Wensinck, 'Muhammed und die Propheten', in *Acta Orientalia* 2 (1924) 169–70.

this category in the Bible.[7] Yet if one studies the environment of the Qur'an in late antiquity more closely, these points are less unusual than they might appear from a modern perspective. Also, the terminological definition of the prophets is far more flexible in the Qur'an than one would realise from enquiring only about the definition of prophecy. The Qur'an does indeed employ very different words for Muhammad and for biblical and non-biblical figures sent, chosen and distinguished by God: prophets (*nabīy, anbiyā', nabīyūn*), messengers/apostles (*rasūl/ rusul*), servants (*'abd, 'ibād*) and those who warn (*naḍīr*). This is related, among other things, to the many developments Christianity, Judaism and their religious environment underwent up until late antiquity and which softened the sharp divisions between these terms before the age of the emergence of the Qur'an.

This evolution does however reach back to biblical times. The Gospels mention prophets and apostles in the same breath. Both groups were persecuted and killed (Luke 11:47–51).[8] Paul's epistles also testify to the actions of prophets alongside apostles (1 Cor. 12:28; Eph. 2:20).[9] In general, biblical figures who do not appear by those names in the Hebrew Bible are often described in early Christianity as prophets and apostle,[10] and throughout late antiquity, there are prophetic movements and figures who are determined less by their denomination than by their claim to prophetic status.[11] There is a tendency here to systematise and universalise God's salvific work through prophets and messengers.

5.1 The early Meccan surahs: eschatological prophecy

Considering the lexical evidence, it is striking that the applicable Arabic term for prophet/prophets (*nabīy, anbiyā', nabīyūn*) does not appear once in the early Meccan surahs, whereas the word for messenger or apostle (*rasūl*) occurs several times (Q 91:13; 73:15–16; 77:11; 51:52; 69:10). The fact that, regardless, one can and must speak of Muhammad's prophetic consciousness in the early phase of the proclamation of the Qur'an is evident from the form and central topoi of the early surahs.

An *eschatological imperative* is inherent in the early Meccan surahs. Faith in

---

7 Ibid.
8 Matthew names scribes, wise men and prophets as being persecuted (Matt. 23:34), but omits apostles. This deviation should be understood in the context of Luke-Acts.
9 Wensinck, op. cit. 173–4.
10 Ibid.
11 Guy Stroumsa, *The Making of the Abrahamic Religions in Late Antiquity*, Oxford 2015, 59–71.

God's Judgement, accompanied by the resurrection of the dead (Q 100; 101; 82, etc.) and the ultimate dissolution of the physical world (Q 99; 81; 84; 80:33–42, etc.) inspire religious and social virtues. Those who deny this judgement, on the other hand, stand out by their ignorance of these virtues and neglect the relevant piousness that comes from specific ritual acts – prayer, vigils, feeding the poor, etc. (Q 107; 90). The early surahs promise consolation for the pious (Q 93; 94; 108), and one is reminded of God's care-filled affection for them (Q 105; 106). As a religio-political counterpart to the 'eschatological kerygma'[12] of the early Meccan surahs, people have invoked the Syriac Christian sermon literature, which already features many topoi of the early Meccan devotional discourse.[13] This pre-Qur'anic literature is very likely to have been present in oral form around the time of the early Qur'anic proclamations.[14]

Admittedly, there are differences not only in content but in form between the early Meccan surahs and Syriac Christian sermon literature.[15] Even in the early surahs the Qur'an speaks with the authority of a divine message to a proclaimer. However, this proclamation of the word of God takes the form of a decidedly *prophetic diction*, linking Muhammad *typologically* to the literary prophets on a formal and a linguistic level. If one is guided by the common distinction for prophetic annunciation by the biblical prophets between *reports* and *words*,[16] then the early Meccan proclamation presents itself *in nuce* as prophecy on both accounts. In terms of formal criticism, the prophetical words contain exclamations of woe, lamentations, warnings, disputations, announcements of calamities, talk of the Last Judgment, etc.[17] This prophetic typology is also found in the early Meccan surahs, although the latter is not linked to a wider narrative about God's interaction with a prophet and his salvific activity in favour of a specific people. The exclamations of woe in the Qur'an are, usually, not directed at actual historical persons or groups (Isa. 5:8–24; 10:1–4; 29:15; 28:1–4: Jer. 22:13–14) but discuss certain paradigmatic patterns of behaviour resulting from false beliefs (about death, etc.) and (social) ideals (Q 104; 83; 77). In the early surahs at least, no concrete historical damnation is announced for a specific iniquity (imminent eschatological expectation) (Isa. 8:5–10; 29:13–14; Ezek. 13:18–22). Rather, there is a threat of judgement at the

---

12 Nicolai Sinai, 'Der Koran', in Rainer Brunner (ed.), *Islam. Einheit und Vielfalt einer Weltreligion*, Stuttgart 2016, 132–66, here 142.
13 Ibid, 142–8; see Tor Andrae, *Der Ursprung des Islams und das Christentum*.
14 Ibid.146–8.
15 See Sinai, op. cit. 146.
16 See Hans Schmoldt, *Das Alte Testament*, Stuttgart 2004, 148–53.
17 Ibid. 150–2.

end of days (transcendent eschatology) for patterns of behaviour that proceed from denial of this judgement (Q 77; 107). In the context of a dispute over beliefs, the early Meccan surahs paint a picture of eschatological disaster. Contrary to the literary prophets' depictions, *God's judgement* is not a settling of accounts with specific peoples (Isa. 41:1–5; 43:8–13) but a transcendent judgement in which God reveals humans' ledgers to them after the resurrection and takes fair stock (Q 82; 81; 84).

Yet the prophetic proclamation is not indifferent to concrete proofs of God's favour in the past. The Quraysh are warned that they owe their prosperity to God's affection (Q 106). Individuals can also be rebuked for their wicked behaviour and admonished with divine punishment (Q 111). These signs of affection are not based on any sophisticated covenant theology. However, there is a reminder in terms of salvific history that God has already intervened on behalf of Muhammad's contemporaries (Q 105) and that he demands an appropriate awareness of this affection and its corresponding duties and beliefs.

The Qur'anic proclamation is qualified even in the early Meccan period as admonishment (*ḏikr/taḏkira*) (Q 81:27; 80:11; 69:12.48; 73:19; 74:49.54). The early Meccan surahs turn out to be warnings that establish a different relation between deed, retribution and return to God that the literary prophets and John the Baptist do. Contrary to the literary prophets' accounts, God does not threaten immediate earthly retribution or an instantaneous intervention on his part (Jer. 21:11–12; Isa. 8:19–20; 26:20–21). Nor, in the early Meccan surahs, is it possible to escape from imminent apocalyptic retribution through baptism. The eschatological kerygma of the early Meccan surahs conjures up dramatic images of transcendent final judgement to counter false ideas and to heighten their fear that resurrection and a settling of accounts will indeed ensue. These eschatological warnings therefore are meant to change beliefs and lead to internalised behaviour. Unlike in the Syriac Christian Church, a pious individual does not speak and preach against his community.[18] The proclaimer has the same aspiration as the literary prophets and is convinced that his message comes from God.

Muhammad first pronounces *words of disputation* starting in the middle Meccan phase, which is when the opponents of the early Muslim community make their first oral appearances.

Alongside the aforementioned repertoire of linguistic forms, the prophetical books of the Hebrew Bible also contain *reports*, which consist primarily of *visions* and *symbolic actions*.[19] However, the Qur'an does not describe symbolic acts

---

18 See Sinai, op. cit. 147–8.
19 See Schmoldt, *Das alte Testament*, 149–50.

by Muhammad, unlike the literary prophets. Muhammad does not perform any symbolic acts portending a future event (Isa. 8:1–4; 20:1–6; Jer. 13:1–11; Ezek. 4:1–2). Instead, the Qur'an develops a theology of signs, which is in a sense an adaptation of an *epistemic* (Neoplatonic thought, Gnosticism, etc.) and *linguistic turn* (names of God, language as a medium for the conveyance of the divine *logos*) to the context of late antiquity. Angelika Neuwirth has already proved for the early surahs of the Qur'an that the creation of humankind is linked to their gift of language and reason, and that God requires humans to use their disposition, so to speak, to be able to recognise His signs.[20] As the Qur'an's theology of signs grows clearer over the course of the middle and late Meccan periods, it is not simply physical creation that emerges as a sign of God's power. Rather, the divine speech proclaimed by Muhammad is itself composed of symbols.[21] This theology of signs is already implicit in the early Meccan surahs:

> Nevertheless, already in the early Meccan period, there is a pronounced
> sensibility for the sign character of the communicated message itself, the *āyāt*
> that are 'recited': *idhā tutlā 'alayhi āyātunā qāla asāṭīru l-awwalīn*, 'When
> our signs are recited to him, he says: fables of the ancients' (Q 83:13; cf. also
> Q 90:19, 78:28, 74:16, 54:42). *Āya* is thus used from the beginning in the two
> meanings of a textual sign (Greek *stoicheion* or *logos*) and a sensory, physical
> sign (Greek *semeion*). Thus, the designation *āya* is in no way confined to
> creation-specific textual units; but is used in general to mean a shorter textual
> unit of the Qur'an not defined in extent. Thus, from the outset, a deictic-
> paraenetic function is acknowledged for the recitation texts.[22]

Contrary to depictions of the literary prophets, Muhammad's *symbolic acts* are the *performance* of his proclamation of the divine speech. These signs have no prospective purpose but demand to be recognised as God's teaching about His creation, His acts and His nature.

Just as with the symbolic actions, there is no element of promise in Muhammad's implied *visions* in early Mecca. However, Muhammad does experience *inaugural visions* as the literary prophets do. Along with the typological reference of a vision to the calling of Moses on Mount Horeb (Q 53:13–18), Muhammad has two visions during the early Meccan period (Q 81:19–29; Q 53:1–12) that are

---

20 See Neuwirth, *The Qur'an and Late Antiquity*, 264–76.
21 Ibid. 274–5.
22 Ibid. 265.

reminiscent of Isaiah's inaugural vision (Isa. 6:1–13). We owe the most recent analysis of Isaiah's reception to Neuwirth.[23] In common with Isaiah's inaugural vision, both Qur'anic visions feature the image of God on His throne (*'inda ḍi l-'arshi makīnin*, 'by the Lord of the Throne'), although the latter is only implied in the later vision (*fa-stawā*, 'on the highest horizon'). In the first vision, it is an angel who conveys God's speech (Q 81:19), whereas later it is God Himself who is seen by Muhammad, God's servant. Unlike Isaiah, Muhammad does not describe from his own perspective his memories of being called by God. The Qur'anic visions actually serve to authorise Muhammad's proclamation as divine speech, not the word of an outcast devil (81:22.25).[24] At the same time, Muhammad is legitimised as a prophet because his experiences of revelation adapt the calling of the literary prophets. Hence Muhammad appears in these visions as God's appointed prophet, his proclamation authorised by God.

The juxtaposition of *reports* and *words*, which refer expressly to elements of the proclamations of the literary prophets, testify to a prophetic density in the early Meccan surahs that is no longer present *in the same way* in the later surahs. We could supply further examples of the adaptation of the use of prophetic vocabulary here (double images, etc.). Individual forms of speech are, of course, generally biblical and found in all the books of the Bible. And yet, the *close combination* of these formal and linguistic proclamation elements clearly refers, despite all their differences, to the books of the literary prophets. We do not know what form and what nature of reception the literary prophets enjoyed among Muhammad's entourage, but numerous prophetic movements and discussion about false and true prophets continued for a long time into late antiquity.[25] The formal and typological adaptation of prophetic language in the early Meccan surahs offers at least an indication that the Arabian Peninsula was not untouched by the reception of the prophetic books. Their form (oral/written) and place in life (liturgy, prayer, etc.) requires further research and elucidation.

5.1.1 Imminent eschatological expectation?

Stephen J. Shoemaker recently drew attention to a long and suppressed research tradition that discerned an imminent eschatological expectation in the early

---

23 Angelika Neuwirth, 'Zur Jesaja-Rezeption im Koran', in Florian Wilk / Peter Gemeinhardt (eds.), *Transmission and Interpretation of the Book of Isaiah in the Context of Intra- and Interreligious Debates*, Leuven 2016, 373–91.
24 Ibid. 379.
25 See Stroumsa, *The Making of the Abrahamic Religions*, 59–71.

Meccan surahs.[26] He wrote that this significant insight had been marginalised in the previous century by a wish to see Muhammad as more of a social reformer or a moral preacher.[27] Shoemaker pleads for the imminent eschatological expectation of the early Meccan surahs to be taken seriously[28] and placed in its religio-historical context. He seeks to do the latter by highlighting the widespread eschatological hopes and beliefs shortly before the emergence of Islam and afterwards.[29] These imminent eschatological expectations can be found in the many new interpretations of the Book of Daniel, expressing themselves in the political conduct of the major powers and their interpretations ('imperial eschatology').[30] Shoemaker then makes the link to Fred M. Donner's theory and states that, being a new religious group, the early Christian movement had no identity of its own and that the early Meccan surahs point to an imminent expectation.[31] The belief that the end of the world was nigh also played an eminent role in the expansion of Islam. Shoemaker compares the eschatological proclamation of the Qur'an with the eschatology of the Gospels, in which there is a tension between present and future eschatology.[32] This tension is also apparent in the Qur'an, Shoemaker says. Although the Qur'an contains no annunciation of the Kingdom of God, it is possible to argue that the Arabic word *'amr* can be translated as 'kingdom', inviting suggestions of a *basileia* annunciation.[33]

In our previous observations, we presented the theory that the early Meccan proclamation should be understood as eschatological prophecy. Contrary to Shoemaker, we are of the opinion that the proclamation of the early Qur'an is not at all *apocalyptic* and does not announce the imminent end of an eon.

The early Meccan surahs lack the form of an apocalyptic text. They contain none of the secret words that characterise prophecies about the future. Of course, that does not preclude the possibility that the early surahs announce apocalyptic thoughts, but the difference in form should at least warn us not to be too quick to consider the eschatological proclamation of the Qur'an as apocalyptic. In contrast, the Gospels clearly paint a picture of Jesus that implies the annunciation of

---

26 See Stephen J. Shoemaker, 'The Reign of God Has Come. Eschatology and Empire in Late Antiquity and Early Islam', in *Arabica* 61 (2014) 514–58, here 515–7.

27 Ibid. 518–20.

28 Ibid. 524–6.

29 Ibid. 535–7.

30 Ibid. 535–7.

31 Ibid. 527–9.

32 Ibid. 524–6.

33 Ibid. 529–31.

apocalyptic ideas through him. Despite the apocalyptic content, his eschatological proclamation is formally prophetic.[34] There are, however, differences between Muhammad and Jesus as eschatological prophets.

The *words of accomplishment* in the Gospels (Matt. 13:16; Luke 16:16; Mark 2:18 ff.), not least, are a sign that Jesus was convinced that the Kingdom of God is at least coming.[35] Also, the many *words of battle and advent* (Luke 10:18; Matt. 12:28; Matt. 12:22; Luke 17:21; Mark 4:26–29) prove that the Kingdom of God has already come and that its presence reveals itself in the triumph of good over evil.[36] At the same time, the Lord's Prayer and the Beatitudes indicate that the rule of God has yet to fully begin.[37] This tension between presence and expectation also characterises Jesus's sermon about the Final Judgement.[38] He does not utter a categorical threat of judgement. The only ones who need fear it are those who reject the Kingdom of God and deny themselves to it.[39] The conditions of entry into the Kingdom of God that Jesus articulates (Mark 10:25) also turn certain expectations on their head. Sinners and the needy can count on entering (Matt. 5:3–5; Luke 6:20–22; Matt. 21:28–32).[40] Only in very rare cases is judgement pronounced in advance on individual cities due to their attitude of denial (Luke 10:13–15).[41] Otherwise, for example in his lamentations about the Scribes (Luke 11:37–39), Jesus refrains from naming their punishment or pronouncing a sentence.[42] It is suggested in some places that the coming Son of Man will sit in judgement and that this role will be taken on by the disciples.[43] The Jesus of the Gospel appears to be sure that a new eon begins with the Kingdom of God and that natural disasters, for instance, are the pains of the transition to this new age.

Muhammad's eschatological proclamation in the early surahs, on the other hand, is not oriented towards imminent expectation, nor is it *apocalyptic*. Rather, the eschatology of the early Meccan surahs is *discursive* and *expressive*. Muhammad's proclamation in the Qur'an is decisively demarcated from the inspiration of the seers, but the Qur'anic speech does have the oath in common with the *style* of

---

34 See Gerd Theissen / Annette Merz, *Der historische Jesus. Ein Lehrbuch*, Göttingen 2001, 229.
35 Ibid. 235–6.
36 Ibid. 236–8.
37 Ibid. 232–3.
38 Ibid. 244–5.
39 Ibid. 242–3.
40 Ibid. 246–7.
41 Ibid. 245.
42 Ibid.
43 Ibid. 243–4.

the seers.[44] Angelika Neuwirth has analysed the new function oaths take on in the Qur'an.[45] These are no longer purely a source of authority with magical and legal implications, but conjure up images whose semantic charge is not resolved by the utterance of an oath but serves as a reference point for the developing reasoning of the surah. Where one might expect a resolution or a prospective reference to coming events, there is a thetic statement bearing no direct relation to the oath. The utterance of the oath might be a general rebuke to humankind (Q 103). The *expressivity* of the surahs here serves the *discourse* about one or more central arguments of the whole surah. The same issue can be shown in the *iḏā* series and the seemingly apocalyptic surahs, which depict a resolution of the world on a cosmic scale (Q 82; 81; 84). They contradict the *denial* of the resurrection and the *facticity* of judgement day in the respective surahs. There is no description here of the imminent end of the world; instead, these expressive images are set against the propositions that there is no resurrection and that people will not be held to account for their deeds. It is thus a debate about certainties and beliefs, not an announcement that the end of the world is nigh. There are no *interim ethics*, no *interim rite* and no overcoming of any powers, let alone of evil, which is already manifesting itself in various phenomena. *Every* human will be raised from the dead, *every* human will have to account for his or her acts and to *every human* will eschatological knowledge be revealed. These universal truths are subjected in the early Meccan surahs to a counter-discourse to a pre-Islamic, ancient Arab world-view. The many doctrinal questions regarding erratic and enigmatic terminology (Q 101; 104:5–9; 83:7–9.18–20; 90:12–14), many of them featuring neologisms, offer vivid evidence of a polemical discourse that revolves around the facticity of basic metaphysical and eschatological statements about the soul, God and the world.

---

44 In a different place, I argue that a potential formal typology is created between Muhammad and pre-Islamic, local Arab prophets though Muhammad's use of oaths (see Zishan Ghaffar, 'Jesus redivivus – Der koranische Jesus im Kontext von Prophetologie', in Thomas Fornet-Ponse (ed.), *Jesus Christus. Von alttestamentlichen Messiasvorstellungen bis zur literarischen Figur*, Münster 2015, 149–62, here 155). The possibility of a positive relation between seer and prophet is a theme of the Book of Samuel, which points out that prophethood grew out of the existence of seers (A Sam. 9:9). Saul is presented as an example of this (1 Sam. 9.15 ff.).

45 See Neuwirth, *The Qur'an and Late Antiquity*, 168–76.

5.2 Middle Meccan surahs: prophetology as a combination of salvation, election and mercy

The proclamation during the early Meccan period is an example of *pure* prophecy. Muhammad's own role emerges through initial references to previous biblical figures, but these individuals are seldom named and nowhere presented *in extenso*. The spotlight is on Muhammad's prophetic acts. He has no need of a title. After all, the majority of the literary prophets did not describe themselves as prophets either. It was subsequent collective reflections about their role, function and proclamation that led to the updating and expansion of the text. Similarly, when the circumstances changed during the middle Meccan period, it became necessary to put greater emphasis on Muhammad's proclamation. If one assumes – as Angelika Neuwirth and Nicolai Sinai have suggested – that there was a process of proclamation that reflected the community's and the proclaimer's need to reassure themselves through the Qur'anic text,[46] then one must particularly eschew false expectations that the nomenclature of the Qur'an will provide individual titles for Muhammad and other protagonists. The Qur'an is not an authorial text. No readymade notions of prophecy and ready theologoumena fall from the heavens. Instead, they emerge over time, overlap, grow clearer or become more ambivalent. The very fact that there has been no smoothing over of the terminology and concepts of the Qur'an as a whole is the best proof that the text reflects the formation of a community. It was only exegetes who harmonised its statements.

It was during the emerging prophetology of the middle Meccan period that Muhammad and other figures came by a multitude of titles (*nabī*, *rasūl*, *nadīr*, *mundir*, *'abd*). These are not clearly defined *ab ovo*; rather, they have a family resemblance, and each develops further. The relationship each bears to the other waxes and wanes over time, sometimes growing clearer, at others becoming more vague. This is not only due to the *developments* in the process of forming a community; it is also part of the basic *typological* structure of the Qur'anic proclamation and of the emerging prophetology. This typology is *existential* to the survival of the community, consolidates its *identity* and gives it *prestige* and *authority* in the discourse it presents to opponents and members of other faiths. That expresses the inherent *tension* in the process of forming a community, which is why the attribution of individual concepts and terms can vary.

---

46 Neuwirth, op. cit. 1–32; Sinai, *Fortschreibung und Auslegung*, 1–22.

5.2.1 The new context of the proclamation in the middle Meccan period and its central topoi

The establishment of a community around Muhammad was integral to the development of a prophetology in the middle Meccan period. It can be assumed that a community of the faithful grew up around the proclaimer in the early Meccan period, but this coalesced into a group that had its own identity and regarded itself as a new *communitas/civitas*. This new development is illustrated by the reference to the early Muslim community as *'ibād*.[47] The servant (*'abd*) or servants (*'ibād*) are addressed sixty-one times in the middle Meccan period. In late Mecca they are mentioned forty-two times, twenty-two times in Medina – and only three times in early Mecca. The frequency with which this new label is used is not the only sign of its centrality and significance for the community in middle Mecca. It is almost exclusively during this period that the *'ibād* are showered with special praise. They are chosen, both as a community and as individuals (*'ibādu l-llāhi l-mukhlaṣīn/iṣṭafā*, Q 37:40.74.128.160; 15:40; 38:83; 27:59), devoted (*al-'ibādu l-mu'minūn*, Q 37:81.111.122. 132; 27:15), sent (*al-'ibādu l-mursalūn*, Q 37:17), grateful (*'abd shakūr*, Q 17:3), pious/righteous (*al-'ibādu al-ṣālihūn*, Q 21:105; 27:19), distinguished (*tafḍīl*, Q 27:15), contrite/penitent (*'abd munīb*, Q 50:8; 38:17.30.44) and admirable (*ni'ma l-'abd*, Q 38:30.44). It is true that the *'ibād* represent the typological mirror of the community's self-assurance in the middle Meccan period and they are contrasted in terms of salvific history and eschatology to the deniers of God's signs. However, as chosen servants (*'ibādu llāhi l-mukhlaṣīn*), Muhammad's followers were already assured of protection from the temptations of Satan in cosmogonic prehistory (Q 15:39–42).

If we remind ourselves at this juncture that Jesus presented himself as a servant for the very first time in Surah Maryam, then this statement takes on a new meaning (Q 19:30). We saw in an earlier chapter that the term 'servant' was one of the first Christological titles and also a name monks and nuns commonly used to refer to themselves. The proclaimer of the Qur'an obviously democratises this term and uses it for all those who respond to his call. In doing so, he relativises the distinction granted to Christ. This is not at all to suggest that describing Jesus as a servant of God represents his demotion. The aim of the Qur'an's prophetology is instead to extend Jesus's grandeur to the Qur'anic community. Just as Christians would say that we are all God's children because Jesus is the Son of God, the proclaimer of the Qur'an can also say that we are all servants of God because Jesus was God's servant. This carries no criticism of Jesus nor any criticism of

---

47 See Neuwirth, op. cit, 282–9.

Christianity, which, as we have already shown in detail, is not yet a target for the Qur'an in Mecca. Instead, this is about bringing the tradition of Jesus, the son of Mary, into the cosmos of the early Qur'anic community.

One of the central topoi of the proclamation in the middle Meccan period is an increasingly explicit theology of signs, which is already implicitly present in the early Meccan period.[48] Now, though, there is a diversification of God's signs (*'āyāt*), which manifest themselves in the creation, in God's historical actions and in the acts or the annunciation of chosen people. This change is clear from the composition of the surahs, which are now endowed with *'āyāt* series to describe the creative power of God.[49] Messengers (*rasūl*) are presented by name, their essential mission being to proclaim the signs of God, and by God's grace a few chosen individuals become signs in their own right. As we saw earlier, Jesus is distinguished in the same fashion (Q 19:21). In view of the notion of signs, which is just as relevant to Christians, one can therefore note that the proclaimer of the Qur'an seeks to appropriate this term and broaden its potential meanings. What is striking is that the list of various messengers in the middle section of the surahs includes not only biblical but also non-biblical/ancient Arab figures (for instance in Q 57; 37; 15; 26). This demonstrates the *inclusive* nature of the Qur'an's apostolic doctrine, which acknowledges the destinies of other peoples and individuals and claims them as part of the Bible's salvific history. The community around Muhammad is also convinced that he too is the proclaimer of signs imparted to him in the form of divine messages. Thus it adheres both to the theology of signs and to the theology of God's servant, expanding the horizons of classical Christological themes. Once more, this should not be construed as a criticism of Christianity but merely as a fresh appropriation of major topical ideas that were being debated on the Arabian Peninsula in late antiquity.

The words and verses of the Qur'an that open many of the surahs of this period claim to be excerpts from divine scripture.[50] The divine provenance of this proclamation is firmly distinguished from other forms of inspiration (poets/seers). The denomination *'abd/ 'ibād* remains the *nomen/genus proprium* of the middle Meccan community. Even figures who are subsequently and clearly introduced as messengers or prophets are initially presented as (faithful) servants (alongside Jesus, these include Muhammad, Noah, Moses, Aaron, Abraham, Solomon and David).

---

48 See above in section 5.1, 'The early Meccan surahs. Eschatological prophecy'.
49 See Angelika Neuwirth, *Studien zur Komposition der mekkanischen Suren. Die literarische Form des Koran – ein Zeugnis seiner Historizität?*, Berlin 2007, 264–90.
50 Neuwirth, *Studien zur Komposition der mekkanischen Suren*, 250–2.

While the servants in the middle Meccan period become synonymous with Muhammad's community, the identity-defining role of the term wanes in the late Meccan and Medinan periods, when *'ibād* is more frequently employed as a collective noun for humanity and can therefore be increasingly translated as 'people'. In the context of creation theology and the economy of salvation, the term *'ibād* now refers to the relationship between God and humankind. God knows what His servants do (Q 40:44; 42:27; 35:31.45; 3:15.20), God shows favour to His servants (Q 30:48; 14:11), wills no injustice on them (Q 40:31), has control over them (Q 6:18.61), leads them along the righteous path (Q 39:16; 42:52; 6:88) if He so wishes, and is willing to forgive them (Q 42:19.25). The middle Meccan definition of the *'ibād* as believers (*al-mu'minūn*) becomes the exclusive *nomen/ genus proprium* of the early Muslim community in Medina. In Medina there is no longer the irrefutable certainity that faithful servants enjoy special protection from Satan. Instead, Satan takes his due share (*naṣīban mafrūḍan*, Q 4:118) of them. The following section shall give a better idea of whether the use of the term 'servant' develops the Christian or Jewish reception of Isaiah's servant songs in the Qur'an, and whether there might be a soteriological dimension to the prophetology of the Qur'an.

5.2.2 The Qur'an's apostolic doctrine in the middle Meccan period

Muhammad's proclamation was vehemently rejected in Mecca. The divine 'prophetic solace', assuring him of his vocation and exhorting him not to be sad and to bear patiently the repudiation of his message, becomes an increasingly typical component of surah endings. The difficulties faced by him and his community are also a reminder of the revelations through earlier messengers or apostles (*rasūl/ rusul*) and their destinies. During the middle Meccan period, an apostolic doctrine emerges within Qur'anic prophetology, which situates the interaction between messengers and their addressees typologically in God's universal and habitual salvific action. It is no surprise that the Arabic word for messenger (*rasūl*), mirroring the name 'apostle' (in Greek, *apóstolos*),[51] is used to evoke the state of the proclamation and the community around Muhammad. After all, the word 'apostle' conveys an inherent sense of stability and universality, and its potential had been demonstrated in the Gospels and especially in apocryphal scripture and the prophetic movements of late antiquity.[52]

---

51 See Josef Horovitz, *Koranische Untersuchungen*, Berlin 1926, 45.
52 See Wensinck, *Muhammad und die Propheten*, 174.

The core of the middle Meccan surah contains several messenger tales recounting the hostile attitude of various peoples to earlier messengers. In all of these stories, God protects his *rasūl* and punishes the relevant peoples for their recalcitrant attitude and their resistance. God's behaviour and the messengers' fates have been correctly analysed as part of a stereotypical pattern. Quoting Horovitz, these are known as 'punishment legends/God's judgements'.[53] It is often suggested that the Qur'an's versions of the prophets' stories are extremely monotonous and uninteresting compared to the lively and ambivalent portrayals in the biblical stories.[54] It is only possible to come to this verdict by misconstruing the typological aspiration of the Qur'anic proclamation. The judgement here does not – as the model of the *punishment legend* requires – involve a crude obsession with projections of the Prophet, who makes a crude and forced analogy between his situation and that of the community with biblical figures and stories. Contrary to what one might imagine of a 'punishment legend', the messenger stories in the Qur'an are not based on a punitive and wrathful image of God. There is a different reason for the seemingly redundant portrayal of earlier messengers and peoples succumbing to the same fate – the Qur'anic typology is *existential*. The motive behind the *punishment legends* is the suffering, the despair, the isolation and the persecution that Muhammad and the community undergo for promulgating God's message and signs. That explains their *mimetic* focus on God's punitive intervention and the saving of earlier messengers from the hardships of their age against the backdrop of their current negative experiences.

Here it is not a matter of ironing out differences between messengers and their individuality, but about the typological amplification of a universal dimension of their proclamation demonstrating God's succour for Muhammad and his community: previous messengers found themselves in desperate straits and their followers were persecuted, and the same trials are now being visited on the early Muslim community. As He did then, God will intervene. God's solace and the litany-like repetition of this certainty were of great existential significance to the early community around Muhammad. If one sticks closely to the meaning of the Greek word *soter* ('saviour'), then it can be said that there is a decidedly *soteriological* dimension to the Qur'anic apostolic doctrine. Yet the Qur'an went on to categorically reject any false association of God's actions with an incarnational soteriology and theology of sin.

The typological stylisation of the apostolic doctrine also loses its monotonous

---

53 See Horovitz, op. cit. 10–12.
54 Ibid. 8–9.

and apparently redundant rhetorical effect when one contrasts it with Christological typologies. The sermons of the Syriac church fathers feature very similar
attempts to define a typology of the same Old Testament stories, interpreting them
all as foreshadowings of Jesus Christ. Even in the absence of close contact with
Christian congregations, one can reasonably assume that such typological interpretations were doing the rounds in late antiquity, and so it would have been
easy for the proclaimer of the Qur'an to reach for this technique and adapt it to
his purposes. In any case, the aim of middle Meccan prophetology is not yet to
forge a discourse with Christian groupings but to offer existential reassurance to
the emerging Qur'anic community in the context of the hostile environment in
Mecca.

The text itself provides evidence to flesh out these preliminary thoughts regarding the apostolic doctrine of the Qur'an. One of the early surahs of the middle
Meccan phase contains a declaration that Muhammad's proclamation asserts the
role of former messengers (ṣaddaqa l-mursalīn) (Q 37:37). Most of the generalis-
ing statements about rusul repeatedly refer to their persecution and rejection: their
message is rejected and rebuffed as slanderous (takḏīb) (Q 50:14; 38:14; 23:44).
They are also mocked and ridiculed (istahza'a/ittakhaḏa huzuwan) (Q 15:11;
36:30; 18:106; 21:41; 25:41). The latter is a reaction to the role of the messenger,
who is to receive the word of God and then proclaim his signs and warn people
(Q 18:56; 17:105; 25:56).[55] The messenger stories of the middle Meccan period
make it clear that God's punitive actions are meant as a warning to the opponents
of the early Muslim community, but of far more crucial importance is the assurance offered to Muhammad and his followers that God is devoted to them despite
all their persecution and rejection and will continue to be devoted to them. This
explains why the messenger stories, which, as it is, refer only very briefly to the
fate of former messengers, refer to the perilous situation of the messengers and
their followers as well as God's interventions.

Probably the earliest surah from the middle Meccan period, The Moon (Q 54),
proclaims five messenger stories, bound together by a common refrain about the
rejection (takḏīb) of the warnings.[56] These early messenger stories of the middle
Meccan period are characterised by a strong typological permeability. The 'ibād
experience the same hardships before and now, which is why none of the stories
in Q 54 names the messengers by name (not even Moses!). What is important is

---

55 The entire terminology about the role of the messenger and of the Qur'an as a warning
(naḏīr/nuḏur/munḏir) largely occurs during the middle and late Meccan periods.
56 See Neuwirth, Der Koran. Vol 2/1: Frühmittelmekkanische Suren, 112–3.

their *shared* fate. The community and Muhammad are so closely connected to the previous messengers that it is not individual nuances or contingent circumstances that count, but their common destiny of slander and rejection. God's punitive interventions are part and parcel of their persecution. Noah and Lot receive God's help and commitment (*naṣr, najāh*) amid the gravest danger (Q 54:9–15.33–40). In the other messenger stories, the focus is on the punishment God metes out when rejected, but this also represents, by ellipsis, the *saving* of the messengers.

The relevant stories are later expanded to present the scale of the rejection, persecution and salvation. This is the case in Surah 37 (al-Saffat), probably the second earliest. The focus in the middle section of the messenger stories here is on the saving acts of God. The individual episodes are introduced by a contrast between the chosen servants and those who reject the warners. The messenger stories are related from the perspective of the *community*, which sees itself typologically as joined in a community of fate with the servants of God who were persecuted in the past: 'Most men in the past went astray, even though We sent messengers to warn them. See how those who were warned met their end! Not so the true servants of God' (Q 37:71–74). God's intervention frees Noah, Moses and Aaron from their perilous situation: 'We saved them and their people from great distress (*wa-najjaināhumā wa-qaumahumā mina l-karbi l-'aẓīm)*' (Q 37:115); 'We saved him and his people from great distress (*wa-najjaināhumā wa-ahlahū mina l-karbi l-'aẓīm)*' (Q 37:76). Abraham too is protected from fire (Q 37:97–98), while Elijah and Lot's families manage to escape persecution. Jonah escapes from his agonies inside the belly of the fish. For their bravery the messengers receive an explicit blessing (Noah, Abraham, Moses, Aaron and Elijah) and an implicit one: 'Peace be upon the messengers (*wa-salāmun 'alā al-mursalīn)*' (Q 37:181).

Muhammad's and the early Muslim community's basic experience of persecution, rejection and the desire for freedom is illustrated in Moses's prominent position in the middle Meccan period and the memory of the Exodus. An entire surah (Q 20) is devoted to the life of Muhammad, and in other ways too his person receives greater attention, both qualitatively and quantitatively, than other messengers. The central point of reference here is the Exodus. God's command to Moses to leave is not explicitly addressed to the Israelites – unlike the mission (Q 20:47; Q 26:16–17) – but to the servants of God (Q 20:77; Q 26:52; Q 44:23). Moses's mission is later reformulated as an instruction to ask the pharaoh to liberate the servants (Q 44:18). Here too, there is significant *typological permeability*: the early Muslim community and the Israelites want to, and will, be set free as servants of God.

The Qur'an's apostolic doctrine during the middle Meccan period reaches its peak in Surah 36, which condenses and focuses previous interpretations of messengers so as to rule out any theological misinterpretation. The surah begins with an oath to the wisdom of the Qur'an, which introduces us to the central theme of the whole surah: 'By the wise Qur'an, you are truly one of the messengers sent on a straight path [...] to warn a people whose forefathers were not warned, and so they were unaware' (Q 36:2–6). Muhammad is for the first time proclaimed a messenger, although Surah 37 previously referred to Elijah, Lot and Jonah by this title. However, the direct identification of Muhammad as a messenger in an oath at the beginning of a surah demonstrates a new degree of self-confidence on the part of Muhammad and his community. God's approval of his role and tasks becomes a reflexive part of his consciousness.

In the opening section of Q 36, Muhammad is offered solace. He should not interpret the rejection and polemics directed at the warnings he has delivered as his failure: 'The verdict has been passed against most of them, for they refuse to believe [...] It is all the same to them whether you warn them or not: they will not believe. You can warn only those who will follow the Qur'an and hold the Merciful One in awe, though they cannot see Him: give such people the glad news of forgiveness and a noble reward' (Q 36:7–11). The actual heart of the surah is formed of a parable (*mathal*) and an *'āyāt* series,[57] which contrast the rejection of the messengers with God's signs. Their prominence in the middle of the surah is noteworthy because this position is usually occupied by cases of biblical and non-biblical narratives in the middle Meccan period.[58] The explicit employment of a parable is striking anyway because nowhere has this category of divine speech been a theme or even employed. Its use here should be seen less as introducing a new formal element than as the reception of a special likeness or parable that aptly exemplifies the Qur'an's apostolic doctrine.

Only a detailed analysis of the Qur'anic *mathal* in the surah can clarify the precise nature of the parable and how the Qur'an makes a link to it:

Give them the example of the people to whose town messengers came. We sent two messengers but they rejected both. Then We reinforced them with a third. They said, 'Truly, we are messengers to you,' but they answered, 'You are only men like ourselves. The Lord of Mercy has sent nothing; you are just lying.' They said, 'Our Lord knows that we have been sent to you. Our duty is only to deliver the message to you,' but they answered, 'We think you are an

---

57 See Neuwirth, *Studien zur Komposition der mekkanischen Suren*, 279–80.
58 See Neuwirth, *The Qur'an and Late Antiquity*, 306–7.

evil omen. If you do not stop, we shall stone you and inflict a painful torment
on you.' The messengers said, 'The evil omen is within yourselves. Why do
you take it as an evil omen when you are reminded of the Truth? You are
going too far!' Then, from the furthest part of the city, a man came running.
He said, 'My people, follow the messengers. Follow them: they are not asking
you to reward them and they are rightly guided. Why should I not worship the
One who created me? Is it to Him that you will be returned. How could I take
besides Him any other gods, whose intercession will not help me and who
would not be able to save me if the Lord of Mercy wished to harm me? Then I
would clearly be in the wrong. I believe in your Lord, so listen to me.'

He was told, 'Enter the Garden', so he said, 'If only my people knew how
my Lord has forgiven me and set me among the honoured.' After him We did
not send any army from heaven against his people, nor were We about to:
there was just one blast, and they fell down lifeless (Q 36:13–29).

The parable describes the sending of two messengers to an unnamed town. They
immediately gain the support of a third messenger when their message is greeted
with hostility. Yet even this triumvirate is unable to win over the town's inhabit-
ants for their cause. The messengers are rejected as being normal people and
threatened with death. Here, an anonymous person enters the scene and exhorts
the townspeople to recognise the messengers and worship the one God. This man
is killed and goes to paradise, while the townsfolk are destroyed. One could see
this parable as a simple representation of the so-called *punishment legend model*:
God's messengers are sent out to different peoples and those who deny their
message are punished. By linking it to the exegetical tradition, the parable could
also be placed in its historical context, and the messengers and town identified.[59]
In fact, though, this interpretation does not live up to the compositional prominence of the parable in the middle section or its use as a substitute for a specific
narrative. Neuwirth has rightly pointed out that we should instead be alive to the
Qur'an appropriating a known parable and giving it a theological makeover to
create a vehicle for its own apostolic doctrine.[60]

The obvious choice is the parable of the vineyard, the oldest version of which
is recorded in Mark:

---

59 The town has been identified as Antioch, although there is some debate as to whether the
messengers were sent by Jesus or by God (see al-Tabari, *Jāmiʿ al-bayan*, vol. 19, 412 ff.).
60 See Neuwirth, *The Qur'an and Late Antiquity*, 305–7.

Then he began to speak to them in parables: 'A man planted a vineyard and set a hedge around it, dug a place for the wine vat and built a tower. And he leased it to vinedressers and went into a far country. Now at vintage-time he sent a servant to the vinedressers, that he might receive some of the fruit of the vineyard from the vinedressers. And they took him and beat him and sent him away empty-handed. Again he sent them another servant, and at him they threw stones, wounded him in the head, and sent him away shamefully treated. And again he sent another, and him they killed; and many others, beating some and killing some. Therefore still having one son, his beloved, he also sent him to them last, saying, "They will respect my son." But those vinedressers said among themselves, "This is the heir. Come, let us kill him, and the inheritance will be ours." So they took him and killed him and cast him out of the vineyard.

'Therefore what will the owner of the vineyard do? He will come and destroy the vinedressers, and give the vineyard to others. [...] And they sought to lay hands on him, but feared the multitude, for they knew he had spoken the parable against them. So they left him and went away' (Mark 12:1–12).

The parable of the vinedressers in Mark is itself an allegory based on the song of the vineyard in Isaiah (Isa. 5:1–7). The servants stand in for the prophets who were sent to the Jewish people and, according to the logic of the parable, suffered rejection, hardship and persecution. The depiction eventually results in the sending of the Son of God, whose killing is a beacon of hope for a new communion with God. The composition of the parable of the vinedressers suggests that it is to be read *soteriologically*. The prophets are shown in distress, but then the killing of the Son of God unleashes the redeeming and salvific force to forge a new covenant with God.

The parable of the *aṣḥāb al-qarya* (the townspeople) in the Qur'an is constructed in opposition to the parable of the vinedressers in terms of its narrative logic, motivations and purpose. The scene is relocated to an urban setting, which removes the reference to the Jewish people. The *rusul* are not sent out *sequentially*, like the servants, but appear *simultaneously*, thus diluting the build-up of tension of the parable of the vinedressers.[61] The messengers do not suffer and when the Son of God is sent and killed in the parable of the vinedressers, an anonymous believer appears in the Qur'anic parable. Even *his* martyrdom is not *explicitly* depicted. The *soteriological* dimension of the parable of the vinedressers

---

61 See Neuwirth, *The Qur'an and Late Antiquity*, 307.

is defused in the Qur'an. According to the Qur'anic apostolic doctrine, the rejection and persecution of the messengers unleashes no redemptive or soteriological power. Instead, the soteriological message here is that *God* intervenes in salvific history to protect His messengers and the believers in a literal sense. It would be possible to misinterpret this in incarnation theological and soteriological terms because the messengers and the prophets in the Qu'ran are sometimes introduced as *'ibād* and rejected and persecuted as *rusul*. The proclaimer of the Qur'an heads off this possibility by means of the *aṣḥāb al-qarya* parable. This is followed in Surah 36 by an *'āyāt* series that creates a numerical parallel between the rejection of the three anonymous messengers and the three *'āyāt*: the organic, cosmic and maritime order created by God is praised as a sign of His favour (Q 36:33–46). Both the parable and the *'āyāt* series conclude with the resigned remark that the messengers are ridiculed and God's signs ignored every time (Q 36:30.46).[62]

5.2.3 The birth of prophecy out of God's mercy

The apostolic doctrine of the Qur'an is one *aspect* of Qur'anic prophetology. As we have previously emphasised, the titles of the Qur'an are not concepts that are set in stone. They evolve and overlap, with Muhammad and the early Muslim community as their typological epicentre.

Our preceding remarks have demonstrated that the messengers in the Qur'an are a means of communicating God's signs. Their historical effects possess an inherently stereotypical dynamic, which the Qur'an then converts into an *existential typology*: the rejection of Muhammad and the persecution of the community are linked to the experiences of previous servants of God and messengers. They and the early Muslim community belong to a single community bound by a common destiny. Put simply, the apostolic doctrine is God's ultimate intervention to protect His faithful servants.

So while, soteriologically, the Qur'an's apostolic doctrine stresses God's salvific intervention to safeguard the believers, the introduction of the title of prophet (*nabīy*) in the middle Meccan period lends an additional dimension to its prophetology: God not only protects His faithful servants but also shows them special favour in their respective difficult positions. Prophethood (*nubūwa*) is a special

---

62 From a literary critical perspective, it is probably necessary to swap verses 46 and 45 around. That is because verse 45 initiates the *idā* disputation series which is then interrupted by verse 46. If one reverses the order of these two verses, then verse 46 – as a parallel to the messenger stories – makes a fitting conclusion to the *'āyāt* series. Verse 46 would therefore actually be the beginning of the disputation series.

honour afforded to individual believers. The title *nabīy* is introduced in Surah Maryam during the middle Meccan period[63] and used in close connection with God's mercy (*raḥma*).[64] The surah opens with the story section and uses God's servant Zachariah to warn listeners to remember God's mercy: 'This is an account of your Lord's grace towards His servant Zachariah' (Q 19:2). As we discussed in the previous chapter, Zachariah, though old and frail, asked God to give him a son so that he might pass on his (priestly) legacy to him. In response, Zachariah receives the glad news of the birth of John, who is presented as a believer who demonstrates special devotion. Mary's tale follows with an exhortation to remember her story: 'Mention in the Qur'an the story of Mary. [...] (*wa-dkur fīl-Kitābi Maryam*)' (Q 19:16). The imperative here has the same root as the verbal noun in the introduction to the whole surah (*dikr*). Furthermore, the subsequent stories are all introduced with the same imperative, which – as formulated in the introduction – stands elliptically here for the *reminder of God's mercy to His servants*. Mary hears the annunciation of Jesus's birth while on her own as a sign of God's mercy (Q 19:21), and Jesus presents himself after his birth as a servant of God and a prophet (Q 19:30–33). This is followed by an account of Abraham being cast out by his father for entertaining doubts about polytheism. He is rewarded for his steadfastness with prophetic descendants (Isaac, Jacob) (Q 19:49). In the next tale, Moses is rewarded by his brother becoming a prophet (Q 19:53). Ishmael, on the other hand, is praised as a faithful prophet and messenger who commanded his household to act righteously (Q 19:54–55). In the final memorial, Idris is called a true prophet who is raised to a high position by God's favour (Q 19:56–57). What all the stories or brief accounts in Surah Maryam have in common is that they associate the status of the *nabīy* with, or as, a special sign of God's favour and mercy. Jesus, himself a sign of God, is clearly described as an *'abd* and *nabīy*. John is not yet called a prophet, but his birth is a merciful gift to God's servant Zachariah.

In the whole of Qur'an, it is in Surah Maryam that the verb describing God's

---

63 Isaac's presentation as a prophet in Q 37:112–113 is a Medinan insertion (see Neuwirth, *Der Koran. Vol. 2/1: Frühmittelmekkanische Suren*, 163), presumably a response to the Christian typological appropriation of Isaac for its Christology, and the Qur'an now develops the concept of prophetology as a counter-discourse to Christology (see section 5.4.4).
64 The early exegete Muqatil b. Sulaiman lists prophethood (*nubūwa*) as an important aspect (*wajh*) of *raḥma* (see Muqatil b. Sulaiman, *al-wujuh wa al-naza'ir fi al-Qur'an al-'Azim*, ed. by Hatim Salih al-Damin, Damaskus 2006/1427, 40); however, he also subsumes *risāla* into it (see *Tafsir Muqatil b. Sulaiman*, ed. by 'Abdallah Mahmud Shihata, vol. 3, Beirut 2002/1423, 637, 794).

affection or gift (*wahaba*) occurs most frequently. It stands for the merciful action of God *per se*. Zachariah prays for God's affection (*hab lī:* 'grant me', Q 19:5). Jesus is given to Mary as a sign of God's mercy (*li-'ahaba laki ghulāman zakīyan:* 'the gift of a pure son', Q 19:19). God grants (*wahabnā*, Q 19:49) Isaac and Jacob to Abraham, and he also affords His grace to them (*wa-wahabnā lahum min raḥmatinā:* 'We granted Our grace to all of them', Q 19:50). This refers to their noble reputation (*wa-ja'alnā lahum lisāna ṣidqin 'alīyan*) as ancestors and prophets. God also grants Moses Aaron as a prophet (*wa-wahabnā lahū min raḥmatinā 'akhāhu hārūna nabīyan:* 'out of Our grace We granted him his brother Aaron as a prophet', Q 19:53). Ishmael and Idris are regarded as prophets because they are loyal men of truth. The status of *nabī* is, according to these stories, a matter of God's grace. He turns with mercy to His faithful servants in their isolation, loneliness and uncertainty.

This sign of God's solace is of great significance to the early Muslim community in a tribal society riven with the discord caused by Muhammad's new religious grouping. The community can derive typologically existential security from the reminder that through God's grace they will be rewarded for their loss of genealogical ties, their uncertainty and steadfastness: the *'anbiyā'* symbolise God's grace. There is no suggestion as yet of a special genealogical bond between the prophets (*ḍurrīya*), although it is implied in verse 58. For literary critical reasons, Angelika Neuwirth, among others, has identified this verse as a later Medinan insertion.[65]

5.2.4 Muhammad as Moses redivivus – the consolidation of Qur'anic prophetology in the middle Meccan period

The evolving Qur'anic understanding of messengers and prophets comes together in Surah 17 (*al-'Isra'*, The Night Journey) with reference to Muhammad. It is already clear from the inauguration of the title of *nabī* in Surah Maryam that the missions of messenger and prophethood are regarded as two potentially overlapping aspects of Qur'anic prophetology; so there is a resemblance between the two terms within the framework of Qur'anic prophetology. These two aspects are explicitly merged in certain individuals: Moses and Ishmael are both messengers and prophets in Surah Maryam (*rasūlan nabīyan*, Q 19:51.54). The crafting of the Qur'an's prophetology reaches its middle Meccan peak in Surah 17. Even if Muhammad is not expressly called *nabī*, in substance he is characterised, like

---

65 See Neuwirth, *Der Koran. Vol. 2/1: Frühmittelmekkanische Suren*, 599–601.

Moses, not only as *rasūl*, but also as *nabīy*. That is also why he receives the same signs of God's favour: as *rasūl*, Moses was the liberator of the Israelites with God's aid (*naṣr*), and his *nabīy* status is confirmed, as Surah 17 describes, by his receiving the Tablets of the Law and the Torah. Both commitments – Exodus and the Decalogue – are now made to Muhammad and the early Muslim community too.[66]

Surah 17 begins with praise for God for having made it possible for His servant to make a divine journey by night from one place of worship to another: 'Glory to Him who made His servant travel by night from the sacred place of worship to the furthest place of worship, whose surroundings We have blessed, to show him some of Our signs' (Q 17:1). The word used here for 'night journey' (*'asrā*) is the Qur'anic term for the Exodus. The locations of this 'journey' are described, however, only in terms of their geographical relation to each other. What is more, the Arabic word *masjid* makes it clear that the starting point and destination of the journey are places of prayer, while the blessing of the second place of worship would suggest the Holy Land. We must indeed go along with Angelika Neuwirth's interpretation that Muhammad is granted a spiritual exodus from Mecca (which is now called *masjid* instead of *bait*) to Jerusalem, marking a change of direction of prayer for the community.[67] The double destruction of the Temple in Jerusalem is a known fact (as is clear from the reflections on these historical events in the following verses, Q 17:4–8), but the Holy Land possesses a spiritual magnetism that inspires the new consciousness of the community as God's people to display special piousness[68] – and the *fātiḥa* is granted to the middle Meccan community as a prayer. This prayer appears to offer every servant of God inner freedom and exodus.[69] Addressing Muhammad as *'abd* illustrates the typological permeability between Muhammad and Moses. Moses also liberated the *'ibād* with God's help, just as Muhammad and his community are granted spiritual renewal and freedom through prayer. As *rasūl*, Moses and Muhammad share the same experience of God rescuing His *'ibād*. That is the divine *sunna* regarding messengers, as Muhammad is assured in Surah 17: 'They planned to scare you off the land, but they would not have lasted for more than a little while after you. Such was Our

---

66 In the Pentateuch, Moses, as a servant (in Hebrew: *'aḇdî* = '*my servant*'), is the most important of all the prophets and defined as having a special proximity to God (Num. 12:6–8; Deut. 34:10). It is this same proximity that God's servant Muhammad now experiences during the spiritual exodus at the beginning of Surah 17.

67 See Angelika Neuwirth, *Der Koran. Vol. 2/2, Handkommentar zu Q 17* (unpublished manuscript).

68 Ibid.

69 Ibid.

way with the messengers We sent before you, and you will find no change in Our ways (*li-sunnatinā*)' (Q 17:76–77).

And yet some of the opponents of the Qur'an do not take Muhammad's spiritual exodus seriously. They demand his physical ascension to heaven (Q 17:90–93). Muhammad's exodus to the Holy Land represents more than a change of ritual direction; he also receives God's signs there. One can – as Neuwirth follows Levenson in arguing – interpret Mount Zion as the *entelechy* of Sinai, and it becomes the emblem of the reception of the revelation.[70] The very beginning of Surah 17 offers a reminder of Moses's reception of the revelation: 'We also gave Moses the Scripture and made it a guide for the Children of Israel' (Q 17:2). The reception of the Decalogue is the primal inspiration for the reception of divine instruction (*hudā*); it is also an expression of Moses's distinguished status as *nabīy*. Surah 17 also notes that prophets can be guided in special fashion and honoured by God (through the sending down of scripture): 'We gave some prophets (*ba'da n-nabīyīna*) more than others: We gave David a book [of Psalms]' (Q 17:55). In the middle section of Surah 17, Muhammad, as a *nabīy*, also now receives – not yet in terminological, but in material terms – a compendium of laws, which, Neuwirth suggests fall into the *decalogue* category (see Q 17:22–39).[71]

The Qur'anic decalogue does not attempt to establish numerically ten commandments but defines itself emphatically (*wa-qadā rabbuka*: 'Your Lord has commanded') as a source of wisdom (*hikma*) for Muhammad and the community. Neuwirth makes a convincing case that the biblical decalogue is not entirely transposed in Surah 17 and that individual rules are modified to suit new devotional practices (of grace).[72] Furthermore, it is noticeable that this sets up a deliberate contrast between Qur'anic laws and pre-Islamic tribal values.[73] It is crucial for Muhammad's prophetic consciousness that he receives a decalogue and is thereby placed on the same typological level – as a *nabīy* – as Moses.

5.3 Late Meccan prophetology: the apology of the messengers

During the late Meccan phase, the prophetological discourse shifts to defending Muhammad's status as a messenger (*rasūl*). His special role as a prophet (*nabīy*) is by then no longer a topic, and it is therefore hardly surprising that the term *nabīy*

---

70 Neuwirth, *Der Koran*, vol. 2/2.

71 Neuwirth, *Die koranische Verzauberung der Welt und ihre Entzauberung in der Geschichte*, 160–5.

72 Ibid.

73 Ibid.

is almost entirely absent from the late Meccan period. Nöldeke highlighted the description of Muhammad as *nabīy ummī* as a Medinan insertion for both semantic and formal reasons.[74]

Whereas the prophetological discourse of the middle Meccan period was part of reassuring Muhammad and the community against suffering, rejection and persecution, the doubts and reproach levelled at Muhammad are now debated in a *positive* tone. This change has an impact on the formal composition of the surahs: the middle section is now increasingly devoted to discussing theological controversies (revelation, eschatology, polytheism, etc.) rather than simply providing a list of specific narratives.[75] Furthermore, God's *ars disputandi* expands to include new forms of address (e.g. parables).[76] The central topoi of the middle Meccan apostolic doctrine such as mockery and rejection of messengers (Q 13:32; 6:43; 6:10; 35:4; 34:45; 40:5) are still present in the late Meccan period. What has changed, however, is that some characteristics of God's interactions with messengers, which were typologically present before yet not always thetically expressed, are now formulated in a universal manner: 'So do not think [Prophet] that God will break His promise to His messengers: He is mighty and capable of retribution (*fa-lā taḥsabanna llāha mukhlifa wa'dihī rusulahū 'inna llāha 'azīzun ḏu ntiqām)*' (Q 14:47); 'When the messengers lost all hope and realised that they had been dismissed as liars, Our help came to them: We saved whoever We pleased, but Our punishment will not be turned away from guilty people (*ḥattā 'iḏa stay'asa r-rusulu wa-ẓannū 'annahum qad kuḏibū jā'ahum naṣrunā fa-nujjiya man nashā'u wa-lā yuraddu ba'sunā 'ani l-qaumi l-mujrimīn)*' (Q 12:110); 'We support Our messengers and believers, in the present life and on the Day when witnesses arrive. On the Day when excuses will not profit the evildoers, their fate will be rejection and they will have the worst of homes (*'innā la- nanṣuru rusulanā wa-llaḏīna 'āmanū fi l-ḥayāti d-dunyā wa-yauma yaqūmu l-'ashhād // yauma lā yanfa'u al-ẓālimīna ma'ḏiratuhum [...])*' (Q 40:51–52); 'In the end We shall save Our messengers and the believers. We take it upon Ourself to save the believers (*ṯumma nunajjī rusulanā wa-llaḏīna 'āmanū ka-ḏālika ḥaqqan 'alainā nunji l-mu'minīn)*' (Q 10:103); '[...] We make it Our duty to help the believers (*wa-kāna ḥaqqan 'alainā naṣru l-mu'minīn)*' (Q 30:47).

At the heart of the prophetological discourse, nonetheless, is Muhammad's authenticity as a messenger. Hostile rhetoric had been directed at him from as

---

74 See Nöldeke, *Geschichte des Korans*, 159–60.
75 See Neuwirth, *Studien zur Komposition der mekkanischen Suren*, 290–314.
76 See Neuwirth, *The Qur'an and Late Antiquity*, 305–12.

early as the middle Meccan period: he was only a human being (not an angel) and was incapable of performing any physical miracles (Q 17:94–96). Alongside the physico-theological term *'āyāt*, evidence for the authenticity of the messengers is now presented as their having been sent with *bayyināt* (proofs): 'Have they not travelled through the land and seen how their predecessors met their end? They [members of earlier generations] were mightier than them: they cultivated the earth more and built more upon it. Their own messengers also come to them with clear signs: God did not wrong them; they wronged themselves [by refusing to accept clear proof and thus putting themselves in the wrong] (*'a-wa-lam yasīrū fī l-'arḍi fa-yanẓurū kaifa kāna 'āqibatu llaḏīna min qablihim kānū 'ashadda minhum quwwatan wa-'aṯārū l-'arḍa wa-'amarūhā 'akṯara mimmā 'amarūhā wa-jā'athum rusuluhum bi-l-bayyināti fa-mā kāna llāhu li-yaẓlimahum wa-lākin kānū 'anfusahum yaẓlimūn)*' (Q 30:9; see also: 30:47; 14:9; 40:22.34. 50.83; 10:13.74; 35:25; 7:101). The *bayyināt* refer in particular to the verbal/linguistic nature of the signs proclaimed by Muhammad. We have already pointed out that Jesus too seems to have been endowed with *bayyināt* in the early Medinan period (Q 2:253). In Jesus's case, however, virtually all exegetes see this as a reference to his miracles, and so it becomes clear once more how the Qur'an sees Jesus's miraculous deeds and signs as being echoed in the verbal signs of the Qur'an.

It is clear that the *bayyināt* as used in the Qur'an can be interpreted in very different ways. The adjectival participle derived from the same root, *mubīn* (clear, evident), comes to mean *scripture* (Q 26:2; 27:1; 43:2; 44:2; 12:1; 28:2, etc.) and its proclamation (*balāq mubīn*, Q 36:17; 16:35.82; 29:18; 64:12; 5:92; 24:54) in middle Mecca. In the late Meccan phase, it is increasingly the autochthonal linguistic nature of the proclamation of each messenger and their strength of evidence that is defended: 'We have never sent a messenger who did not use his own people's language to make things clear for them. But still God leaves whoever He will to stray, and guides whoever He will: He is the Almighty, the All Wise (*wa-mā 'arsalnā min rasūlin 'illā bi-lisāni qaumihī li-yubayyina lahum fa-yuḍillu llāhu man yashā'u wa-yahdī man yashā'u wa-huwa l-'azīzu l-ḥakīm)*' (Q 14:4; also see: 41:3.44; 16:103; 12:2; 39:28; 42:7; 46:12; 13:37). Many who hear Muhammad's proclamation demand more than the linguistic testimony of the Qur'an to prove that he is a trustworthy messenger. Yet he vociferously declines to do so: 'Say, "I am nothing new among God's messengers. I do not know what will be done with me or you; I only follow what is revealed to me; I only reveal plainly" (*qul mā kuntu bid'an mina r-rusuli wa-mā 'adrī mā yuf'alu bī wa-lā bikum 'in 'attabi'u 'illā mā yūḥā 'ilayya wa-mā 'ana 'illā naḏīrun mubīn)*' (Q 46:9). Instead, the *bayyināt* are used to prove the *tertium comparationis* of the

Qur'anic proclamation and the miraculous proofs offered by other messengers (e.g. to Moses's authentifying miracles in Q 40): they are the means of conferring authority upon the messengers and safeguarding their superiority. The *taḥaddī* verses (Q 10:38; 11:13, but also other early and middle Meccan verses: Q 52:34; 17:88) also allude to this superiority. It is noted that Muhammad's *bayyināt* enjoy similar status to earlier biblical books: '[...] messengers came to them with clear signs, scriptures, and enlightening revelation (*jā'athum rusuluhum bi-l-bayyināti wa-bi-z-zuburi wa-bi-l-kitābi l-munīr*)' (Q 35:25). The conjunction *wa* has both an additive and an explicative function here.

The incessant challenging of Muhammad's *bayyināt* leads to the clarification that the messengers only proclaim and perform their signs (*'āyāt*; *bayyināt*) with God's permission (Q 40:78). In general, Muhammad's verbal proclamation cannot contain every single messenger story (Q 40:78) and serves as a warning, a reminder and an encouragement (Q 11:120).

The Qur'anic typology during the middle Meccan period was *existential*, which explains why references to former messengers and prophets were extremely permeable categories. The names and individual characteristics of past figures could be presented so vaguely that it was sometimes hard to tell the difference between the early Muslim community around Muhammad and earlier tribes with their respective messengers. The nature of these typological references changes in the late Meccan phase in line with Muhammad's increasing self-assurance as a messenger. They become only *semi-permeable*, which is not to say that there were fewer typological classifications. This can be attributed to the early Christian community increasingly forging an identity for itself, which opens up typological relational definitions that went beyond simple analogies. Thus, in the late Meccan phase, the Qur'an highlights that every *umma* has a messenger (Q 16:36), who is sent to the relevant town (7:101; 28:59) or *qaum* (Q 30:47; 14:9) with clear proofs. The early Muslim community's environment is forcing it to situate its own identity in a specific time and place. This process speeds up and only reaches completion during the Medinan phase. We must therefore speak in terms of *typological semi-permeability* in the late Meccan period because some narrative references remain highly permeable. One example of this can be found in Surah 12, in which the classification of Yusuf as a chosen servant (*'innahū min 'ibādina l-mukhlaṣīna*) reveals the typological permeability of the entire story.

5.4 Qur'anic prophetology in Medina

There is no comprehensive formal and literary critique of the Medinan surahs, and so we can only undertake a preliminary study of the evolution of Qur'anic prophetology in Medina.[77] Overall, the Medinan surahs highlight a fundamental change in the context of the proclamation in Mecca. Nicolai Sinai has branded this the 'Medinan constellation' in a preliminary overview of the Medinan textual corpus.[78] The decisive turning point for the community's new circumstances is the exodus (*hijra*) of the early Muslim community to Medina. This changes the discursive constellation, as new named interlocutors appear on the scene. The first essential factor in the development of Qur'anic prophetology is that the heirs of the biblical tradition are now present (*alladīna hādū, al-yahūd, al-naṣārā*) and challenge the Qur'anic proclamation to date. Second, exile in Medina shakes up the existing *topographia sacra*. The forced change of location and the need for self-assertion towards the new interlocutors from the biblical tradition promotes a fresh yearning for Mecca and the sanctuary there, and this is also expressed by the change in the direction of prayer (Q 2:142–145).

5.4.1 From existential to textual typology

The existential dimension of Qur'anic prophetology in the middle and late Meccan phases requires the use of an *a priori* perfect: the messengers have *always* been persecuted; God has *always* shown His servants special favour; etc. In Medina, the Muslim community's own textual historical memory challenges this existential reference to biblical and non-biblical salvific history of Jewish and Christian groups. The early Muslim community and Muhammad now face the challenge of negotiating their previously God-conveyed understanding of themselves as a new religious community as part of a new scriptural discourse with their neighbours' biblical tradition. It is this step that ultimately helps them to establish a fixed identity. The nature of the typological references changes: they become increasingly *impermeable*. This is the only way that the community and Muhammad can carve out a positive, autonomous role for themselves in God's salvific plan. Situating themselves in history presupposes typological *alterity*: Muhammad and the early Muslim community are not the same as what came before ('When God sent them a messenger confirming the Scriptures they already had, some of those who had received the Scripture before threw the Book of God over their shoulders as if

---

77 We are unable to examine all the changes in Qur'anic prophetology in Medina (e.g. the fact that prophets were also killed, etc.).

78 See Nicolai Sinai, 'The Unknown Known: Some Groundwork for Interpreting the Medinan Qur'an', in *Mélanges de l'Université Saint-Joseph* 66 (2015/16) 54–61.

they had no knowledge', Q 2:101). They also accomplish what was previously announced and can even stake a claim to a superior status. So it is now possible that Abraham and Ishmael lay the foundations of the Ka'ba and asked for Muhammad to be sent to them in their inaugural prayer:

> As Abraham and Ishmael built up the foundations of the House [they prayed],
> 'Our Lord, accept [this] from us. You are the All Hearing, the All Knowing.
> Our Lord, make us devoted to You; make our descendants into a community
> devoted to You. Show us how to worship and accept our repentance, for You
> are the Ever Relenting, the Most Merciful. Our Lord, make a messenger of
> their own rise up from among them, to recite Your revelations to them, teach
> them the Scripture and wisdom, and purify them: You are the Mighty, the
> Wise' (Q 2:127–129).

Muhammad's arrival is the answer to Abraham's prayer. Jesus has also announced the coming of Muhammad:

> Jesus, son of Mary, said, 'Children of Israel, I am sent to you by God,
> confirming the Torah that came before me and bringing good news of a
> messenger to follow me whose name will be Ahmad' (Q 61:6).

In general, the references to biblical narratives start to take on a politically discursive dimension. Individual theologoumena (e.g. *the Trinity*) and theological claims (e.g. *election*) are debated afresh.

5.4.2 From community of fate to the universal community of the covenant: Qur'anic prophetology between universality and exclusivity

From the middle Meccan period onwards, the Qur'an's apostolic doctrine assumed that God had always sent out His messengers to proclaim the *'āyāt*. In doing so, He held His sheltering hand over His faithful servants and as a sign of God's special favour, gave them the gift of prophecy. In the Medinan period, however, certain groups understand God's affection and election (*iṣṭifā'*) as *exclusive*, and claim this status down through the generations, because individual prophets were granted God's grace and election for their descendants (*ḍurrīya*) too, forming a special covenant between God and them (*'ahd/mīthāq*). The exclusivity of this theological covenant is debated in Medina as part of Qur'anic prophetology. By the end of the late Meccan period, God's sealing of the covenant is pushed back into the mists of time and therefore encompasses the whole of humanity as descendants (*durrīya*) of Adam:

> When your Lord took out the offspring from the loins of the Children of Adam and made them bear witness about themselves, He said, 'Am I not your Lord?' and they replied, 'Yes, we bear witness.' So you cannot say on the Day of Resurrection, 'We were not aware of this' (Q 7:172).

There is a thoroughgoing ambivalence about the further development of Qur'anic prophetology in Medina. On the one hand, there is now an attempt to take account of God's real historical alliances with Moses, Jesus and others and to claim them for the early Muslim community and Muhammad too. On the other hand, the exclusivity of these alliances is neutralised by classifying all human beings as being included in God's universal covenant. This development is demonstrated by the broad alignment of the status of messengers (*rasūl*) and prophets (*nabīy*). Or at least the special favours granted in the form of prophecy and to the prophets are also nominally claimed for the messengers:

> We favoured some of these messengers above others. God spoke to some; others He raised in rank; We gave Jesus, son of Mary, Our clear signs and strengthened him with the holy spirit. If God had so willed, their successors would not have fought each other after they had been brought clear signs. But they disagreed: some believed and some disbelieved. If God had so willed, they would not have fought each other, but God does what He will (Q 2:253).

In Medina, however, it remains the case that – with the exception of Muhammad – only biblical figures can be called prophets (*nabīy*). At the same time, it is stressed that these special favours have no bearing on the significance and dignity of the respective messenger – they are all equal in faith (Q 2:285). The proclaimer of the Qur'an is very obviously seeking to honour the special status of certain prophets and of Jesus, yet does not wish to leave any doubt that they all play an equal part in God's salvific plan.

It is no coincidence that the form of God's special affection and of His covenant with the prophets is made explicit in Surah 3 (Al 'Imran), which we discussed earlier. As we mentioned, this represents a new reading of Surah Maryam, in which prophecy is introduced as a sign of God's mercy. There, however, it carried no covenant-theological and genealogical implications, and so Ishmael was declared a prophet separately from Abraham. Surah 3, on the other hand, takes account of the covenant-theological implications of prophecy. The first section immediately reminds readers of God's choosing of certain prophets and their offspring: 'God chose Adam, Noah, Abraham's family, and the family of 'Imran, over all other people, in one line of descent – God hears and knows all. 'Imran's wife said, "Lord, I have dedicated what is growing in my womb entirely to You; so accept this from me. You are the one who hears and knows all"' (Q 3:33–34). Neuwirth has demonstrated superbly how in Surah 3 the Christian 'Holy Family' constitutes a highly pious community that is contrasted with the 'House of Abraham'.[79] Each represents a special type of servant of God, and each also stands for different conceptions of revelation theology. The remainder of the surah now unites these two differing covenants sealed by God into a universal prophetic covenant:

> God took a pledge from the prophets saying, 'If, after I have bestowed
> Scripture and wisdom upon you, a messenger comes confirming what you
> have been given, you must believe in him and support him. Do you affirm this
> and accept My pledge as binding on you?' They said, 'We do.' He said, 'Then
> bear witness and I too will bear witness' (Q 3:81).

The universal prophetic covenant (*mīthāq al-nabiyyīn*) is to be interpreted here as a *genetivus obiectivus* and a *genetivus subiectivus*. The first refers to the universality and continuity of God's covenant with the prophets. No one may lay claim to a special, exclusive status here. This also implicates God's concrete covenants in history, of which the covenant with the Prophet Muhammad is now one:

> We took a solemn pledge from the prophets – from you [Muhammad], from
> Noah, from Abraham, from Moses, from Jesus, son of Mary. We took a
> solemn pledge from all of them (Q 33:7).

What the Prophet Muhammad lacks, however, is the scriptural heritage and genealogy of past prophets. This is made up for with a reference to the covenant with Abraham:

> Who but a fool would forsake the religion of Abraham? We have chosen him
> in this world and he will rank among the righteous in the Hereafter (Q 2:130).

---

79 See Neuwirth, *The Qur'an and Late Antiquity*, 327-30.

This covenant with Abraham includes no unconditional affection from God for Abraham's offspring:

> When Abraham's Lord tested him with certain commandments, which he fulfilled, He said, 'I will make you a leader of people.' Abraham asked, 'And will You make leaders my descendants too?' God answered, 'My pledge does not hold for those who do evil' (Q 2:124).

As a 'pagan prophet' (*nabīy ummīy*) Muhammad has no genealogical relationship with past prophets, but in salvific historical terms he does:

> [Those] who follow the Messenger – the unlettered prophet they find described in the Torah that is with them, and in the Gospel – who commands them to do right and forbids them to do wrong, who makes good things lawful to them and bad things unlawful, and relieves them of their burdens, and the iron collars that were on them. So it is those who believe them, honour and help Him, and who follow the light which has been sent down with Him, who will succeed (Q 7:157).

5.4.3 The Messenger Muhammad as lawmaker and his special prestige as a prophetic dignitary

Unlike the Meccan period, the Medinan text corpus contains a large number of very detailed legal guidelines.[80] This change in the nature of the proclamation is now reflected in descriptions of the Messenger Muhammad. Not only does he proclaim the scripture, but he also teaches wisdom (*ḥikma*) (Q 2:129.151; 62:2; 3:164). In this context, one needs to classify the vehemence with which obedience to God and the Messenger is now demanded (Q 58:12; 24:56.62; 47:33; 33:66; 4:64; 9:71; 8:1.20.46; 3:32.132; 5:92). Observance towards God is even equated with obedience to Muhammad (Q 4:80). Those who show obedience to the Messenger are promised great rewards (Q 24:52; 57:21; 4:13.69; 33:71; 48:17). As a lawmaker, Muhammad occupies a typologically similar position to Jesus, who has an ambivalent relationship with Jewish law and demands his followers' obedience:

> I have come to confirm the truth of the Torah which preceded me, and to make

---

80 See Sinai, *The Unknown Known*, 66–7.

some things lawful to you which used to be forbidden. I have come to you
with a sign from your Lord, so serve Him (Q 3:50).

The Qur'an's *legal culture* shows its links to the Christian tradition here.[81]

During the middle Meccan period, Muhammad's status as a prophet (*nabīy*)
shone through due to the typological permeability of the Qur'anic stories. He is
a nominally referred to as *nabīy* in Medina too. Particular dignity is conferred
on Muhammad as a messenger and a prophet, and this is expressed in the rules
governing interactions with him:

> Believers, do not enter the Prophet's apartments for a meal unless you are
> given permission to do so; do not linger until [a meal] is ready. When you are
> invited, go in; then, when you have taken your meal, leave. Do not stay on and
> talk, for that would offend the Prophet, though he would shrink from asking
> you to leave. God does not shrink from the truth. When you ask his wives for
> something, do so from behind a screen: this is purer both for your hearts and
> for theirs. It is not right for you to offend God's Messenger, just as you should
> never marry his wives after him: that would be grievous in God's eyes (Q
> 33:53).

Interactions with Muhammad are organised in a particularly ritualised manner.
One should give alms before conversing with him (Q 58:12) and speak with him
in a soft voice (Q 49:2–3). Nicolai Sinai has pointed out that the Qur'an's require-
ments for dealings with the Prophet are reminiscent of the corresponding formulations about contacts with episcopal and priestly dignitaries,[82] in spite of the
Qur'an's sharp criticism of the god-like reverence for clerics (Q 9:131). This is a
warning to the early Muslim community not to exaggerate the Prophet's special
status. At the same time, however, this honouring of the Prophet acknowledges
that the belief in prophets and messengers has become an integral part of their
faith (Q 2:285; 64:8; 3:179; 4:136, etc.).

5.4.4 Prophetology as a counter-discourse to Christology?

We noted above that the title of prophet (*nabīy*) first occurs in Surah Maryam, and
so the mercy that is the theme of this surah appears as the instigator of Qur'anic

---

81 Zellentin, *The Qur'an's Legal Culture.*
82 Sinai, op. cit. 68–70.

prophetology – at least, that is, if we understand prophetology in its narrower sense. At the same time, Jesus is the first person described as a prophet (*nabīy*), and all the other prophet descriptions in the surah refer to him.[83] Furthermore, none of the persons described as a prophet in the middle Meccan surahs are considered a prophet in the Christian or Jewish traditions. At any rate, Abraham, Isaac and Jacob, for instance, are regarded as patriarchs or fathers outside the Muslim tradition, but not as prophets.

If one considers what all of those named, from Abraham to Idris/Enoch – most of whom are mentioned again in Surah Al 'Imran – have in common, it is that all of them are typologically related to Jesus in Syriac patristic exegesis. The term 'prophet' (*nabīy*) is therefore the new link connecting all of these figures, and so in Medina at the latest, prophetology – once more in the terminologically narrower sense described above – becomes a counter-discourse to Christology.

This is not to say that prophetology should be viewed entirely as a counter-discourse. In developing his prophetology, the proclaimer of the Qur'an focuses on constructive aspects, not just critical ones. That is why we have devoted a large part of this chapter to explaining these aspects. This does not, however, alter the fact that this prophetology takes an overwhelmingly critical stance regarding this book's main theme – Christology.

It is obviously important to the proclaimer of the Qur'an to make it clear that the title of prophet does not distinguish Jesus but instead binds him into the tradition that preceded him. In Q 3:84 he implicitly labels Jesus a prophet in a line that includes Abraham, Ishmael, Isaac, Jacob and Moses, and insists that we must not distinguish between them. According to his conception, prophets should not be taken as lords (Q 3:80), nor should the gift of prophethood cause anyone to become the servant of a prophet (Q 3:79). It is easy to detect the underlying criticism of Christianity in these statements, as Jesus Christ is of course recognised as Lord and Christians obey him. It is also striking that here, as in Surah Maryam, the Qur'an picks out figures that otherwise feature in Christological typology. This is the case with the patriarchs Abraham, Isaac and Jacob at least, but it also applies to Moses. Aaron and Ishmael, on the other hand, might feature in their roles as patriarchs and Aaron simply because he fights with Moses against the pharaoh. With Idris, a lot depends on how one classifies him. The Muslim tradition always identifies him with Enoch in reference to Gen. 5:24 and attributes the first jihad

---

83 By that we mean that all the prophets mentioned in Q 19 can be interpreted as being Jesus Christ in a Christian reception, as we already alluded to in our exegesis.

to him, in the battle against the children of Cain.[84] Since the Bible relates Enoch's direct elevation to God's side, then mentioning his name is also a reference to Christ's fate.

What is particularly interesting is that Surah 37, which introduces a whole host of messengers and therefore represents a great prophetological leap, refers to Isaac as a prophet. This description is presumably an insertion from the Medinan phase, and our thesis that prophetology is a counter-discourse to Christology is therefore only valid for that period. However, Isaac's sacrifice is one of the most conspicuous scenes to be interpreted typologically, first in the New Testament and then again and again by the Church Fathers, in terms of Jesus's death on the cross. The aim of the proclaimer of the Qur'an is clearly to appropriate this typology and reinterpret it. It is not Christ's sacrificial death that is prefigured by the offering of Isaac, but the fate of the Prophet, who is shielded and blessed. The Qur'an does not make any pronouncement as to whether it is actually Isaac whom Abraham is to sacrifice, and the exchanging of Abraham's sons is also used to contradict the Christian narrative.

It therefore strikes us as a plausible hypothesis, despite the range of terminology used in the Qur'an, that the term 'prophet' (nabī) in the Qur'an is increasingly assigned the task of offering a counter-discourse to Christology. The aim of the proclaimer of the Qur'an is to develop an instrument that is capable of naming the specificity of the Prophet on the one hand (see Q 17:55) and, on the other, of cracking open its Christological interpretation.[85] The specificity of every individual prophet is illustrated by the fact that some prophets have particular and highly personal characteristics in the Qur'an. Thus Abraham is the friend of God (Q 4:125), and Moses is described as being pure (Q 19:51), as a man with whom God had a special proximity (Q 19:52) and with whom He spoke face to face (Q 4:164). God took a solemn pledge from Muhammad, Noah, Abraham, Moses and Jesus (Q 33:7).

It is surely no accident that the Qur'an stresses in the case of David that his

---

84 Erder, 'Idris', 484. If Idris really is Enoch, then it is interesting that the Book of Enoch came down to us only in Ethiopian, even though there was substantial reception of the Ethiopian scriptures in Syriac territory.

85 As we noted earlier, we assume that the Qur'an's conflict with Christianity only came to a head in the Medinan period. That does not alter the fact, however, that prophetology was already equipping itself during the Meccan period with means that could then be used in Medina to put forward prophetology as an alternative to Christology. The special profile we describe here already partially existed in Mecca and so, in the following section, we shall repeatedly illustrate our position with verses.

specificity as a prophet was that he received the psalter from God (see Q 4:163). That is because David's messianic role was of particular importance to the Church Fathers for proving the legitimacy of Christology. Rather than picking up on this strand, however, the proclaimer of the Qur'an focuses on David as the recipient of the psalter, acknowledging his crucial role in one of the major biblical texts of late antiquity, which featured very heavily in the Christian liturgy. So one of David's essential character traits is picked up on here. This demonstrates that prophetology is entirely capable of appropriately highlighting the particularities of individual prophetic figures. On the other hand, the Qur'anic depiction of David's specificity offers no opportunity for him to be typologically linked to Christ, even though that was how patristic exegesis commonly interpreted his role. Once more, prophetology appears to constitute a counter-discourse to Christianity and offers proof of more appropriate honouring of biblical figures. Since we are discussing biblical figures, we shall discreetly point out another major aspect of Qur'anic prophetology we alluded to earlier. Although non-biblical figures are called messengers or apostles, in the whole Qur'an only biblical figures are fortunate enough to be named prophets – with the sole exception of Muhammad. This distinction only comes about during the Meccan proclamation, perhaps even only in Medina. A prophetology centred on the notion of prophets does not initially set out to distinguish Muhammad and only becomes associated with his person as its contours take shape. At first, the focus is on the prophetological statements of Jesus, son of Mary, and in their middle Meccan form these are meant to prepare the way for announcing his specificity in such a way that the statements honour him and his mission without endowing prophetology with a messianic charge. Interestingly, it is only at a very late stage that Jesus is addressed as a messenger in this context, and this occurs in the late middle Meccan verse Q 23:51. Indeed, Jesus is only included in the line of messengers late in the Medinan period (Q 2:253 and then, most importantly, Q 3:49.53).

Our thesis therefore runs that the title of prophet (*nabīy*) is initially a specifically biblical term, which is used in the Qur'an to honour individual figures and protagonists from the biblical tradition and, as such, is employed to relativise Christology. In the Medinan period comes a warning not to deduce any redemptive exclusivity from the specificity of individual persons, and so the prophets are increasingly addressed as messengers. This elevates the prophetological design, insofar as the messenger title now ranks more highly than that of prophet during the Medinan period. If, for instance, Muhammad is criticised, it is only as a prophet, never as a messenger. Also, only prophets can be killed – not messengers. The title of prophet suggests a certain degree of ambiguity.

It is this ambiguity, however, that makes for an interesting dialogue between prophetology and Christology. In spite of all God's support for the prophets, the proclaimer of the Qur'an has no doubt about their fates. They are mocked (Q 15:11), called liars (Q 3:184; 22:42; 23:44; 35:25), muddled dreamers and poets (Q 21:5), and their message is rejected (Q 11:59). They are also branded sorcerers and madmen (Q 51:52). They endured persecution and banishment (Q 14:13) and were killed by their own people (Q 2:61.91). It is surely not coincidental that the theme discussed in the greatest depth in the surah centred on a discussion of Christianity and Jesus Christ is the killing of the prophets by disbelievers (see Q 3:21.112.181 and also, interestingly, Q 4:155, i.e. in close proximity to the verse on the Crucifixion). We shall have occasion to reflect again on this ultimate, drastic consequence of the prophetic mission when we search in the next chapter for functional equivalents of soteriology in the Qur'an. It is, however, worth pointing out clearly at this juncture that the proclaimer of the Qur'an is, in the Medinan period especially, by no means a proponent of the naïve idea that God preserves His messengers and prophets from all ills. He does, however, refuse to interpret the general fate of many prophets in relation to Jesus or to see his suffering as the culmination of this problem.

6

The Work of Jesus Christ and the Qur'an: A Forensic Search for Functional Equivalents

In the Christian perception of Jesus Christ, it is not just his person that counts but also his work. Christians profess that they are reconciled with God though him, with him and in him. This involves, first of all, the belief that in Jesus Christ they are meeting God Himself and thus God's love of humanity becomes tangible reality in Jesus. From this insight, Christians have proceeded, at least since the nineteenth century, to speak of God's self-revelation in the context of a model of revelation influenced by communication theory, and so the decisive dimension of the revelation lies not in propositional truths but in the presence of God Himself. This concept is often expressed on the Christian side in terms of the modern philosophy of freedom, and we shall therefore test the applicability of this thinking to Islamic theology.

We already saw in Chapter 3 that it has often been the philosophy of freedom and subject philosophy that have, since Schleiermacher, defined the framework for Christological theories among Christians. In addition, an insight that has gained currency in modern Christian theology is that the freely communicated presence of God is in itself already the work of salvation. In the Eastern Christian tradition, therefore, salvation means nothing other than the deification of human beings. Deification here means the salvific communion of humans with God. Fourthly and lastly, the special significance of the cross of Jesus Christ lies in the fact that this cross reveals that God allows Himself to be affected and moved by people's pain, and we therefore know through the cross that God does not abandon us in our suffering but shows solidarity with us. From this perspective, Jesus Christ's work consists of making tangible and real the affection God shows us in all areas of our lives, including in our feelings of being God-forsaken, our despair and our suffering.

In enquiring in the this chapter about functional equivalents for Jesus's work in the Qur'an, we wish to consider whether there are equivalents in Islam to the aforementioned functions of Christology. Yet we also intend to highlight enduring objections to and shifts in the relevant questions. We shall therefore contemplate whether one can also say of the Qur'an that God shows Himself in His love of humankind in Jesus (6.1) and whether God enters into a free relational dialogue with human beings (6.2). We also wish to check whether the Qur'an also makes God's presence a tangible reality (6.3) and whether we can recognise through the Qur'an that God enters into our passion stories and suffers with us (6.4). In doing so, we should pay particular attention to the issue of whether, from the Qur'an's perspective, emotions such as love or compassion can be conceived of in conjunction with God (6.5). On none of these points do we expect equality, but we want to look for equivalents and similarities and also lasting differences, which exist merely on a regulatory level because the bridge that assumes the corresponding functions for the relationship between God and the world is, from Islam's perspective, not Jesus Christ. Despite all the respect he has for Jesus Christ, the proclaimer of the Qur'an does not consider him God-man, but is thought of in radically human terms and an integral part of the Qur'an's previously explained, newly developed prophetology. The position that Jesus Christ occupies in the Christian tradition is already taken in the Qur'an – largely by the Qur'an itself. This constitutive difference obviously shifts the constellations of problems, and so it is important to remain alert to enduring differences between the two religions.[1]

All five of these sets of issues have prompted such wide-ranging debates in modern Christian theology that we can do no more than provide an introductory schematic overview here. Yet we do hope that it will become clear from a first level of reflection that the Qur'an offers possibilities in all the aforementioned respects to be understood in terms of Jesus Christ's interpretative system and to enter into a fruitful dialogue with it. Our impression is that the Qur'an adopts and transforms the central achievements of Christology and soteriology for performative purposes, rather than simply denying them. Being able to claim this in a modern theological context depends on understanding the Qur'an as an event of

---

1 In drawing such prominent parallels between Jesus Christ and the Qur'an, we naturally have no intention of denigrating the significance of the Bible or of Muhammad. Without the Bible there is no approach to Jesus Christ and, accordingly, the Bible is the living Word of God, but ultimately conveyed by Christ. And without Muhammad and his way of life there is no Qur'an and he is accordingly and repeatedly called the living Qur'an. Yet our understanding of Muhammad finds its ultimate definition in the Qur'an, not the other way around.

God's presence and thus presenting a Qur'anic concept in which God imparts His own being or allows His own being to become an event.

6.1 God's self-revelation in the Islamic tradition?[2]

To our minds, Islamic revelation theology has many means of developing theories of a perfect, substantial and free divine self-revelation or God's *supreme self-communication* in a philosophically and theologically consistent fashion. This is not to claim that we humans, in our limited cognisance, are able to recognise and explicate this self-communication in consummate fashion. It is self-evident that God is never available to human beings and always remains a mystery. Yet talk of a communication of God's being changes nothing about this realisation; indeed, to be precise, talk of self-revelation is the crucial clue that it is an enduring mystery that is being revealed here – namely, God Himself, not some form of propositional truths. Yet God Himself is by definition a reality surpassing our understanding and hence a mystery.

We think that a useful starting point for theological contemplation of the topic of God's self-communication would be to present a transcendental-logical reflection because this is an appropriate means of contemplating the irruption of the absolute into the contingent which is reflected in revelation theology. The transcendental-logical approach recognises the condition of possibility to conceive God's revelation as self-communication in the explanation of a certain relationship. It is a relationship between God and humans which has to be explained ontologically and terminologically as a meeting point between transcendent-essential communication and immanent-essential reception (which is also sensitive to transcendence).

A first approach is to reflect on an examination of God's self-communication in the message of the sound of the Qur'an. This proves to be the aesthetic, mediatory *eikon* of absolute unconditionality, i.e. its beauty is the imparting of a sense of God Himself and ultimately of God's very presence. From a communication theory perspective, the entire revelatory reality constitutes a radical dialogical event in the relationship between God and human beings. In this respect humans are represented as the hearers of the voice of the Qur'an, and also as those called to respond to this voice. The implication is that of a theological-anthropological hermeneutics which is central to understanding this relationship as a whole. The

---

2 Important passages in sections 6.1 and 6.3 were written by our project assistant, Darius Asghar-Zadeh.

main difficulty lies in interpreting the *theological-anthropological* dimension of the revelational context and its analysis.

In accordance with the Christological logic of incarnation, Christian theology seeks a mediatory figure. Even if this mediatory figure is criticised by the Qur'an for reasons of ambiguity, one could consider whether its achievements cannot also be understood by the Qur'an. Thus Muslims too can say of the Qur'an that since it is in Arabic, it represents a truly human word without its divine origin being called into question. Even the Qur'an's self-analysis emphasises that, on the one hand, God's word becomes audible, proving that it is accessible to human beings; the hearer's humanity is therefore repeatedly stressed. On the other hand, that selfsame word is also the unfathomable word that transcends all human realities. Its beauty surpasses anything human, all too human, and expands human horizons towards a reality that surpasses human understanding.

In terms of the salvation economy, God is experienced according to revelatory logic in the iconic nature of the sound of the Qur'an and of the *Creation*, and as a continuum of the sound, this experience may absolutely be described as *pneumatologically perpetuated*. By the power of God's spiritual actuality, God's presence is therefore not only to be experienced in the beauty of the recitation of the Qur'an but also in every sign of the Creation. There is thus a truly soteriological dimension to the sound of the Qur'an because it is an aesthetic expression of the instructions to human beings created in image of the Perfect One and with the purpose of striving towards Him. In the recitation of the Qur'an, therefore, we are able to experience how God has already come close to us in all reality, and so we need only to remember His salvific reality as we look back over our lives.

Bound up with the semantics of God's revelation of Himself is the understanding of the explication of God's power in the benevolence that Islamic theology ascribes to God when it acknowledges Him as the continuously active upholder of the world He created and regards Him as the Almighty (*al-Jabbār*, Q 59:23) and, in the Qur'anic tradition, as the Provider (*al-Razzāq*, Q 51:58), the giver of life (*al-Muhyi*, 41:39), the Most Forgiving and Most Merciful (*al-Ghafūr*, Q 12:98; *al-Tawwāb*, Q 2:128) and the Judge (*al-Muqsit*, see Q 5:42).[3]

This is where the particular issue of the status of God's love becomes urgent, as it can include not only the Qur'anic terminologies[4] of *hubb/mahabba* (love) and *wudd* (friendship) but also the mystical *'ishq* (desire). It is no coincidence that the idea of God as love, in particular, is the guiding principle of the entire theology of

---

3 See also Lutz Berger, *Islamische Theologie*, Vienna 2010, 172.
4 See Q 3:31; 3:134; 11:90; 20:39.

self-revelation in the Christian tradition. It is precisely by conceiving of God as love that the form of His message to us (in the form, and by means, of love) can be said to be Himself (i.e. love). Regarding the aforementioned aesthetic context, one might consider whether God's affection and beauty are not also made tangible in the beauty of His address to humankind.

It is beneficial in the context of this philosophical and theological debate to consult the thinking of the polymath Ibn Sina (980–1037), Avicenna in Latin. Ibn Sina, of Neoplatonic and Qur'anic training, perceives the one and only God to be the source of life, beauty, good, knowledge and love, indeed of pure love itself, and identifies God's self-love as the most perfect form of love.[5] Pure love, as the absolutely constitutive element of God's essence,[6] deserves to be studied as a topic in the 'science of God's sovereignty' ('ilm al-rubūbīya) and therefore as a principle of philosophical theology (al-'ilm al-ilāhī) in the sense of a theologically normative term.[7] Hence Ibn Sina elucidates a theory of emanation, which is criticised by traditional theology but relevant to our context. This goes back to Platonic philosophy, and Ibn Sina largely adopted it from his predecessor al-Farabi. What is important here, though, is to realise that Ibn Sina tries to combine his conception of a creation ex nihilo (here: ibdā') with the doctrine of the emanation of all created things from God in order to guarantee an ontological but not chronological supremacy of the Creator over Creation. In doing so, he aims to liberate God in people's minds from any notion of His being bound by time, and consequently and ultimately to sustain the idea of God's total transcendence in a profoundly religious sense.

This is precisely the framework in which the Persian scholar is concerned with the link between ontology and cosmogony, which assigns to the perfect Supreme Being (al-mawjūd al-'ālī), as the highest subject and object of love, a love born of boundless wisdom that overflows on to the earth (ḥikma). God therefore emanates this love as an everlasting reaffirmation of his divine reign (see the term

---

5 We are aware that Ibn Sina's conception of love is often 'downplayed' as the mere adoption of a Hellenistic (and above all [Neo]platonic) teleology, causal logic and relation ontology. It is, however, a fundamental mistake to ignore the religiously directed components and their monotheistic conception of a personal God, which ultimately influenced Ibn Sina as well, by depicting him exclusively as a Hellenist. It is therefore not only legitimate to attempt a speculative theological interpretation of the thinking of the (Islamic!) genius Ibn Sina; it is necessary and hermeneutically profitable.
6 See Maha El Kaisy-Friemuth, *God and Humans in Islamic Thought. Abd al-Jabbār, Ibn Sīnā and al-Ghazālī*, New York 2006, 83.
7 Also see Etin Anwar, 'Ibn Sina's Philosophical Theology of Love. A Study of the Risālah fī al-'Ishq', in *Islamic Studies* 42 (2003) 331–345, here 332.

al-mudabbir).[8] Ibn Sina's metaphysical thought here incorporates a love-centred original theology[9] where God – pure goodness (al-khayr al-maḥḍ), original goodness (al-khayr al-awwal) and absolute goodness (al-khayr al-muṭlaq) – is identified as original love, perfect in itself.[10]

In this context one should also take into account, incidentally, that in spite of his necessitaristic cosmology, Ibn Sina does not omit an intensive conception of the force of God's free will. Ibn Sina differentiates this free will (irāda or ikhtiyār) sharply from human will and in its primary, everlasting nature, it is a will devoid of any other motive than divine selfhood per se.[11] If one follows Ibn Sina in also assuming a radical coincidence of divine will, knowledge and God's being,[12] then one must also accept – linked to a conception of creation by emanation – an ontologically everlasting (mediated) effect of the divine being, will and knowledge in cosmic reality. Thus the idea of God's self-revelation is made metaphysically and theologically apparent in the reality of Creation.

These preliminary considerations are of particular interest for the development of an understanding of revelation based on love, in which one may speak of divine self-communication as living love. This theory is valid if one considers that in Ibn Sina's eyes, the relationship between God and the world or between God and humans is understood as a part of Creation's dependence on God and the universal ordering love emanating from Him. In this line of thinking, God reveals Himself in His divine assistance to humans and in His mystically understood manifestation or 'revelation' (tajallī), which must above all be proved.[13] This love that shapes the world order must be seen as the culmination of this manifestation. The word tajallī is accordingly translated with revelatory terms such as 'self-unveiling', 'theophany' or obviously 'self-revelation'.[14]

---

8 See Anwar, Ibn Sina's Philosophical Theology, 335.
9 Maria De Cillis, Free Will and Predestination in Islamic Thought: Theoretical Compromises in the Works of Avicenna, al-Ghazālī and Ibn 'Arabī, London 2014, 79.
10 See Anwar, op. cit. 334–8; El Kaisy-Friemuth, God and Humans, 79, 83.
11 See Ibn Sina, al-Ta'līqāt, edited and with an introduction by 'Abd al-Rahman Badawi, Cairo 1973, 50–1.
12 On this see Ibn Sina, Kitab al-shifa': al-Ilahiyat VIII 7 (= Ibn Sina, Kitab al-shifa': al-Ilahiyat, vol. 2, eds. Muhammad Yusuf Musa / Sulayman Dunya / Sa'id Zayid, Cairo 1960 [ND Qom 1983], 366–7); Muhammad Yusuf Musa, The Metaphysica of Avicenna (ibn Sina). A Critical Translation-Commentary and Analysis of the Fundamental Arguments in Avicenna's Metaphysica in the Danish Nama-i 'ala'i (The Book of Scientific Knowledge), ed. Parviz Morewedge, New York 1973, 67.
13 See El Kaisy-Friemuth, God and Humans, 117.
14 See Hamid Parsania, Existence and the Fall. Spiritual Anthropology of Islam., tr. Shuja Ali Mirza, London 2006, 191; Haifaa Jawad, 'A Muslim Response to the Christian Theology

We now come to the issue of the extent to which this mystical conception of a divine revelatedness stands up in terms of revelation theology. Ultimately, the efficacy of such an approach depends on whether it can be handled and explained in a systematic theological way. To do this, we must not relinquish the concept of *tajallī* occurrences to an exaggerated Sufic amalgamation of the kind that mystic concepts occasionally and unhelpfully develop. It is preferable to discuss revelation through the prism of the relationship between God and humankind.

This reflexive strength is due to the fact that human beings gain in significance in this concept (without God's significance being degraded). Through its decisive assertion of the existence of God and His Creation in the face of 'nothingness' or 'non-being' (*'adam*), Ibn Sina's existential philosophy is a significant intellectual enhancement of creatureliness and thus of humanity.[15] This is continued in the very potential for emphasis of the human components as part of the profound *relationship* between God and humankind. The importance of human beings in the revelatory occurrence is emphasised by their relevance as recipients of the divine *logos*.

The fundamental structure of this receptive relevance is indexed to Ibn Sina's intellectual and inspirational doctrine. Human reception of the divine *tajallī* presupposes intensive spiritual activity which, as the scholar emphasises, reaches its peak in so-called 'intuition' (*ḥads*), the highest category of knowledge of which humans are capable. First, he highlights a special ability in terms of both 'imaginative revelation' and 'intellect-related revelation'. In imaginative revelation, prophetic knowledge is disclosed by heavenly souls to the so-called 'imaginative capability' (*quwwa mutakhayyila*). Intellectual revelation encompasses intuitive insights in the sense of syllogism achieved through reason. It is the special combination of intensive imaginative and intellectual epistemics that produces the highest prophetical form of reception of the revelation (*waḥy*).[16]

---

of Religions', in Elizabeth Harris / Paul Hedges / Shanthikumar Hettiarachchi (eds.), *Twenty-First Century Theologies of Religions. Retrospection and Future Prospects*, Leiden 2016, 328–58, here 355. On previous Ibn Sina interpretation, see also Darius Asghar-Zadeh, 'Menschsein im Angesicht des Absoluten. Theologische Anthropologie in der Perspektive christlich-muslimischer Komparativer Theologie' (*Beiträge zur Komparativen Theologie*; 29), Paderborn 2017, 160–1, 390, 395.

15 See Tilmann Nagel, *Islam: Die Heilsbotschaft des Korans und ihre Konsequenzen*, Westhofen 2001, 72–3.

16 On this see Frank Griffel, 'Philosophy and Prophecy', in Richard C. Taylor / Luis Xavier López-Farjeat (eds.), *The Routledge Companion to Islamic Philosophy*, London 2016, 385–98, here 392–3; Griffel, 'Muslim Philosophers' Rationalist Explanation of Muḥammad's Prophecy', in Jonathan E. Brockopp (ed.), *The Cambridge Companion to Muḥammad*,

Ibn Sina admittedly ascribes the most perfect form of intuitive knowledge to the prophets, proceeding along this prophetological path according to a consciously orthodox conception of faith. Nevertheless, this plays a remarkable role in a conception of revelation that serves the pneumatological self-communicational dialogue between Islam and Christianity in the sense that Ibn Sina explicitly talks about the efficacy of the 'holy spirit' (al-rūḥ al-qudsī or al-rūḥ al-qudsīya) in the said spirit-induced revelatory occurrence.[17]

This process is not limited to an anthropomental capacity for knowledge but, given the revelatory context, clearly involves the activity of the divine spirit as well. When one focuses on this activating role of God's spirit, then the obvious question with regard to the Qur'an is whether one might not speak here of a carrier of the *divine self*. Going further, this approach is of epistemological significance to the debate – closely related to revelation theology – about God's actions in the world. This significance also becomes clear if we think 'of actions or interventions by God on the intramental level [...]' in the human-free subject. Maybe we can talk here of the 'possibility of an immanent conscious, proclaiming, guiding and liberating experience of God's reality', indeed the 'sense of being led and safe'.[18] At this point it is sufficiently hermeneutically comprehensible with 'guidance' (hudā) in this pneumatological conception of revelation.

One further philosophical and theological element of revelation epistemology that merits closer examination is the so-called *tashkīk* principle. This concept, which is primarily associated with the Persion theosophist Sadr al-Din al-Shirazi (1572–1640), also known as Mulla Sadra, can be ultimately – and at least indirectly – analysed with reference to the (emanation-logical) multilevel thinking of Ibn Sina.[19] The notion of *tashkīk*, whose meaning is highly complex and extremely

---

Cambridge 2010, 158–79, here 172. The term 'intellectual revelation' comes from the study by Fazlur Rahman, *Prophecy in Islam*, London 1958, 30 onwards.

17 Frank Griffel, *Philosophy and Prophecy*, 392. For example, see Ibn Sina, Avicenna's *De Anima* (Arabic text), ed. Fazlur Rahman, London 1959, 249. The inspirational revelation model can be supported in the Qur'an by Q 15:29: 'When I have fashioned him and breathed My spirit into him [nafakhtu fīhi min rūḥī]'; Q 16:102: 'Say that the Holy Spirit [rūḥu l-qudusi] has brought the Revelation with the Truth, [...]'; or Q 40:15: 'He sends revelations [yulqī al-rūḥa] with His teachings.'

18 Stosch, *Systematische Theologie*, 92; for context, see ibid. 87–94.

19 Ibn Sina used the term *tashkīk* or *mushakkak* long before Mulla Sadra did, although not in the same specific hermeneutic sense one sees with Mulla Sadra. See Tiana Koutzarova, *Das Transzendentale bei Ibn Sina. Zur Metaphysik als Wissenschaft erster Begriffs- und Urteilsprinzipien*, Leiden 2009, 425, 428; Sajjad H. Rizvi, *Mulla Sadra and Metaphysics: Modulation of Being*, London 2009, 44–7. On its use by Mulla Sadra, see Sadr al-Din Muhammad ibn Ibrahim al-Shirazi (= Mulla Sadra), *al-Hikma al-muta'aliya fi l-asfar*

nuanced, has been used in more recent Islamic theology, especially by Mehdi Hairi Yazdi (1923–99) in his 'pyramidal ontology'[20] and translated as 'existential variance',[21] 'gradation of being', 'equivocal being', 'the systematic ambiguity of existence',[22] and 'modulation of being'.[23] We could also offer an additional translation of 'multi-level spectrum of existence'. The *tashkīk* principle is an expression that allows for an ontological conception of the *differentiality* that arrives from divine union by means of its idea of a multi-level and diverse form of the reality of the Creation emanating from God. *Tashkīk* is often explained by metaphors of light, in the sense that the ontological pyramidal structure it expresses is compared to the effect of a strong light source (e.g. the Sun) and the rays it emits. In this phenomenon, the rays (the being that emanates from God) appear as prismatic forms, levels and layers in a range of different intensities, gradings, qualities and thus infinite variety with increasing distance from the light source (the divine), and yet they all originate from the same source.[24]

According to the *tashkīk* principle, God's relation to Creation and God's actions in the world can be understood in a completely process-theological conception as *creatio continua*, as actions that are tangible, imparted through creation and immanent to consciousness. *Tashkīk* means a reality of (whole) being, a 'continuum of being',[25] at the top of which is God as the source and creative origin of everything

---

al 'aqliya al-arba'a (=al-Asfar), eds. Rida Lutfi & Muhammad Rida Muzaffar, Qom 1387/1967), vol. 1, 36, 423–46; vol. 2, 104; vol. 4, 3–5. The etymological root of *tashkīk* is the Arabic verb *shakka*, but due to its philosophically elaborate semantics, it should not be confused with its original meaning of 'to doubt', as it is only distantly related to this in terms of the differential nature of 'ambiguity' (and the 'doubt' that comes from ambiguity). The philosophical approach relies on the graded semantics of *tashkīk* (on this, see Ayatollah Ghaemmaghami, 'Einheit und Vielfalt im Gottesgedanken', in: Muna Tatari / Klaus von Stosch (eds.), *Trinität – Anstoß für das islamisch-christliche Gespräch* (*Beiträge zur komparativen Theologie*; 7), Paderborn 2013, 171–93, here 185, 187; Reza Hajatpour, *Vom Gottesentwurf zum Selbstentwurf. Die Idee der Perfektibilität in der islamischen Existenzphilosophie*, Freiburg 2013, 47 note 90).

20 See Mahdi Ha'iri Yazdi, *Hiram-i hasti: tahlili az mabadi-i hastishinasi-i tatbiqi*, Tehran 1980.

21 Farzin Vahdat, 'Mehdi Haeri Yazdi and the Discourse of Modernity', in Ramin Jahanbegloo (ed.), *Iran Between Tradition and Modernity*, Lanham 2004, 51–70, here 55.

22 Hajj Muhammad Legenhausen, 'Mulla Sadra's Critique of Apophatic Mysticism and Pantheism', in Bernhard Nitsche / Klaus von Stosch / Muna Tatari (eds.), *Gott – jenseits von Monismus und Theismus?* (*Beiträge zur komparativen Theologie*; 23), Paderborn 2017, 309–21, here 315.

23 Rizvi, *Mulla Sadra and Metaphysics*, 27–9.

24 On this, see also Ghaemmaghami, *Einheit und Vielfalt*; Hajatpour, *Mehdi Hairi Yazdi*, 56–7.

25 Hajatpour, *Mehdi Hairi Yazdi*, 55.

without subsuming all being, but in which He should be conceived as producing and simultaneously encompassing everything.[26] In this reality, the entities that come from God – or, to use Ibn Sina's terminology, creatively emanate from God – are apparitions from God, yet distinct from Him. Human acts that correspond to God's will take place within and from the ontological *tashkīk* process and are therefore part of the reality of God's revelation and action. This is not least a solid basis for arguing for a manifestation of God both in making His mercy immanent in the work and in Creation, without having to lapse into a pantheistic position. Such talk requires a conception of God's action (including His self-revelation in the world) in *creatio continua*.

The *tashkīk* principle allows for the expressibility of a creative, transcendent and immanent occurrence, along with transcendent occurrence within immanence, through the idea of a continuum of being (being in becoming; becoming in being). We can appropriately express our complete relatedness to God in our complete difference from God by referring back to the idea of the 'pyramidal structure' of being that is implied in the *tashkīk* dictum. This concept conveys the intensity of the interrelatedness of the divine and creative dynamics in an extremely plausible form, because humans' motion towards God (towards perfection), which Mulla Sadra highlights as the theory of transsubstantial motion (*al-ḥaraka al-jawharīya*),[27] is to be understood as a consequence and a procedural continuum of the entire process of being that emanates from the transcendent origin.

We have so far sought to approach the notion of self-revelation primarily from the position of the classical Islamic philosophical tradition and have therefore engaged in ontological reflections reliant on ontological commitments that are not uncontroversial nowadays. So we now wish to have another go at our topic by referring to a greater extent to concepts and terminology from modern philosophy of freedom. In doing so, we wish to at least indicate that the idea of self-revelation is not related to a second metaphysical paradigm but can be attained through a variety of forms of language and thought, for each of which a Muslim variant can be formulated.

---

26 This ontological, all-encompassing character of God is vividly captured in the Qur'an's title for God as 'Lord of the Worlds' (*rabb al-'ālamīn*, Q 1:2) and the Qur'anic reference to Him as 'all pervading' (*al-Wasi'*, Q 2:115).

27 On this see Hajatpour, *Vom Gottesentwurf zum Selbstentwurf*, 113–23.

6.2 The relation between God and humankind as a liberating relationship

If one seeks to provide an overall appreciation of the Qur'an, then one can say that it invites all people to have a relationship with God. At the same time, from a Muslim perspective the Qur'an is the Word of God itself, and so it powerfully imparts the presence of God of which it invites people to partake in. God's presence, into which the Qur'an invites us, appeared not with the revelation of the Qur'an but has shaped Creation from the very beginning. Hence God does not need to join the world in His revelation; God encompasses the world from its very first instant. The Qur'an therefore underlines the fact that God is not outside the world but embracing it in His mercy (see Q 7:156) and at the same time closer to us than our own jugular vein (Q 50:16).

In the Qur'an's view, God chose humans so as to give them the chance to devote their lives to Him. In doing so, God opened Himself up to humankind. This boundless, fundamental openness is the condition and basis for freedom. Freedom, on the other hand, is inconceivable without self-determination,[28] and so God cannot deny humankind this self-determination if He wishes to designate it free.

Human freedom is accomplished in the realm of the contingent and is therefore first and foremost contingent. However, if it is genuinely supposed to be free, then it is, transcendentally speaking, non-contingent. This means that if freedom is to be genuinely free, it cannot be completely explained by the conditions in which it is accomplished. Naturally, freedom is shaped by environmental influences and genetic dispositions, but if humans are a mere product of these, they cannot be described as 'free'. So the condition for the possibility of asserting one's freedom is a moment of non-contingency in the accomplishment of human freedom. This non-contingency or unconditionality does not challenge the idea that human freedom is always accomplished under specific conditions and is therefore never free of contingency. From a formal perspective, though, these contingencies must not completely condition freedom if it is to be itself.

Within the school of the Catholic theologian Thomas Pröpper, it has become usual at this point to talk, like Hermann Krings, of a transcendental or even formal unconditionality of freedom.[29] Although we do not wish to evalutate this

---

28 See Hermann Krings, 'Freiheit. Ein Versuch, Gott zu denken', in Krings (ed.), *System und Freiheit. Gesammelte Aufsätze* (in the collection 'Praktische Philosophie'; 12), Freiburg 1980, 161–84, here 171.

29 For a classical source, see Thomas Pröpper, *Erlösungsglaube und Freiheitsgeschichte. Eine Skizze zur Soteriologie*, Munich 1991, 183–5.

phraseology here, it at least makes it clear that the philosophy of freedom offers
a possibility of developing a concept of unconditionality that enables people to
test the claims of the unconditional against a set of criteria.[30] It also gives direction to freedom, since the philosophy of freedom demonstrates that freedom is
only achieved if it is based on freedom; the fulfilling substance of freedom can be
nothing other than freedom itself.[31] Only in the affirmation of freedom is freedom
fulfilled.

However, the implication of this for God's absolute freedom, which of course
is not only formal – unlike finite freedom – but materially unconditional, is that it
is fulfilled in Creation through the affirmation of human freedom. In other words,
God revealed Himself to humankind in freedom and thereby asserted humankind's freedom. If God were to restrict humans' freedom, this would restrict the
freedom of God Himself, since freedom is fulfilled by opening up to another form
of freedom, allowing it and encouraging it to be free.

Might it be possible to suggest the philosophy of freedom as a basis for the
Muslim definition of the relationship between God and humankind? In his book
The Problem of Freedom, following his criticism of Spinoza and Spinoza's ideas
about humans' lack of freedom from God, the Egyptian philosopher Zachria
Ibrahim (1924–76) enquires:

> What prevents us from presuming that God Himself wanted there to be free
> creatures who act of their own accord in the sense that they are endowed with
> their own will which is independent of the will of God? Why can we not say
> that precisely because it is impossible that things exist contrary to God's will,
> that it is possible for God to creat a creature that is endowed with its own free
> will? [...] Truly, this kind of autonomous power that God creates of His own
> accord through the gift of another will, may appear to be an imperfection of
> God's omnipotence. May we not say, however, that the absolute omnipotence
> of God appears more perfectly and more clearly if it actually brings forth
> mighty creatures rather than incapable creatures which neither possess their
> own power nor are capable of self-determination? What kind of divine might

---

30 The Christian author of this book has tried elsewhere to formulate the concept of the
unconditional differently. See Stosch, *Offenbarung*, 74–81. This is only to say that there
are different ways of defining the concept of the unconditional in contemporary Christian
theology, and we prefer not to nail ourselves down to any particular concept at this point. It
should however be noted that these kinds of terminological derivations raise opportunities to
test claims of unconditionality according to certain criteria.
31 Krings, *Freiheit*, 174.

is it that can bring forth only puppets? Is such a conception not far from our conception of the absolute omnipotence of God? So why do we not say that the greater the aunomous power and genuine motion that God gives to His Creation, the more perfect and visible is His omnipotence? For the greatness of the gift points to the greatness of the bestower of this gift. Is not our freedom the truest sign of God's absolute omnipotence?[32]

Ibrahim traces resistance to the philosophy of freedom back to latent pantheistic ideas in the Islamic tradition, and his thinking is sympathetic to the position of the Schelling-influenced Swiss philosopher Charles Secrétan (died 1895). In Ibrahim's reconstruction of his thought, Secrétan construes God as absolute freedom,[33] and He is free in relation to Himself. Secrétan argues that God has also freely decided on His own perfection. Were God to be perfect in His essence, this would constitute an inherent contradiction, because a pre-existing perfect God – i.e. a God who comes to Himself already perfect – would be less perfect than a God who freely bestows perfection upon Himself.[34] God cannot be subject to a particular nature imposed upon Him. Conceiving of God as absolute freedom would mean that He had freely opted for His own perfection.[35] Secrétan sees – as before in Ibrahim's reconstruction – the Creation as God's free decision in accordance with His own free will. Thus God created a being on whom He freely bestowed autonomy. God does not do this to demonstrate His splendour and greatness, but without any preconditions or specific purpose – if not, the Creation would be necessary and no longer God's free decision. Rather, God wants humankind unconditionally; God wants to bestow upon them the gift of His love. That is why God wants free human beings who are not merely the purpose of His intentions, but a purpose in themselves.[36]

The influence of such consideration of modern philosophy of freedom on Ibrahim is obvious. Our aim is not to delve into the subject any further here, but rather to test whether it is compatible with traditional Islamic scholastic theology. It is, however, extremely interesting that both the Ash'ari and Maturidiyya schools

---

32 Zakariyya Ibrahim, *Mushkilat al-hurriyya*, Cairo 1972, 136–7.

33 Zakariyya Ibrahim, op. cit. 137.

34 Charles Secretan, *La Philosophie de la liberté. Cours de philosophie morale fait à Lausanne*, Lausanne 1849. Quoted in its Arabic translation in Ibrahim, *Mushkilat al-hurriyya*, 137.

35 Emile Boutroux, *Nouvelles études d'histoire de la philosophie*, Paris 1927, 324. Quoted in its Arabic translation in Ibrahim, *Mushkilat al-hurriyya*, 137.

36 Ibrahim, *Mushkilat al-hurriyya*, 138.

agreed that God's original, core characteristic is His *irāda* ('will'). Al-Taftazani,[37] like many other scholars, takes the stance that *irāda* requires no motive; it is the motive of all motives in God. *Irāda* means nothing other than God's absolute freedom, in a sense His original self-determination. According to classical Sunni scholastic theology, God is absolutely independent and free to do or not do whatever He pleases.

This tradition also views God's mercy as the expression of God's will[38] and not as God's essence as classical scholastic theology and metaphysics see it. The statement that God is absolute freedom is therefore in line with the traditional Islamic conception. We can therefore say that God freely defined Himself as merciful. The Qur'an itself underlines this in two places (Q 6:12 and 6:54) when it says the God took it on Himself to be merciful. In this reading, therefore, mercy does not have to be a description of God's being before all Creation; it is not ontologically necessary in God, but freely chosen by God. If God Himself were ontological mercy or endowed with mercy as a necessary essential characteristic, then the Qur'an could not need to mention and stress that He had taken it on Himself to be merciful. Humans can rely, and stake their lives and deaths, on the fact that God is merciful because God has made that promise to them.

Hence it is easy to reconcile the idea of God as freedom with traditional scholastic theology; indeed, it is the obvious conclusion. We do not, however, mean to say that this idea is imperative. We are not even sure whether we ought to adopt it. After all, the Qur'an makes a clear distinction between two different forms of mercy, and so one could certainly consider whether there is not also a form of mercy that has always been ingrained in God's being, guiding His freedom. This ingrained mercy has nothing to do with the authority to pardon we think of when we use this term nowadays. Instead, if one takes seriously the sense of the word in the Semitic languages, it describes God's visceral concern. This is an image of God being profoundly moved by people's distress. God does not first have to choose to be moved, nor can God distance Himself from it without betraying His nature.

If one accepts this idea, then freedom would not be so frequently understood as absolute self-determination but rather as God being true to Himself in His love of humankind. There is no need to answer this question here, though; we simply

---

37 Sa'd al-Din al-Taftazani, *Sharh al-Maqasid*.
38 Both the Ash'ari and Maturadiyya schools recognise that mercy depends on God's will. See, for example, Muhammad Al-Baqillani, *Tamhid al-awa'il wa-talkhis al-dala'il*, ed. 'Imad al-Din Haydar, Bayrut 1987, 299. See al-Baqillani, *Tamhid*, 47–8.

wanted to think about God in terms of freedom in an Islamic context too. The Muslim author of this book will examine elsewhere the potential effects of such thinking on spelling out a theology of mercy and how that relates to a theology of freedom.

Although the possibility of thinking of God in categories of freedom is clear in Islam, it is controversial whether human beings can also enter into a relationship of freedom with God, and the same theological traditions that emphasise God's freedom are sceptical about it. On the other hand, the Mu'tazila tradition and, even earlier, the ideas of the Qadarites are good examples of the fact that options of a strong idea of human freedom were considered in classic Islamic theological debates.[39] The insistence of the modern philosophy of freedom that the relationship between God and humans should be thought of as one of freedom and mutual determination is not without precedent in Islamic scholastic theology. It can also hark back to mystical currents in popular devotion, as there are countless texts defining the relationship between God and humans as one of love. First and foremost, however, the Qur'an offers a definition of the relationship between God and man – in what is presumed to be the final surah, moreover, and one that we have studied in detail and discusses Christology in depth – that has so far not been adequately exploited in the formation of Islamic theological theory. Here, God speaks of 'people He loves and who love Him' (Q 5:54) and whom He calls to be witnesses for those who might go back on their faith. God obviously has a special trust in those people with whom He has a loving relationship. So it does not strike us as particularly far-fetched to assume that the proclaimer of the Qur'an sees this relationship of mutual love as an important aspect of the perfection of human existence.

If God does invite people into a relationship of love, however, He must respect their freedom. From an anthropological point of view, freedom is the law of love, and without freedom there can be no sincere love of God. With slight overemphasis, one may therefore say that God sent the prophets and their tidings to people because He did indeed wish to invite them into a relationship of love. This is precisely why the Qur'an sees the call to Islam as an invitation (da'wa). An invitation can only be freely accepted if it facilitates the realisation of love. If His intention is to preserve and protect human freedom, then God will only intervene in the world in a way that does not destroy this freedom. So God invites people to be free in

---

39 As an introduction, see Ulrich Schoen, 'Gottes Allmacht und die Freiheit des Menschen. Gemeinsames Problem von Islam und Christentum', with an introduction by K. Hock and an updated afterword by the author (*Christentum und Islam im Dialog*; 2), Münster 2003.

order to make freedom possible. It is human beings, first and foremost, who accomplish God's plan of love and mercy, making it a tangible reality in the here and now. This is the highest honour for human beings. They are God's partners – *calif* in the language of the Qur'an – in turning His intention into reality. So one should not see divine and human behaviour as competing with one another. On the contrary: the more humans strive to release freedom, the more God's intention is accomplished. Human efforts to release freedom find fulfilment in behaviour that promotes love and mercy, and so both of these must become the goal of human actions.

If, following these thoughts on the relationship between God and man as one of love, we turn back to the Qur'an, it becomes clear that for Muslims the Qur'an is the realisation of God's consent to enter into a relationship with human beings. It is proof of God's love of humankind and His mercy. The Qur'an is God's 'yes' to humankind. In order to be able to trust absolutely in this 'yes', Muslims believe that one need not hypostatise it, merely take seriously that it expresses the authentic will and being of God. God invites humans to devote their lives to Him and promises that He will always reach out to them, again and again (as it is clear from the word *hudā*, which is generally translated as 'guidance' and can therefore easily end up sounding purely legalistic, although it is actually about God's aid for the fundamental direction of people's lives).

In this conception, the Qur'an is a medium for communication between God and human beings – and not simply for the Qur'an's initial seventh-century audience on the Arabian Peninsula. Instead, it is an offer of communication to all people and simultaneously God's relational commitment. And it is precisely this offer of communication and this relational commitment through the Qur'an, which is the expression of God's mercy understood as God's unconditional affection and commitment, that is the true content of the Qur'an. It would therefore be the task of a hermeneutics of the Qur'an that takes account of God's mercy to examine its statements for God's offer of communication and His relational commitment, which are first and foremost intended as historical signs that allow people to strike up a trusting relationship with God.

The Qur'an does talk about the word of God, but in the sense of *God's direct spoken word*. By that we do not mean the word that we humans hear. Rather, the Qur'an uses this category of God's speech as a medium for the fulfilment of God's will/freedom, which is why it says in the Qur'an: 'When We will something to happen, all that We say is, "Be" and it is' (Q 18:40). And since God takes it freely upon Himself to be merciful, He has decided to define His word in terms of mercy. This word manifests itself in the Creation, but also in God's various revelations. It is in this sense that the Qur'an is the word of God.

Ash'ari theology has always differentiated between the transcendent and the immanent sides of the Qur'an. Its transcendent, uncreated side is an expression of its unconditionality as God's self-communication, whereas its immanent, created side is an expression of its contingency in its linguisticality. It was also clear to the Ash'aris that God did not speak Arabic before the creation of the world, but that the concrete morphogenesis of the Qur'an in intelligible Arabic can become a reality only in the Creation. And yet it was important to the Ash'aris that this immanent verbalisation of God's eternal self-communication truly captured the message in human words. Based on the Ash'ari position, we can therefore say that the Qur'an represents God's self-communication, which has entered the contingent world as the spoken or recited word. This dual nature of the Qur'an as described by the Ash'aris, with one unconditional, transcendent side – the Ash'aris speak here of God's inner speech, the *kalām nafsī*[40] – and one contingent, immanent side, immediately raises the question of how the transcendent may be recognised in the immanent.

Here we encounter epistemological issues, and there is insufficient time to clarify them in this study. Suffice it to say that the special aesthetics of the Qur'an might be key to being able to define the Qur'an as a manifestation of God's self-communication. The Qur'an explicitly teaches and defends its own beauty (Q 39:23; 12:3; 25:33) and this became an ever more important dimension in the course of Islamic theological history, as Navid Kermani, for instance, has pointed out in his PhD thesis.[41] The Qur'an itself highlights its miraculous nature, of which its inimitability is a sign. That is why the Qur'an wagers that it would be impossible to copy, let alone better it (see Q 11/13 and Q 10:38).

Muslim scholars have paid a great deal of attention to the theme of the Qur'an's inimitability and miraculous nature in order to demonstrate its rhetorical superiority to the works of the poets.[42] They thought that it was important to show that:

[S]uch a book could not possibly have been produced by a human author,
Muslim scholars from the early ninth century on went to great lengths to
demonstrate its thematic profundity and its formal perfection. They developed
literary theories and poetic standards and compared their holy book again and
again with the works of the poets, and continue to do so in our time.[43]

---

40 Sayf al-Din, Al-Amidi, *Abkar al-afkar fi usul al-din*, vol. 1, Cairo 2004, 353–5.
41 See Navid Kermani, *God is Beautiful. The Aesthetic Experience of the Qur'an*, tr. Tony Crawford, London 2015.
42 Ibid. 191.
43 Ibid. 190.

Their endeavours are highly reminiscent of attempts by the early Christian apolo-
giae's to justify Jesus's divinity on the basis of his miracles. We saw earlier that
this kind of response to faith has become obsolete in the modern age, and we can
therefore make only limited use of it here.

Yet we do wish to pursue the path Kermani lays out in order to link categories of the philosophy of freedom with this aesthetic theory. So let us return to
Kermani's reconstruction. He mentions the examples of some Muslim scholars
who underscore the miraculous nature of the Qur'an:

> A person who hears the Qur'an, al-Baqillani wrote, knows that it is God's
> own speech: the same certainty arises in him that came over Moses when he
> heard the voice behind the thorn bush. And only the Qur'an has this quality;
> the miracles of the Torah and the Gospels lie only in secondary properties,
> such as their 'messages about the unseen' (akhbār 'an al-qayb), not in the
> linguistic composition itself. Al-Suyuti later added that Muhammad's miracle
> was greater and more permanent than those of his prophetic predecessors,
> such as the camel that was given to Salih according to verse 7:73, or the staff
> that Moses transformed into a snake. Those signs were merely outward, and
> visible only to the eyes; but Muhammad's proof, because it is experienced
> inwardly and 'seen by the heart', is verifiable at all times, he wrote.[44]

The beauty of the Qur'an obviously is not manifest merely in the linguistic form
of the Qur'an and its aesthetic uniqueness, but also in the great emotional response
that its recitation arouses. It is not possible to recognise its specificity if one objec-
tifies the Qur'an and removes it from its structural ties to the Muslim community,
but only if one reads it as a relational commitment and hears how it resonates with
people. Only by studying the Qur'an in the context of relational events can the
free relationship between God and humans become tangible reality. From a transcendental point of view too, the relational principle is the fundamental condition
if any kind of reciprocal and free revelation between God and humans is to occur.

Neither singling out subjective experience nor the objective beauty of the
Qur'an can help us to capture its revelatory claim epistemologically. The focus
must constantly be on the relational event, which always remains a mystery
because it confronts people with the absolute and therefore surpasses our understanding. By starting from the formal unconditionality of freedom, we can, as
explained above, form a conception of the absolute that prevents us from trusting

---

44 Ibid. 191.

blindly in God's relational commitment. Yet even if we once more test the terminology of the Qur'an's pledge to see if it fits with the philosophy of freedom,
its reality and thus the reality of the unconditional exceeds any possible terminological guarantee. We are therefore unable to provide at this juncture any positive
form of analysis of faith, only a rapprochement *ex negativo*.

In the Islamic tradition it is the beauty of the Qur'an that provides a bridge to
the absolute. That dovetails nicely with the aesthetics of Schiller, who also saw
beauty as the bridge between the sensory and extrasensory worlds.[45] Of particular
interest for our freedom-theological appropriation of thinking about revelation is
the fact that Schiller sees beauty as the expression of human freedom. For Schiller, beauty is realised when a person is not exposed to any external purposes and
pressures, rules and heteronomy, but exists freely and autonomously in accordance with her or his own essential nature as a human being. However, if beauty
genuinely can be regarded as an expression of freedom, then it also becomes
easier to recognise God's freedom in the beauty of the Qur'an and, with it, His
freely chosen love for humankind.

For Schiller, beauty is firstly an essential part of human nature and opens
human hearts to freedom. But beauty also seems to him to be the grand plan
of self-determination manifest in particular characteristics of nature.[46] With its
notion of self-determination, Schiller's writing provides an extremely interesting
criterion for what is *beautiful*. An object seems to him to be beautiful if it appears
in the sensory world as if freely and entirely obeying its own autonomous law.
Again, this insight is only theologically interesting because it makes it clear that
the beauty of the Qur'an may offer proof of the beauty of God when it simultaneously expresses God's sovereignty and inner autonomy. It is therefore obvious
that God's relational commitment can never be construed as God making Himself
reliant on humans. God's beauty obtains precisely because He does not need
human beings, but decides of His own volition to permit humankind to be free.

To briefly sum up our arguments so far: the background inspiration is that God
freely determines Himself to be present in the recitation of the Qur'an. When
God gifts us the experience of His presence in the recitation of the Qur'an, the
experience of hearing makes His mercy and love for humankind a reality. God
can be heard in His beauty whenever we make His voice ring out in the Qur'an. It

---

45 Friedrich Schiller, *Aesthetical and Philosophical Essays*, trans. Nathan Haskell Dole,
Boston 1902, 62.
46 See Friedrich Schiller, Letters to Gottfried Körner. Letter dated 19th February 1793,
Schillers Briefwechsel mit Körner, Berlin 1859, 41–3, here 42.

therefore seems obvious to us that the Qur'an constitutes a functional equivalent to Jesus Christ, insofar as the Qur'an also makes it tangible that God desires to be there for us and to enter into a relationship with us.

Simultaneously, however, the first differences become visible between the mode of givenness of the revelation in both religions. While talk of self-revelation on the Christian side led to the establishment of the Trinity and talk of Jesus Christ as the Word of God expresses belief in his hypostatic union with God, Islam conceives of God's proximity in the word of the Qur'an, making such logical implications superfluous. This makes it easier for Islam to open up to the thought that God's word does not only become an event in the Qur'an but is extended to humans in other words and signs.

In modern Christian theologies such as the one proposed by Karl Rahner, it is indeed clear that Christians also see God's self-communication not only in Jesus Christ; every person is an event of God's self-communication.[47] Even these modern theologies, however, would insist that God's address is only revealed and made intelligible to us in every person through Jesus Christ.

We hesitate at this juncture to speak of an equally prominent role in the Qur'an for revelation theology. One can nonetheless say that Muslims would not deny that God speaks to us in other ways than through the Qur'an. Indeed, they would even go so far as to say that there are signs throughout God's creation, and so God speaks to us, and is present, in every particle of this world. However – and this would be the functional equivalent of Christology – it is the Qur'an alone that reveals the salutary meaning of this connection and that the Qur'an too can be recognised as evidence that makes God's love of humankind a tangible reality. We must now consider anew whether this evidence is soteriologically relevant.

6.3 On the soteriological relevance of the Qur'an

Salvation is frequently understood in modern Christian theology to mean that God's unconditional love became complete historical reality in Jesus Christ. In the midst of the ambivalence and fragmentedness of our freedom, Jesus brought the unconditional 'yes' of the love of God to us, and so we too are empowered to symbolically grant our unconditional 'yes' to one another by availing ourselves of His love. Thus God reveals Himself in Jesus's life, death and resurrection as

---

47 See for example Rahner, *Foundations of Christian Faith*, 116 (chapter heading).

unconditional love.[48] And as unconditional love, God unconditionally forgives all sins and pronounces His 'yes' amid the ambivalence of human freedom. I may therefore claim God's 'yes' in my affirmation of another person and thus symbolically promise a reality I cannot bring about, one that is guaranteed to the other person by the Absolute Himself as the final death-defying reality:

> So Jesus's death and resurrection proves and makes definitively visible what began with Jesus's annunciation: God's self-revelation as unconditional love for humankind. And this revelation is our salvation – provided only that one comprehends revelation as the event of freedom in which God's self-determination in favour of humankind becomes reality for us through Jesus's corresponding freedom.[49]

In the present, this salvation can become visible in people's representative actions, for love is only reality when it happens, meaning that God's love can only reach us and stay with us through other people – that is the logic of Christian soteriology as reconstructed in modern philosophy of freedom.[50] The attempts to fulfil this, however, are always merely a symbolic utilisation of what finally burst forth in Jesus Christ and which is still longed for in eschatological hope and expectation – God's unconditional and historically all-pervading self-love.[51]

However much modern Christian soteriology draws on the philosophy of freedom, it does not ignore human guilt. Pröpper, for example, stresses that Christ has broken the power of guilt 'because forgiveness is vouchsafed to all who are willing to recognise it',[52] and the distress of a distant God is also abolished by Jesus's relationship to his Father. Yet the release from guilt appears here not as a prerequisite but as a consequence of the message of salvation. Even a person who does not suffer from his or her guilt can receive this message in the ambivalence of her or his freedom. The target of this message is, as Dietrich Bonhoeffer declared,

---

48 See for example Pröpper, *Erlösungsglaube und Freiheitsgeschichte*, 197.
49 Pröpper, *Erlösungsglaube und Freiheitsgeschichte*, 59.
50 Ibid. 210. Of course, creation can also be appreciated as the sign of God's love and of course angels can be messengers of this love, but love can only become an experiential event through human love, i.e. no other creatural event can be understood as a sign of love without this human testimony.
51 Ibid. 215–7.
52 Ibid. 207. Like Thomas Pröpper, we assume in the following section that there is no guilt that is not simultaneously sin – just as there is no sin that is not simultaneously guilt. For an explanation of this link, see Thomas Pröpper, *Theologische Anthropologie*, Freiburg 2011, 680–735.

not human weakness and guilt, but human strength and pride – their freedom and capacity for love.[53]

We have talked so far as if there were a single modern Christian soteriology, but we must now qualify this. Obviously, we are only presenting a particular version of soteriology here, indeed one that is heavily inspired by modern philosophy of freedom and sees salvation in God's approach to human beings. We have deliberately excluded the question of crucifixion theology so that we may consider it separately in the next section. Even with this exception, however, it is clear that here we are only noting one specific strand of soteriology, a strand that has distanced itself considerably from the Roman Catholic satisfaction theory of atonement. If we consciously proceed in a slightly one-sided manner, then this is not to facilitate for Christian soteriology to dialogue with Islam, but because this form of soteriology strikes the Christian author as especially convincing and here, as elsewhere, it is his own Christology that he uses as the basis for forging a dialogue with the Qur'an.

So how does the Qur'an respond to this Christian interpretation of the work of Jesus Christ? Can one say that it too makes God's affection for humankind and love experiential reality? This interpretation is complicated by the fact that a modern Christian theological approach sets great store by the compatibility of the salvific message and its medium. The substance of Christian faith in salvation is, as we have said, God's love, intended for all people. This message becomes tangible in the human affection of Jesus Christ and its attestation through the Church. Because Jesus bestows unconditional love, and because the Church is a symbol of this love, the substance of the Christian message becomes an event through its propagation.

If one wished to make the same claim for the Qur'an, one would not only have to say that the substance of the Qur'an is God's affection for humankind. This book's Muslim author has repeatedly taken up this position and tried to formulate it in terms of God wanting and being nothing other than merciful affection for humans.[54] Indeed, the proclaimer of the Qur'an tirelessly emphasises how forgiving and friendly God is to humans.

---

53 See Dietrich Bonhoeffer, *Prisoner for God: Letters and Papers from Prison*, ed. Eberhard Bethge, tr. Reginald H. Fuller, New York 1959, 122, 124 (entry for 30.4.1944): 'Are we to fall upon one or two unhappy people in their weakest moment and force upon them a sort of religious coercion? [...] I should like to speak of God not on the borders of life but at its centre, not in weakness but in strength, not, therefore, in man's suffering and death but in his life and prosperity.'

54 See Mouhanad Khorchide, *Islam ist Barmherzigkeit*, Freiburg 2012.

Regarding the discussion about the identity of the substance and the act of revelation by God imparting Himself as love, one should note from an Islamic perspective that the substance of revelation here does not involve an actual person, as is the case for the concept of incarnatory self-communication in the Christian understanding of divine revelation. One must also consider, however, that God's revelation, enacted by an undeniable personality and endured by an undeniable personality, calling an indubitable personality decisively to (inter-)personal activity, is entirely unaffected by the lack of clearly personalised way of thinking. This bestows great importance to the personality of the prophetic intermediary and the believers in terms of their respective 'functions' in the Muslim conception of the revelatory event, but it also plays a crucial role for the intense substance of a decidedly theological and anthropological basis for thought.

When faced in debate with a legitimate query about the extent to which Islamic theology approaches revelation from a transcendental point of view, or whether revelation can be conceived as the actual purpose of freedom,[55] it is imperative to expand this postulated purpose hermeneutically when deciding on a transcendental channelling of the Muslim conception of revelation. There is a good case for including the aesthetic approach to the overall theme as we have outlined and advocating a strict framework of understanding which reflects the logic of existence.

With regard to the concept of believers being struck by the revelatory beauty (or to put it more intensely: struck to the core by the revelatory beauty) of the sound of the Qur'an, beauty must be accepted as an indivisible part of existential decision-making. The acceptance of belief and the recipient of the revelation's resulting actions are existential events, i.e. ontologically speaking, revelation, reception and answer are the actuality of existence. On the basis of transcategorical ontology, the consequence is a need to conceive of revelation first and foremost as an actual definition of relation, and indeed, before any claim, to form an autonomous idea of the moment of contact and thus of the relation between the absolute and the contingent. This requires an ontological basis because, from the standpoint of the entire contextual explanation of revelation and being struck by the revelation, this is the existential question. Relation – which must logically include the fundamental category of freedom – is the principal intellectual prerequisite for all thought about the revelatory complex around God as the revelatory sender, the Qur'an as the revelatory medium, the Prophet as the revelatory intermediary, and humans as the revelatory recipients.

---

55 See Aaron Langenfeld, 'Das Schweigen brechen. Christliche Soteriologie im Kontext islamischer Theologie' (*Beiträge zur komarativen Theologie*; 22), Paderborn 2016, 381–3.

On the other hand, it is still difficult to claim that a text itself is the event of God's self-love or of His love. Of course a text can express love, affection or mercy, but only to a limited extent can it make them become real. Texts cannot embrace or caress us, but they can build us up and console us. The text's sender can become tangible in the text, and His love can touch us. Think of love poems, for example, which convey the intensity of the poet's love through their aesthetic form. Might one therefore understand the Qur'an in the same way as a declaration of love for humankind through whose recitation God kindles our love and enthuses us? Does the Qur'an too mean to show that communion with God and being filled with God are the objective and vocation of human life? Can one say that humans may experience in the Qur'an that God accepts them despite their ambivalence and also that He wishes to perfect them by His merciful affection? Does the Qur'an state that humans are created and construed for the sake of God's affection?

It is not only the Qur'an but also the tradition of Islamic mysticism that contains a series of indications that the answer to the above questions is yes. One aspect deserving of special attention is the fact that *fiṭra* theology[56] is exceedingly fertile ground for associated soteriological thinking, as long as its implications for the provenance and destination of humankind is taken seriously in a soteriological sense. A soteriological clarification does however require a pertinent new formulation of most of the earlier *fiṭra* hermeneutics including a clear expansion of the components of the radical independence – explained in creation theological terms – of the God-created human being. This expansion involves actively incorporating the (salvific) components of humans' unquestioned acceptance and everlasting sojourn as God's creatures into the condition of freedom bestowed upon them. With regard to a Muslim theology of salvation understood in terms of revelatory logic, the *fiṭra* should be designated as the first (natural) principle of human *receptivity* to revelation and thus humans' fundamental *relation* to revelation. One crucial step in this direction is the illumination-inspired ideas of the contemporary theologian Hamid Parsaniya about the salvific return to the *fiṭra*[57] which may, in the final analysis, be thought of as a soterial liberation movement.

---

56 The Muslim theology of *fiṭra*, i.e. the natural disposition of humans to devote themselves to God, can be persuasively linked to Karl Rahner's idea of the 'transcendental existential' and with Wolfhart Pannenberg's theory of *humankind's fundamental openness to God*. On *fiṭra* see Q 30:30: 'So [Prophet] as a man of pure faith, stand firm and true in your devotion to your religions. This is the natural disposition God instilled in mankind [... *fiṭrata llāhi llatī faṭara al-nāsa 'alayhā*]'

57 See Parsania, *Existence and the Fall*, 134.

Hypotheses postulating that God encompasses the whole of existence[58] can be developed – as long as they are reshaped in the spirit of a theology of grace and one seeks to perceive the original and eternal status of grace that is ontologically explicated in God's comprehension of all existence – as an interesting option for neometaphysical, soteriological theory.

Admittedly, we then have to imagine the question as to the possibility of a coherent concept, based on the theology of grace, of the pre-cosmic love of God defined as mercy, as contemplation of grace will quickly produce the intellectual problem of an asymmetric complex. Starting from modern Western moral philosophy, if one assumes the superiority of the merciful over the one who receives the mercy, and thus an asymmetry at the heart of the concept of mercy, then one must take issue with the Islamic semantics of mercy, which are weighted slightly differently. On the basis of hermeneutic findings regarding the Qur'an and the hadith,[59] a speculative theological study of terminological usage recognises the need to understand God's mercy (*rahma*) as such an all-encompassing, all-surpassing dimension of *rahmān* (see, for example, Q 6:12; 7:156; 11:90) that it may be conceived – especially in relation to God's status as the Lord (*rabb*) in the sense of solicitude[60] – as nothing other than a loving (not serving!) *being-there* for God and hence as constitutive of human life itself. The word *rahma*, meaning All-Merciful, should be conceived, especially in view of central connotations such as *riqqa* ('gentle of heart') and *ihsān* (translated here as 'goodness'),[61] as originating absolutely from God *without any asymmetry* and therefore as *love itself*. If one sees God's grace in its absoluteness in the context of the theology of grace, i.e. as a grace that is categorically not owed, and if one sees God's original, eternal and

---

58 See for example Hamid Parsania, ibid., 50–1. Or Mahdi Ha'iri Yazdi's propagation of a *Seinsganzen (muṭlaq-i hastī* or *muṭlaq-i wujūd)* (on this, see Ha'iri Yazdi, *Hiram-i hasti* and Reza Hajatpour, *Mehdi Hairi Yazdi*, 34–40, 54–61, 87. This context may generate controversial debate about the aspected of *monism* and *pan(en)theism*.

59 See Mouhanad Khorchide, 'Anstöße zu einer Theologie der Barhmherzigkeit', in Khorchide / Milad Karimi / Klaus von Stosch (eds.), *Theologie der Barmherzigkeit? Zeitgemäße Fragen und Antworten des Kalām*, Münster 2014, 15–36, here 17–20, or the opinion of Andreas Renz, *Der Mensch unter dem An-Spruch Gottes. Offenbarungsverständnis und Menschenbild des Islam im Urteil gegenwärtiger christlicher Theologie*, Würzburg 2002, 493–4.

60 See the etymological derivation from *rabbā:* 'bring up', 'educate', 'sustain', 'care for' (on this, see Amina Boumaaiz / Bernd Feiningener / Jörg Imran Schröter '"Bin Ich nicht Euer Herr?" [Surah 7:172]. Aspekte zum Menschenbild im Islam', in Katja Boehme (ed.) *'Wer ist der Mensch?' Anthopologie im interreligiösen Lernen und Lehren*, Berlin 2013, 101–43, here 115).

61 See Khorchide, *Anstöße*, 16.

encompassing salvific will, even without the accomplishment of the Creation, as a sign of His merciful nature, then even a pre-cosmic *actuality of grace* is imaginable. This is particularly valid for Ibn Sina's position that God's self-love is the most perfect form of love, because it already incorporates the perfect reality of salvation and mercy.

A discursive expansion of the *fiṭra* theology, which takes serious account of the point of view of human dignity (in freedom) placed in God's salvation, will furthermore prove its fruitfulness if – starting from the significance of the subject in the freely knowing transcendental existential[62] – one looks for the position of knowledge and of consciousness within the status of *fiṭra*. This desired status can be conveyed by the testimonial, devotional God-consciousness (*taqwā*)[63] and in the corresponding life-regulating mentioning of God (*ḍikr*),[64] or ultimately in the reactional moment of actualisation of a conscious *fiṭra*-led reality of life. This position requires, in general, the basic metaphysical assumption of *eventfulness in processuality* and hence a constant reciprocal bond between ontology and event, which strengthens talk of the continuity of a salvific liberation event. This talk of continuity is supported from the point of view of the theology of grace by a soteriological theology of guidance (*hudā*).

Aside from that, a *fiṭra* concept that sees the dispositional orientation of the human creature as embedded in grace (as the reality of God's dominion) and therefore utterly encompassed by it, illuminates the idea of an innovative inclusion of nature in grace.[65] A recognition of the virtually dual dispositional status of human beings, as the bearers of both *fiṭra* and *taqwā* consciousness in the debate about the relationship between nature and grace, indicates the close connection between *nature* and *grace*. One should note that the said dispositional status (whatever the person's own accompanying activity) may be understood as the grace of creation in the sense of a dynamic and processual reality, in particular in being approached by God's pledge of salvation (revelation, recognition of 'servanthood' [*'ubūdīya*], guidance).

If one assumes that Islamic thought, especially in its theological-anthropological approach, obeys a fundamental principle of (self-)perfectioning, i.e. of human

---

62 On this theological-anthropological context in Christian theology, see Rahner, *Foundations of Christian Faith*, 39–41.

63 See, for example, Q 30:31; 48:26.

64 See, for example, Q 3:191; 4:103.

65 On this idea that follows on from Luther, see Johanna Rahner, *Creatura Evangelii. Zum Verhältnis von Rechtfertigung und Kirche*, Freiburg 2005, 66.

'perfectibility',[66] then it stands to reason that both the revelation-theological and the soteriological-intellectual context are inseparable from this, and that the theological idea of humans' capacity and duty to perfect themselves, as God's will, necessarily takes the form of something like the pronouncement of a *soteriology of perfectibility*, which could be explained as being closely related to the Oriental Church's thinking about salvation described earlier.

Since such a concept must immediately set off alarm bells in Christians and Muslims about the risk of pathological self-optimising and self-redeeming forces, we should underline the unquestioned relatedness of this soteriology of perfectibility to talk of lasting radical dependence on God and reliance on God's grace. This not least gives the option of establishing a soteriologically reinterpreted concept of human power and capacity that is conceived in every respect as not only coming from God but moving towards God, and this is by no means a self-absolutising, but a God-fearing orientation (of all desire, effort and capacity) towards the transcendent, which ultimately includes the soteriological and eschatological certainty of resurrection.[67]

This emphasis on the link to the Oriental Church's soteriological traditions clearly demonstrates the limitations of our attempt to mediate. Our goal is not to claim that there is a convergence between Islam and Christianity. Nor do we mean to suggest that the two religions wrestle with the same references in their philosophies of freedom and salvation. We have therefore decided not to explore the complicated subject of the theology of original sin.[68] We merely want to make clear that there is a form of salvation theory, deeply rooted in Christian tradition and compatible with modern thought, which can be applied to the Qur'an and can productively challenge Islamic theology. The aim of our theory is merely to show that there is a legitimate form of Christian soteriology for which there is a functional equivalent in the Qur'an. We are unable to demonstrate in detail within the scope of this study how this soteriology might square with the obvious multiplicity of traditional and present-day Christian salvation theories in the New Testament.[69]

---

66 On this, see Hajatpour, *Gottesentwurf*, especially 19–31, by way of an introduction; Babak Shamshiri, *Tarhi naw dar insanshinasi-i islami*, Tehran 1395/2016, 145–64.

67 The preceding sections adopt various formulations from Asghar-Zadeh, 448–9, 467 and 474–8.

68 As a first approach to the problem see Klaus von Stosch, 'Streit um die Erbsünde?', in Jürgen Werbrick (ed.) *Sühne, Martyrium und Erlösung? Opfergedanke und Glaubensgewissheit in Judentum, Chrsitentum und Islam*, Paderborn 2013, 81–96.

69 We rely heavily on our previous soteriological comments on Thomas Pröpper's approach,

If our remarks are to touch a nerve in Christian soteriology, however, then they cannot ignore the extremely staurocentric nature of Western salvation theory. That is why, following this very rough outline of Muslim equivalents of Christian soteriology, we shall now turn to perhaps the thorniest aspects of Jesus Christ's work for an Islamic audience – the issue of the Passion and the Crucifixion of Jesus Christ.

6.4 Can God suffer?

We have already noted that the proclaimer of the Qur'an avoids talking about Jesus Christ's Passion and Crucifixion. Our exegetical efforts have demonstrated that the Qur'an by no means denies Jesus Christ's death on the cross, although that is the common assumption. At the same time, though, there can be no doubt that the proclaimer of the Qur'an has no interest in the idea of Jesus's suffering or finds it of little use.

Considering how heavily charged the theology of the cross is with axioms of exclusivity, one should be wary about drawing premature conclusions on the matter. As we have seen, the Qur'an does not associate any exclusive salvific power with Jesus Christ. However much the Qur'an honours Jesus's redemptive powers and acknowledges that Jesus is God's word of acceptance made flesh, it is not at all willing to restrict God's affection to Jesus. Instead, it is clear that the the Qur'an only wishes to assert God's passionate relation with humankind and His involvement in history in general – and that includes all the prophets to which the Qur'an attests. The Qur'an's blindspot for the suffering of Jesus therefore does not necessarily mean that it disputes God's ability to suffer. The aim may also be to question Jesus's salvific exclusivity and the salvific significance of the Crucifix-ion. We therefore feel that it is not particularly productive to scour the Qur'an for references to Jesus's suffering. It is far more important to see whether the Qur'an reflexively attests that his delivering himself up to humans is a moment in God's Passion. Given the humans' rejection of the Qur'an, is it possible to speak of the Qur'an bearing witness to the Passion of God?

This idea is of course at odds with the whole of Islamic philosophy, which has always insisted on the immutability and transcendence of God. Yet this fact should

---

who enjoys a certain renown in contemporary Catholic theology for this treatise on dogmatics, and so we hope that our suggestions will not simply fuel marginal positions. For analysis of Pröpper's approach to the dialogue with Islam, see Langenfeld, *Das Schweigen brechen.*

not really concern us because the same can be also said of the Christian tradition, which from its origins also took shape around central themes of God's incapacity for suffering and His immutability. The background to this was Christianity's and Islam's adoption of Greek philosophical axioms which consider it simply inconceivable that the One True God might change and be influenced by anything finite. In this conception, mutability is regarded as a weakness and a sign of a lack of perfection. Suffering is seen as a creatural flaw, and may not be associated with God considering His majesty and grandeur. The scholastic theology of both religions appropriated these axioms and they have shaped its thinking until modern times.

Two very grave reasons caused a crisis in this form of scholastic theology in Christian thought. The first reason is that the unspeakable horror of the Holocaust made talk of God's inability to suffer seem aporetic. How, in the face of the atrocities of Auschwitz, can one continue to believe in a God who is unaffected by this event and imperviously watches His creatures suffer from a distance? It is obvious that it was the epoch-ending occurrence of Auschwitz that led to a reformulation of Christian theology as theodically sensitive, in particular, to cleanse the idea of God of its conspicuous apathy.[70]

The second reason for the crisis of traditional metaphysics resides in its being challenged by modern philosophy of freedom and its late-modern continuations and interruptions. In Germany there is an existing current of thought that seeks to develop a notion of God in keeping with the philosophy of freedom. When Thomas Pröpper and his pupils, among others, forge the concept of God – as we alluded to in 6.2 – from the formal unconditionality of freedom,[71] this produces a dynamic of new openness for the Bible's and the Qur'an's testimony of God.

Both of these points have lent fresh impetus to present-day Christian theology and call into question the traditional message of God's incapacity for suffering. It is instructive in the context of our Christian-Muslim dialogue that neither of the two reasons for the crisis of traditional scholastic theology is driven by a specifically Christian motivation. They can therefore be unreservedly applied to the Muslim tradition too. Indeed, perhaps we *must* do so, if Islamic scholarship wishes to engage with the specific context of Germany's spiritual history. Just as it is only in recent decades that Christian theology has registered the full and radical implications of staurology for its image of God, provoking a new reading of the

---

70 See Johann Baptist Metz, 'Theologie als Theodizee?', in Willi Oelmüller (ed.), *Theodizee – Gott vor Gericht? With articles by C.-F. Geyer and others*, Munich 1990, 103–18, here 103–4.

71 See Thomas Pröpper, *Evangelium und freie Vernunft. Konturen einer theologischen Hermeneutik*, Freiburg 2001; Krings, *Freiheit*, 161–84.

Bible, Islamic theology can also study the implications for the Qur'an if it is no longer read through the lense of Greek philosophy.

A new way of reading the Qur'an has particularly exciting consequences with regard to God's Passion and His abandonment among humans, as the Australian Jesuit Daniel Madigan pointed out in his own fashion. In order adequately to appreciate the shock of this discovery, then we ought to sum up what we have endeavoured to make clear in our preceding remarks in this chapter. God pronounces Himself in the Qur'an; in its recitation He becomes experiential reality and fills us with His presence through, in and with the Qur'an. However, that also means that God cannot be indifferent to how people receive the pledge He gives in the Qur'an nor to their response. God's presence becomes tangible in the recitation of the verses of the Qur'an; He exposes Himself to humankind in these signs.

With these preliminary hermeneutic remarks in mind, let us now turn to Madigan's discovery.[72] Madigan observes that virtually all the terms applied to Jesus in the accounts of the Passion are also to be found in the Qur'an – as the story of the passion of the signs of the Qur'an. God's signs (meaning the 'āyāt and therefore the verses of the Qur'an as well) are denied and ridiculed (Q 4:140); opponents make jokes about God and His signs (Q 9:65) and mock them (Q 37:14). They sell the signs of God for a low price (Q 9:9) and wrongfully reject them (Q 7:9.103). They turn away from them (Q 6:4; 21:32) and call them lies (Q 6:157; 7:36.40.136). They treat them with arrogance (Q 6:93; 7:36.40) and spread false rumours about them (Q 41:40). They scheme against them (Q 10:21), they work against them and seek to undermine them (Q 34:5.38). They dispute God's signs (Q 40:4.35.56.69; 42:35) and scorn them (Q 6:68); people try to oppose them (Q 22/51) and to forget them (Q 20:126). People slough God's signs off (Q 7:175) and pay them no heed (Q 7:136; 10:7.92). It is truly astonishing how closely the reactions of the Qur'an's opponents mirror the reactions of Jesus's opponents and how an authentic Passion story is being told here. Madigan is therefore absolutely correct when he notes:

> One might say that God's revelation has a kind of passion even if not a death.
> It is rejected and accused of making false claims to a divine origin, it is
> dismissed as nothing more than poetry, lies, old wives' tales or the product of
> a conspiracy with foreigners.[73]

---

72 See Madigan, *God's Word to the World*, 143–58.
73 Ibid. 151.

Thus in His revelation, God exposes Himself to suffering and is affected by the rejection of the Qur'an. This diagnosis is supplemented by the great significance accorded to the theme of suffering in Qur'anic prophetology, as shown earlier in Chapter 5. Altogether, there can be no doubt that the Qur'an too contains references to the suffering of God and His prophets.

What we have not yet identified, however, is how God reacts to the ridiculing of His commitment. There are some clues that God repays in kind those who mock, and there is no mention of God suffering physical harm. We are therefore entitled to ask whether God really does show solidarity in suffering.[74] Madigan therefore asks what price the Muslim God pays for His involvement in human existence; he sees no consequence of the ultimate, physical abandonment of God in the Qur'an's thinking. To understand his insistence on this point, we need to return once more to Christian soteriology. Why do Christians set so much store in modern theology by the fact that God Himself truly suffers and is affected by Jesus's pain?

It is important if we are to see more clearly here that we realise how passionately some people reject God's merciful commitment to humankind because they find it unfair. The Russian author Fyodor Dostoyevsky paints a particularly drastic picture of this problem when he allows his hero Ivan Karamasov to say of the death of a hunted child that he refuses to accept the entry ticket to a process of reconciliation after death.[75] Admittedly, this figure is highly stylised and has less dignity than someone who has been visited by suffering him- or herself, but there are enough Holocaust survivors who have said that they will never forgive the harm done to them.[76] What of those who, given the atrocities perpetrated against them, do not want and are not able to forgive? The miracle of reconciliation occurs time and time again, and we hope for nothing more than for this miracle to become all-encompassing reality. And yet the unsettling question must be allowed: what happens if the victim refuses reconciliation with the perpetrator? Is God not permitted to forgive the perpetrator? And, conversely, would the victim be unable to enter into communion with the unconditionally loving God due to his or her fixation on the perpetrator's guilt, because he or she refuses the act of the forgiving pledge that only he or she and no one else can freely speak? Is one genuinely to

---

74 Ibid. 152.

75 Fyodor Dostoyevsky, *The Brothers Karamazov*, Part II. tr. David McDuff, London 1993.

76 See Elie Wiesel, *All Rivers Run to the Sea: Memoirs*, tr. Marion Wiesel, New York 1995, 78: 'I see them now, and I still curse the killers, their accomplices, the indifferent spectators who knew and kept silent, and Creation itself, Creation and those who perverted and distorted it. I feel like screaming, howling like a madman so that the world, the world of murderers, might know it will never be forgiven.'

assume that a Jewish man or woman will not enter into heaven until he or she is able to forgive the SS soldier who murdered his or her entire family?

Obviously such an assumption would be cynical. But how then is one to sustain the all-important idea of an unconditionally forgiving God for a soteriology of categories of freedom if one takes seriously the possibility that there is no escha-tological guarantee that people will not reconcile, autonomously, of their own free will? How can one conceive that the victim of violence shall experience reconciliation in the love of God, even if he or she is not willing to forgive? And how can God forgive the perpetrator if the victim refuses this forgiveness? Indeed, from the perspective of Ivan Karamazov's quoted protest – does God even have the right to promise such forgiveness, or must one not accuse Him of making it all too easy for Himself? For 'the crime leaves Him unscathed, whereas it robs me of my integrity, harms me and can even kill me'.[77] The precondition for forgiveness is therefore 'that one was affected by the injustice',[78] and it also makes a great difference whether one was physically affected by the pain or not.[79] 'If God did not actually experience the severity of the guilt "firsthand", then His forgiveness would basically be as superficial as the "forgiveness" of people who do not take evil seriously anyway'.[80]

The soteriology in categories of freedom is plagued by a problem for solving which the Christian tradition had the ready idea of atonement by the God-man deputising for humankind, and perhaps it should examine more closely than hith-erto the thought that, despite all problems, accompanies Anselm of Canterbury's satisfaction theory of atonement. How, from the perspective of the Christian tradi-tion, would one seek to resolve the problem raised by Ivan Karamazov, and how could one reformulate this solution in accordance with the emancipatory potential of the philosophy of freedom?

The tradition's answer to these questions resides quite obviously in the ref-erence to Jesus Christ's representative atonement. 'God exposes Himself to the effects of sin to be able to forgive. God did everything, indeed "He spared not

---

77 Harald Schöndorf, 'Warum musste Jesus leiden?', in *Zeitschrift für katholische Theologie* 124 (2002) 440–67, here 455.
78 Ibid. 454.
79 'The true dimension of forgiveness only becomes clear when someone has to feel and experience the consequences of a despicable act. The same is true for the understanding of pain: someone who has not suffered cannot imagine what suffering means. But to be affected by a malevolent act is to suffer. And this is double suffering because it is not only a physical suffering but also a suffering caused by the knowledge of the deliberate nature of the deed' (Ibid. 453).
80 Ibid. 457–8.

His own son, but delivered him up for us all" (Rom. 8:32) in order to be able to forgive us in an effective and credible way.'[81] By God becoming a human being and exposing Himself to people's sins and also physically suffering among them, God's forgiveness becomes forgiveness by a 'man who is affected through and through by the consequences of evil',[82] and is therefore able to sue for reconciliation with the authority of the suffering.

It is not our objective to build Jesus up into a 'super-sufferer' nor do we mean to revive the idea that Jesus takes all the sins of the world upon himself. It is completely unclear to us how a man can ever come to shoulder all the sins of the world. Rather, our goal is that according to the logic of Christian soteriology, it is revealed in Jesus Christ that God endures suffering Himself and thus cracks it open and transforms it from the inside. God not only suffers with humankind but out of this suffering opens up creative possibilities for forgiveness and a new beginning. In the tradition of the Late Old Testment wisdom literature, one might speak here of an initiatory approach by God which – in biblical terms – redeems us of our sins. God renews His solidarity in the deepest depths of godlessness, thereby breaking the power of humans cutting them off from Him. God interrupts any further proliferation of sin and in so doing, liberates us from the ultimate chasms of human suffering. To put it more pointedly, one could say that God goes into death with us in order, by His presence, to transform this final perdition. In everything, therefore, it is God's uplifting approach that puts humans on the right path. This takes human form in Jesus Christ, but the Qur'an testifies to it as the saving closeness of God.

If, for example, a woman suffers physically and psychologically to this day from the abuse to which her father subjected her as a girl, then this suffering is not the suffering Jesus of Nazareth suffered on the cross. Nevertheless, according to the logic of the idea we have just outlined, God has the authority to forgive this woman's tormentor only if He allows Himself to be affected both physically and psychologically by the after-effects of that torment. Since God by definition does not possess a body because a body would limit God, there seems to be no resolution here. Even God being made flesh does not solve this, as the suffering of the One God cannot of itself absorb the pain of all, however great that suffering may have been.

And yet the fact that God was made flesh offers an opening, as long as it is not interpreted as being exclusive but *inclusive*. If something is revealed in Jesus of

---

81 Ibid. 462.
82 Ibid. 455.

Nazareth that is valid in the rest of history, then this problem can be resolved. If God becomes flesh in all of us, if, as Karl Rahner put it, God's self-communication is there inside every human being,[83] and if God reveals Himself especially in the suffering person and is therefore there in him (Matt. 25), then the effects of every torment would indeed affect God Himself. And God could then, by virtue of His Holy Spirit, facilitate from inside a creative new beginning in the depths of godlessness.

This thought does not require us to hold the absurd notion that the world or humankind are God's body. It is a sufficient idea, from a Christian point of view, that God enjoys the same relationship to the Logos and to the Spirit as we do to our bodies.[84] If one takes the idea seriously that God's Logos is present in every person who suffers and thereby becomes God's assertion to me, and that it is God's Spirit that enables us to register this affirmation of the unconditional in our contingent interlocutor,[85] then this idea has a notable consequence: God would suffer in the same way physically and psychologically from the sins and torments of this world as we do, and would therefore have the authority for the forgiveness we attribute only to the suffering themselves. Above all, though, God's innovative power of mercy would be able to enter into the despair of those who are far from God and could change them from inside.

From a Christian point of view, this structure of the God-world relationship would be revealed in Jesus of Nazareth and it would be legible from his physical and psychological suffering how God responds to the sins of the world. Yet he would also be the one through whom God redeems us of our sins and through whom He grants us renewed hope. He would be the one who transforms the distress of the godless from within and makes God's salvific presence tangible for humankind in the utmost godlessness. From this perspective, the cross would be the visible sign of how God allows Himself to be touched by human suffering in every corner of the world and attempts to transform it from within where no outside salvation would succeed. From this perspective, Jesus's suffering and dying alone reveal that God genuinely does suffer with everyone who suffers – precisely because the Logos is present with a completely different self-revelatory purpose than in its taking shape within us. This form of salvific exclusivity is non-negotiable for Christians and will remain a lasting obstacle to Islamic-Christian dialogue. From

---

83 Rahner, *Foundations of Christian Faith*, 126.
84 In defence of the proportionality-analogue conception targeted here, see Stosch, *Gott – Macht – Geschichte*, 48–9.
85 Ibid. 355–99.

a Christian point of view, it is Jesus Christ and no one else by whom it is revealed and made tangible to us that God has broken open and transformed even the greatest distress of those far from God. Through him Christians can also recognise God's salvific solidarity in the prophets and in any person of good will.

Yet although Christian faith is fuelled by the belief that there is 'no other name under heaven given among men, whereby we must be saved' (Acts 4:12) and that no other person makes God's relationship experiential reality for humankind, it does not dismiss other forms of imparting the presence of God. Considering the cross can therefore help us to comprehend the forgiveness that is guaranteed to all by God through His actions in the Logos and in the Spirit. He wishes to draw us into an all-encompassing inclusiveness, but this by no means excludes a complementary inclusive movement out of a different form of divine self-sacrifice. It is precisely the physicality of the pain of the crucified Jesus that demonstrates God's unconditional willingness to suffer and to love, and that can empower us in such a redemptive fashion to attune ourselves to His reconciling love.

Yet God's love is not reliant on our free approval for the performance of its eschatological purpose. Rather, by virtue of His suffering, it has the authority to grant forgiveness even to people to whom we are not capable of granting it on a lasting basis. And He grants it to each and every one of us, regardless of our actions, regardless too of our own capacity to forgive. So the only precondition for God's redeeming love to become a reality for us is that we are ready to welcome His unconditional and liberating love – a precondition that stems from the fact that love requires freely granted approval for it to be possible. Anything else (including our willingness to forgive) is not the *presumed* prerequisite for salvation but its *desired* outcome.

In Christian terms, given the suffering in the world, salvation therefore requires not only God to be made man but also the suffering of the Logos in man: therein, the tradition is correct. And yet it takes place without pre- and post-conditions, and it is not necessary for God's sake (and His honour or the order of the world) but for the humankind's sake – that is the enduring value of modern soteriology, reformulated in terms of the philosophy of freedom.

What does this explication mean for our search for functional equivalents of the work of Jesus Christ in the Qur'an? We have already seen that Christians can by no means claim that Jesus is God's body and that He suffers exclusively in him. We also conceded that it is nonsense to speak literalistically of God's physical pain. If we seek an analogy for God's suffering, then it is absolutely possible to ask from a Muslim point of view whether God's relationship with His word of acceptance in the Qur'an corresponds to our relationship with our body; and then one might also contemplate what it might mean for God to be rejected and ridiculed for His word. For Christians, the crucial question would then be whether one can make out in the Qur'an that God is moved, affected and changed by human suffering, and whether He is capable of transforming it from within, unleashing creative processes of forgiveness.

6.5 Qur'anic stimuli for conceiving of emotions in God

To begin, one can at least say that there are several clues in the Qur'an that God is not indifferent to humans' rejection of His word of acceptance and that His threats of retribution are only one facet of His response to this refusal. The Qur'an portrays God as a being who is personally and unconditionally devoted to humans. God presents Himself in the Qur'an as being on the side of humans and interested in humans and who rejoices for them and with them and bears people's cares.

When examining the Qur'an, it is therefore quite obvious that God is affected by human suffering. In Surah 93, Muhammad and, with him, all believers are offered solace:

> Your Lord has not forsaken you [Prophet], nor does He hate you [...] Your
> Lord is sure to give you so much that you will be well satisfied. Did He not
> find you an orphan and shelter you? Did He not find you lost and guide you?
> Did He not find you in need and make you self-sufficient? So do not be harsh
> with the orphan and do not chide the one who asks for help (Q 93:3.5–10).

This consoling message to Muhammad continues in the next surah, Surah 94:

> Did We not relieve your heart for you [Prophet], and remove the burden that
> weighed so heavily on your back, and raise your reputation high? So truly
> where there is hardship there is also ease. The moment you are freed [of one
> task] work on, and turn to your Lord for everything (Q 94:1–8).

God makes His concern for Muhammad known. He takes care of his needs and hardships, and is also worried about him; i.e. He shows emotion towards His creature.

This relationship also shapes the later surahs of the Qur'an. God always shows sympathy towards His messenger and says to Muhammad, for instance: 'But [Prophet] are you going to worry yourself to death over them if they do not believe in this message?' (Q 18:6). God tries to raise Muhammad's spirits and give new direction to his actions. Elsewhere we read:

It is only the disbelievers who dispute God's revelations. [Prophet], do not be dazzled by their movements back and forth across the land. Before them the people of Noah rejected the truth and so did those who formed the opposition after them: every community schemed to destroy its messenger and strove to refute truth with falsehood; but it was I who destroyed them. How terrible My punishment was! (Q 40:4–5)

Also, when the Prophet Muhammad missed his hometown of Mecca, from which he had been driven out, and wished to change the direction of prayer to Mecca, the Qur'an provides an image of an empathetic God: 'Many a time We have seen you [Prophet] turn your face towards Heaven, so We are turning you towards a prayer direction that pleases you. Turn your face in the direction of the Sacred Mosque' (Q 2:144).

It is important to God that not only He be satisfied with His messenger, but also that His messenger be satisfied with Him (see Q 93:5). This paradigm can be extended as a general rule to the relationship between God and human beings, especially if we focus on their eschatological calling. In all four places where the Qur'an says that God is satisfied with those who act honestly, it goes on to say: 'God is pleased with them and they with Him' (see Q 5:119; 9:100; 58:22; 98:8). Even if the Qur'an first calls to mind an eschatological context, it paints a picture of a God to whom human needs are important and who sets store by humans being satisfied with Him. Even if, in the Qur'an, this is an expectation of what the relationship between God and man will be in paradise, one may assume that God is also concerned by human hardships and worries in this world and wishes to make humans content. In any case, at no point in the Qur'an does it say that God alone is pleased with humans without mentioning that they should also be pleased with Him.

In addition, the proclaimer of the Qur'an does not tire of wrangling with those who reject and refuse to accept God's signs. Here we can only pick out a few examples of passages in the Qur'an highlighting that God is not indifferent to whether His words are accepted or not. Surah 53, for instance, appeals vehemently to the Meccans[86] who have rebuffed Muhammad's proclamation. This warning begins with a rhetorical question addressed to Muhammad: '[Prophet], consider that man who turned away: he only gave a little and then he stopped?' (Q 53:33–34). This man is now reminded of the eschatological consequences of his acts:

---

86 Muslim exegetes name al-Walid b. al-Muqira as the addressee of this warning (see for example al-Tabari, *Jami' al-bayan*, vol. 22, 71–2.

Has he not been told what was written in the Scriptures of Moses [...] that
no soul shall bear the burden of another; that man will only have what he has
worked towards; that his labour will be seen and that in the end he will be
repaid in full for it; that the final goal is your Lord; that it is He who makes
people laugh and weep; that it is He who gives death and life [...] Which then
of your Lord's blessings do you deny?' (Q 53:36.38–44.55).

No immediate testimony for God's suffering may be derived from this reaction
of the Qur'an to the rejection of God's offer, but this reaction still shows that the
God of the Qur'an is not indifferent and that people's reception of His word does
not leave Him unmoved. The divine signs ('āyāt) by which humans are called
to God are an expression of the divine emotion which the Qur'an describes with
God's gentleness and mercy to bring people onto His path: 'It is He who has sent
down clear revelations to His Servant, so that He may bring you from the depths
of darkness into light; God is truly kind and merciful to you' (Q 57:9). As we
noted earlier, this mercy is a power within God that affects Him, signalling God's
presence to those in distress, far from God. And where the poor and the needy are
concerned, God identifies with their suffering and He even begs for a donation or
a loan for Himself:

Who will make God a good loan? He will double it for him and reward him
generously [...] Charitable men and women who make God a good loan will
have it doubled and have a generous reward (Q 57:11.18).[87]

This explains the recurring warning in the Qur'an that people should be good to
orphans and the needy (see Q 93:9–10; 89:17–18). Anyone who rebuffs orphans
and does not stop to feed the poor does not believe in an encounter with God (see
Q 107:1–3). In the Qur'an too, there are clues that it is among the suffering and
the needy that we particularly encounter God.

---

87 God's identification with the poor and the needy is reminiscent of the hadith where
Muhammad says: 'In the afterlife, God will ask a man, "I was sick and you did not visit
Me, I was hungry and you did not give Me food, and I was thirsty and you did not give Me
anything to drink." To this the man will answer in astonishment: "But You are God, how
can You be sick, thirsty or hungry?!" God will answer: "On such and such a day, someone
you know was sick and you did not visit him; had you visited him, you would have found Me
there with him. One day someone you know was hungry and you did not give him food, and
one day someone you know was thirsty and you did not give him a drink"' (Source: Muslim
author).

God is not left unmoved by the rejection of His word, and the Qur'an describes this as an act of spite against God and His prophets: 'Those who insult God and His Messenger will be rejected by God in this world and the next – He has prepared a humiliating torment for them' (Q 33:57). This threat of punishment should be understood as a sign of God's hurt. God allows Himself to be affected by humankind's rejection; it hurts him.

Often we pay attention only to the threats the Qur'an pronounces in such situations. However, these recurring threats should be interpreted as an expression of the fact that it *does* matter to God whether human beings accept His pledge or not. God is aware of what we do (Q 63:11) and calls on people to change course (Q 63:5). He threatens those who will not place their trust in Him with retribution, reminding them that all the power is His (Q 63:8). If they do not wish to be among the losers, they must think of God and give alms (Q 63:9–10). If one examines the literary fuction of these verses, it becomes clear that they are attempts to persuade people to convert. According to Karen Bauer's analysis, the proclaimer of the Qur'an seeks to bring about this conversion through descriptions of emotions. The emotional plots he uses present 'specific series of emotions that lead the listener from one emotional state into another emotional state, achieving an emotional transformation'.[88] Two of these plots, which Bauer defines with the use of several examples, are on the one hand the plot 'that passes through fear or despair and ends in mercy' and on the other, the plot which begins with 'arrogance, disdain, or any of a number of emotions, and [ends] in destruction or damnation'. In the process, 'the emotional plot [...] describes the arc of feelings in the believer who is being threatened with damnation, promised great reward, exhorted to do the right thing, or told a story of past peoples whose fates were either salvation or damnation.'[89]

The draconian punishments God repeatedly threatens to mete out should not be read as expressions of God's brutality and propensity for violence, but as a sign of the seriousness of His endeavours on behalf of humankind. Their aim is not to damn those who have turned away from God but to call them insistently to change their lives – a change that puts God at the centre of their lives and demonstrates solidarity with those who need our help. This is how al-Ghazali interprets the paradise and the hell that the Qur'an describes. He sees ultimate bliss (the true condition of paradise) as being close to God, i.e. in reaching His presence: 'Bliss

---

88 Karen Bauer, 'Emotion in the Qur'an: An Overview', in *Journal of Qur'anic Studies* 19:2 (2017) 1–30, here 17.
89 Ibid. 17–8.

in the afterworld consists of being close to God and looking at His face.'[90] On the contrary, separation from God is the true nature of hell. Al-Ghazali speaks of the 'fire of separation'.[91] The Qur'anic images of paradise and punishment in hell are, for al-Ghazali, merely metaphors that attempt to represent these two conditions of being near or close to God: 'But it is inconceivable that the spiritual world [the afterlife] could be explained in the earthly world by anything other than metaphors. That is why God said: "Such are the comparisons We draw for people, though only the wise can grasp them" (Q 29:43).'[92] In al-Ghazali's understanding, hell begins as a condition here on earth when a person opts for hatred and arrogance over love and mercy.

The Qur'an is often accused of adopting an aggressive tone, especially when it comes to injustices. The proclaimer of the Qur'an even goes so far as to allow people to take up arms to ward off injustices if there is no other option, although this is always within a strict framework of rules (Q 2:190–193). This is not the place to reflect on such passages' potential for violence.[93] We only wish to bring them into the discussion as examples that even such ambivalent passages can be read as expressions of God's emotions. God does mind if people are unjustly treated, and He urgently entreats us to help make this world a more humane and fairer place. The first point in the Qur'an that allows Muslims to practise military self-defence says:

> Those who have been attacked are permitted to take up arms because they
> have been wronged – God has the power to help them – those who have been
> driven unjustly from their homes only for saying 'Our Lord is God' [...]
> God is sure to help those who help His cause – God is strong and mighty' (Q
> 22:39–40).

God calls us to stand up for His justice and joins battle on our side. God identifies with those who have suffered injustice and who are in need of help. God thus

---

90 Richard Gramlich, *Muhammad Al-Gazzalis Lehre von den Stufen zur Gottesliebe*, Wiesbaden 1984, 67.
91 Ibid.
92 Ibid, 62–3.
93 On this see Hamideh Mohagheghi, '"Tötet sie, wo ihr sie trifft." Eine Auslegung zu Q 2:190–195', in Mohagheghi / Klaus von Stosch (eds.), *Gewalt in den Heiligen Schriften von Islam und Christentum (Beiträge zur Komparativen Theologie*; 10), Paderborn 2014, 73–91; Klaus von Stosch, *Herausforderung Islam. Christliche Annäherungen*, Paderborn 2017, 139–45.

appears as the one who comes to their aid and wishes to enlist this aid to root out injustice.[94]

God repeatedly appeals to us through His signs. However, the greatest injustice is to dismiss God's signs ('āyāt), because by doing so one not only damages one's own life but obscures God's good instructions for all humankind in history: 'Who does greater wrong than someone who fabricates a lie against God or denies His revelation?' (Q 6:21). The grounds for God's warning are that those who commit injustices corrupt God's Creation and make it hard for people to trust the Creator of all things and devote themselves to the origin of all meaning and all life. But He clearly wants His good will to be fulfilled in us or – to cleave more closely to the Islamic formulation – God wants us to want and fulfil His good will. If that were not the case, why would it be so bad for us to lie about His signs? God obviously counts on us to make His signs intelligible to the world, and He wishes to use us to make His message comprehensible. If we refuse to do so and even deliberately obscure God's commitment to humankind, then God cannot remain indifferent and shows what we may, by analogy, call emotions.[95]

In various places, the Qur'an mentions God's positive and negative emotions. Thus God does not love deniers (Q 3:32) or those who overstep the limits (Q 2:190); He does not love the arrogant (Q 4:36), traitors (Q 8:58) and those who spread corruption (Q 28:77). All these verses pinpoint specific examples of human behaviour and state that God does not love people if they display this behaviour. God's love obviously reaches its limits in the face of human rejection.[96] God therefore wants to find an echo to His approach to human beings and makes His affection dependent, in a sense, on humans' response. God does not shower humans blindly with His love, but approaches them with a willingness and an invitation to engage in dialogue.[97]

In the same spirit, the Qur'an testifies that God loves those who do good (Q 2:195). God loves those who show remorse and who turn to Him (Q 2:222), those

94 It says in Q 47:7: 'If you help God, He will help you.'
95 This is not the place to go into the analogy doctrine in detail. We would merely like to make a brief reference to it so as to clarify that mention of God's emotions should not be taken to mean that God has the same relation to His emotions as we do to ours. God surpasses our understanding, and we should therefore be careful not to seek to know too much about God. On the other hand, Qur'anic and biblical testimony speak so clearly of a God who feels with and cares for humankind that we feel it would be a mistake to ignore the topic of God's emotiveness as too anthropomorphic.
96 This does not lead to a restriction of God or of His love, merely to an exclusion from this love of people whom God does not love because they close themselves off.
97 See Bauer, Emotion, 10.

who are mindful of Him (Q 3:76) and the just (Q 5:42). This does not mean that
people could or must earn God's love. It makes it clear that God wishes to enter
into a reciprocal relationship of love and freedom with humans. We discussed this
fact earlier in relation to the Qur'anic verse 'people He loves and who love Him'
(Q 5:54). The scholar Ibn Taymiyya uses this same verse in order to criticise theologians who interpret God's love in the narrow sense of His desire to be good.[98] He
writes: 'He, the Sublime One, loves what He has provided and loves His faithful
servants. That is the position of the ancestors and of the eminent scholars.'[99] So
here is another opinion, which cannot be suspected of the slightest modernist bent,
that God truly does love. Ibn Taymiyya reflects on this fact in a different passage
and writes: 'Love is a characteristic that belongs to God's perfection. It forms the
core and the root of God's will [...] The creation of His creatures was the product
of His intentional beloved wisdom (cause).'[100]

So love is the starting point for God's affection and His free relationship with
humankind, not only in the Qur'an but also in Qur'anic scholastic theology. The
Qur'an explains that God is close, He hears the call of those who call Him (Q
2:186) and God is with them wherever they are, right here and right now (Q 57:4).
When Moses and Aaron voiced their fears before their meeting with the pharaoh,
an empathetic and compassionate God spoke to them to give them strength: 'Do
not be afraid! I am with you both, hearing and seeing everything' (Q 20:46). God
is not indifferent to human suffering (Q 4:28). God knows humans' weaknesses
and He is always willing to support them on their path.

Yet this support does not lead to the disenfranchisement of human beings and
it does not release them from their responsibility. As we argued earlier, God grants
people freedom; God Himself determined that He would be determined by them,
and that is why He takes the risk of leaving the relationship open. God therefore
links the accomplishment of His good will to the cooperation of human beings
and invites them to become accomplices of His will: 'God does not change the
condition of a people [for the worse] unless they change what is in themselves'
(Q 13:11).

God and humans find themselves in a dialogue, and God proves Himself to be a
God who responds to people's concerns and consistently and efficaciously stands
by their side: 'Everyone in heaven and earth entreats Him; every day He is at

98 Al-Nasafi, for example, writes about the meaning of God's love in Q 5:54: 'He is pleased
with their actions and rewards them for them', in Al-Nasafi, *Madarik*, vol. 1, 270.
99 Taqi al-Din Ibn Taymiyya, *Sharh al-isfahaniya*, Riyadh 1995, 27.
100 Taqi al-Din Ibn Taymiyya, *Minhaq al-sunna al-nabawiya*, vol. 3, ed. Muhammad
Salim, Bulaq 1904, 100.

work' (Q 55:29). When the fifth surah reminds believers about the commandment regarding prayer and ritual cleansing, the Qur'an lists in the same verse alternatives for the sick, travellers and others who have no access to water, and at the end of the verse paints the picture of an empathetic God who has great understanding for the relevant circumstances and explains almost apologetically: 'God does not wish to place any burden on you: He only wishes to cleanse you and perfect His blessing on you, so that you may be thankful' (Q 5:6).

This Qur'anic evidence corresponds to the image that the Prophet Muhammad conveyed in his proclamation – the image of the personal God who allows humans to touch His emotions. Even when people sin, God remains available for them, for His mercy is unconditional and absolute. That is why the Prophet Muhammad says: 'Verily, God Almighty stretches out His hand by night to accept the repentance of those who sin by day, and He stretches out His hand by day to accept the repentance of those who sin by night, until the sun rises from the west.'[101] This picture of a merciful God, who wants to give human beings hope, matches the image of God that one meets in the Qur'an when it says: 'Say [God says], My servants who have harmed yourselves by your own excess, do not despair of God's mercy. God forgives all sins: He is truly the Most Forgiving, the Most Merciful' (Q 39:53).

Many hadiths state that it is humans who close themselves off from God, humans who turn their backs on God, not God on humans. Hence talk of God's emotions should not call His loyalty and consistency into question. God calls humans, stirs them and waits for them. God wants to facilitate a new beginning for people and endows them with the requisite energy. The Prophet Muhammad gives a vivid description of God's joy about every person who comes back to Him:

> Imagine that someone is travelling alone through the desert with his camel and suddenly the camel runs away with all the man's food and drink. When the man gives up looking for his camel and lies down on the ground in resignation to await his death, his camel is suddenly standing beside him. Imagine the man's joy! Thus is God overjoyed at every person who has turned away and then back to Him, more than that man in desert about his camel.[102]

It is interesting to note how this prophetic account radically changes the biblical image of God's affection for humankind. In the Gospel, God the good shepherd

---

101 Source: Muslim author.
102 Quoted by Muslim author from hadith no 2744.

goes after the one lost sheep to bring it back to the flock (Luke 15:3–7), even though he still has ninety-nine other sheep, and the merciful father in the Gospel is overjoyed by the return of the prodigal son, even though his other son is still with him (Luke 15:11–32), but Muhammad revolutionises the imagery. God only has the one person on whom He can rely and whose return gives Him new hope. There is after all only one camel, and that camel is crucial to its owner's survival. So God needs each and every one of us to transform His good will into reality, and God counts on us – a truly radical statement.

God's reliance on us does not mean, though, that He leaves us alone. No, God also responds to our slightest movement towards Him with His enormous mercy and love. Another hadith says:

> God the Most High says, 'I am as My servant thinks I am. I am with him when he mentions Me. If he mentions Me to himself, I mention him to Myself; and if he mentions Me in an assembly, I mention him in an assembly greater than it. If he draws near to Me at a hand's length, I draw near to him at an arm's length. And if he comes to Me walking, I go to him at speed.'[103]

This hadith shows the extent to which God engages in a reciprocal relationship with humankind, although there is at the same time a fundamental asymmetry in this relationship. God always remains the more merciful, because as He loves absolutely, God can continually create new chances for humans and keeps on expanding His possibilities.

If one gives the definition of this relationship a soteriological spin, then it becomes clear that for Muslims there can be no salvation that discounts people's freedom. God never discharges humans from their responsibility; there is no one and nothing to stand in for them. At the same time, though, God is moved by human suffering. God courts human beings by revealing Himself in His vulnerability and weakness. This 'weakness for men'[104] will probably only become clear if we take the Qur'an seriously in its performative guise as God's self-revelation. If we do this, however, it becomes ever clearer how greatly God exposes Himself to humans and allows Himself to be moved by them, and thus on a soteriological level, the Qur'an is less dissimilar to the message of Jesus Christ than has hitherto

---

103 Quoted from Abu Huraira (*Buch über das Gedenken, die Bittgebete, die Reue und die Bitte um Vergebung. Unterkapitel: Die Veranlassung zum Gottgedenken*).

104 Schelling, *Philosophie der Offenbarung*, 26, making the link to 1 Cor. 1:25, discusses the fact that due to this weakness, God is 'stronger than men', and so His heart is capable of anything for the good of humankind. We are grateful to Jürgen Werbick for this tip.

frequently been assumed. And yet despite all the similarities that our studies have identified, it is nevertheless clear that the Qur'an does not cultivate its own theology of the cross, and the Christian thinking associated with the cross can never be fully transposed onto Qur'anic theological remarks. Yet it was never our aim to produce any complete transposition, convergence or even complementarity. We merely wanted to suggest how the seemingly insurmountable barriers between our two religions might be overcome, and how the life and work of Jesus Christ can constitute a particularly fruitful stimulus for Muslim-Christian dialogue.

7

New Perspectives on the Qur'an

We already explained in the introduction that we planned to round off our book with separate intratheological concluding remarks. After striving throughout the whole book to produce a single text combining the Muslim and Christian perspectives, our intention now is to take a stance on what we have achieved thus far from the perspective of our individual relations. In doing so, we would like to ask ourselves what new lessons we have taken for our own theology from the experience of working with theologians from the other religion. From a Christian point of view, the central question is whether we can gain illuminating insights for Christology from the Qur'an. On the Muslim side, it is a matter of whether the Christian-guided enquiries about analysis of the Qur'an and interreligious study of its meaning can contribute to deeper Qur'anic exegesis. However, there is also a more systematic question as to whether modern Christological approaches might provide impetus for productive intellectual movements within Islamic theology.

7.1 Systematic conclusions from a Christian perspective

As a general conclusion to this book I would like to list six lessons for Christology that I have drawn from the detailed Qur'anic exegesis. First, the Qur'an has reminded me with great clarity of the enormous dangers of deifying Jesus at the expense of his humanity. If Jesus is disassociated from humankind and his human nature is no longer recognised as an integral whole, then the Christian message of salvation is ruined. The proclaimer of the Qur'an raises a painful subject for a Christology that obscures the true humanness and humanity of Jesus, and is therefore no longer able to explain how we can be saved through the proof of God's affection in Jesus Christ. For salvation to be possible, God must be fully present in the human dimension and transform it from within. I see the Qur'an's accusations not only as legitimate criticism of seventh-century monotheletic Christology and as a justifiable correction of a version of Christianity shaped by Julianism, but also as a lasting query of modern Christologies which constantly risk obscuring Jesus Christ's true humanity in defence of his ontological specificity.

One aspect of this subject that I find especially moving is the strong connection between Jesus's personal fate and Mary's. The portrayal of Jesus as the son of Mary and his only gradual emergence from her shadow in Surah Maryam demonstrates his authentic humanity and reminds me of Jesus's mother's great influence on his path in life. The Qur'an also chooses an exciting way of expressing his special status from the very beginning through the metaphor of the speaking infant Jesus and by suggesting that the relationship between the two of them was based on a challenging asymmetry. The Qur'an emphatically depicts Mary not only in the distress of her birth pangs but also in her plight after Jesus's birth out of wedlock, and she is presented unadorned in all her hardship. Jesus is then introduced as the one who is able to help her before anyone else. So Jesus, who for Christianity is the saviour of all humankind, stands by his mother from the very beginning and is clearly a blessing for her in her need. Whereas the biblical conflicts between Jesus and Mary are the subject of a great deal of debate in modern exegesis, and the Nazarene is regarded as being insignificant at first in his own family and his hometown, in the Qur'an Jesus's singularity is first recognised by his mother and he initially develops his prophetic vocation within his family. In John's Gospel it is Mary of course who is the first to point to Jesus, paving the way for his public acts (see John 2:5). Yet here Jesus's redemptive closeness to Mary is not mentioned and is only brought to our attention by the Qur'an. This alerts me to Mary's weakness and to the gentleness of Jesus's strength. Even as an infant he is able to give her strength – a thought that makes theological sense to me when I recall how babies give us enormous encouragement in life and, by their mere existence, a sense of meaning and hope. The prophetic infant Jesus is clearly more capable here, resolving the greatest distress in miraculous fashion. Jesus already participates in God's creative power as a child. All these details about Jesus's childhood – described in detail in the Apocrypha – are presented by means of a few quick allusions in the Qur'an, and yet they raise the prospect of an almost Christmas-like theology of the child that strikes me as a first exciting dimension of meaning that the Qur'anic message about Jesus holds for Christians too.

The Qur'an's titles for Christ offer a second innovative and productive approach to Christology. I do not primarily mean the well-known titles of Christ, which are reformatted here and freshly illuminated. It is naturally touching to hear Jesus described in the Qur'an as *Christ*, the *Word of God* and the *servant of*

God. I am however more excited about the titles I had not heard before and which highlight new dimensions of the reality of Jesus Christ. I have already mentioned Jesus being called the *son of Mary*. More unusual by far is his description as the *Spirit of God* and *the one brought nearest to God*. Jesus's closeness to God, his immediate intimacy with Him and his utter relatedness to God is, for Christians, a special key with which to approach the secret of Jesus's life. Anyone who comes into contact with Jesus is confronted with God's mystery because he is so close to God that I cannot help but encounter God if I open myself up to Jesus Christ and trust in him. The notion of Jesus being the Spirit not only rectifies the separation of Christology from pneumatology, it is also an attempt to capture in words the pneumatological intensity of any meeting with him. I am still struggling to come to an adequate understanding of this and am glad that our project assistant Cornelia Dockter expands upon it in her PhD thesis.[1]

Yet it is not only the Qur'an's innovations and adaptations that raise questions but, thirdly, its omissions. These are particularly apparent with regard to the Passion and Crucifixion of Jesus Christ. We contemplated earlier the fact that the Qur'an has no room for either of these theologoumena. As we saw during our analysis of functional equivalents in the preceding chapter, the Qur'an's aim in doing so is by no means to claim that God is incapable of suffering or to marginalise the issue of suffering. Yet the proclaimer of the Qur'an is obviously concerned that the emphasis on the Passion and the Crucifixion of Jesus Christ lead theologically to assertions of exclusivity, obscuring the position that God is vulnerable and susceptible in His statements generally and that He enters into dialogue with humankind in this spirit. The Qur'an's omissions are therefore the most significant indication of how the Qur'an modifies Christology.

The decisive point here is neither revision nor dilution; it is more about expansion and democratisation. This is vividly highlighted in Qur'anic prophetology and theology of signs. Jesus appears as a sign of God's presence in the Qur'an too, but there are a large number, indeed a very large number, of signs of this presence. The inclusion of Jesus in the line of messengers, prophets and servants of God is not meant to relativise the importance of these figures nor to downgrade Jesus Christ's mission, but simply to classify it in salvation theological terms. What is unsatisfactory from a Christian perspective is that the normative and guiding power of Jesus Christ's example are underdetermined here. On the other hand, though, the Qur'an can challenge us to receive Jesus's mission not exclusively

---

1 See Cornelia Dockter, *Geist im Wort. Zur Bedeutung Jesu Christi in Christentum und Islam* (unpublished).

as a determination of the mystery of his person, but inclusively as an exemplary declaration of God's love for and closeness to humankind.

The Qur'an's emphasis on the democratisation of Christology is only possible because it is not just Jesus but the Qur'an itself that is seen as the word of God. The result – and this is my fourth conclusion from the Qur'an's discussion of Jesus – is a formal and material pluralism of God's self-expression that does not arise from Christology, but towards which Christology ought to shift. It is evident that, as a Christian, I am only partially able to take this step, insofar as I fear that this broadening of God's self-expression is too vague. Nevertheless, I can accept and even find it very noteworthy that Christology should not be understood in an exclusive manner but invites us instead to acknowledge the particular dignity of every human being. I believe that such an inclusive form of Christology does exist in the modern, fresh appropriations of Christology we discussed in the relevant chapter.

For Christians, though, this inclusion can succeed only if it is based on a certainty about God's self-revelation in Jesus Christ. Fifth, it is striking in this regard that the proclaimer of the Qur'an – if our exegetical observations above are correct – acknowledges the significance of the Eucharist as a reassurance to Christians and an essential cornerstone of the Christian faith. The proclaimer of the Qur'an is fully aware that the symbolic function of demonstrations of power and miracles of all kinds is always open to misinterpretation. As a rule, the Qur'anic theology of signs and the ambiguity of the Qur'anic style means that the certainty of faith is repeatedly questioned and this is indeed a theme of the Qur'an itself. It is touching that the proclaimer of the Qur'an recognises the celebration of the Eucharist as a response to Christians' insecurity. It is not Jesus's miracles that provide a solid basis for the faith of Jesus's disciples, but his enduring presence in the communion. God's gift of the Eucharist table is thereby acknowledged as the Christian basis for the reaffirmation of the faith, and so people are also open to the establishment of the Christian faith in Jesus's presence. How wonderful therefore, from a diachronic point of view, that the establishment of the Eucharist is practically the final good tidings that Jesus delivers to his community (Q 5:114). It is nonetheless framed by a rejection of John's conception of reciprocal intimacy and knowledge between Jesus and the Father (Q 5:116 versus John 10:15). The proclaimer of the Qur'an obviously wants to warn people against placing the mortal Jesus in an overly reciprocal relationship with God. Naturally, Christians will not be able to go along with the Qur'an on this point. Yet they will also be able to acknowledge the legitimacy of the proclaimer of the Qur'an's concern that this form of Christology can lead to a distancing of Jesus from humankind rather than allowing God in His everlasting unfathomability to move closer to us.

Finally, I would like to cite a sixth and final point whose importance the Qur'anic criticism of Christianity has brought home to me in a new way. For the proclaimer of the Qur'an a strong argument against the beliefs of the Jews and the Christians is that they so frequently engage in fierce disputes with each other. He takes aim equally at intra-Christian quarrels over Christology and at the frequently bloody conflicts between Christianity and Judaism. He appeals for unity and mutual understanding instead.

If we contemplate the state of our world with a modicum of realism, it is clear that we are in desperate need of this kind of testimony. We need proof of a God who desires justice for all His creatures and also for His severely endangered Creation. For all the significance of its quest for truth and all its earnestness regarding the correct form of faith, the Qur'an's irritation with Christological quarrels is an important sign that we should always be aware of the nature of our calling in this world and of the object of our testimony. Here the Qur'an criticises any form of self-righteousness and issues a warning about the dangers of a martial definition of relations between the religions. So I view the Qur'an's message as an emphatic appeal to us Christians to finally fulfil Jesus's wish that we should be one (John 17:22) and to strive tirelessly for a visible ecumenism of all Churches. Just as in Trinitarian theology the Father and the Son form a union-in-difference based on their enduring distinctions, so we Christians are summoned in our diversity to worship the one God.

This unity must not be achieved at the expense of the Jewish testimony but ought to open paths towards recognition of the Jews as elder siblings in faith in the one God. And lastly it requires the inclusion of Muslims in this community of believers, which, whatever the distinctions between specific articles of faith, should be seen more as a shared testimony in favour of one God – the one loving God of the Qur'an and the Bible who stands by us in His steadfast mercy.

7.2 Systematic conclusions from a Muslim perspective

There is an overwhelming tendency in traditional Muslim exegesis and in the traditional positions of Muslim scholars to display an apologetic attitude towards Christianity, which has led in the past and even now to regular interpretations of the passages in the Qur'an where Jesus is mentioned as anti-Christian rhetoric. There is no question that the Qur'an voices criticism of particular Christian positions at various points. However, the result of our intensive joint discussion of these passages shows that the Qur'an's criticism of Christianity is explicitly levelled at specific groupings rather than at the religion as a whole. Thus verses addressing the People of the Book without any such explicit restriction are to be understood as targeted at particular groups. In some places the Qur'an warns about some extreme forms of belief and raises problems found in specific group-ings. But it does not name these groupings, since the aim of the proclaimer of the Qur'an is obviously not to criticise one group or another, but to issue a general warning against false beliefs and practices such as the deification of humans and scholars leading to one religious belief being privileged over others and thus ques-tioning God's omnipotence. This rebuke is directed at Muslims too.

Our findings regarding Qur'anic representations of Jesus invite us to challenge some positions that many Muslims – and many non-Muslims too – regard as *the* Islamic positions on Jesus. As we have noted in our previous remarks, the Qur'an contains far less anti-Christian rhetoric than previously assumed. In what follows, I would like to pick out six main themes that, in my opinion, are deserving of more energetic debate within a broad-based intra-Islamic discourse.

The first theme fundamentally involves the issue of Jesus's nature. There is a strong tendency nowadays to read all the passages in the Qur'an stating that God does not have a son, e.g. Q 19:35, as anti-Christian polemics. We have seen, however, that in its criticism of the suggestion that Jesus is the son of God, the Qur'an generally uses the word '*walad*' and not the Christian term '*ibn*'. This rejection of God's having a biological son is not primarily directed at Christians but, as we have demonstrated, at pagan Arabs. It was obviously the pagan Arabs who regarded Jesus as God's biological son. Even if the Qur'an is addressing this warning directly to the pagan Arabs, however, it can also be understood as being directed at Christians, not as a polemic against Christianity but as a warning to certain Christian groups not to exaggerate their views of Jesus.

The second point concerns the role of Jesus. Our examination of the Qur'anic Jesus shows that the Qur'an depicts Jesus as more than simply the bearer of a message; it sees Jesus himself, his life and his work as the content of this message too. It therefore does not surprise me that the Qur'an draws parallels between itself and Jesus: both are signs that God has given people as proof of His mercy. Both are the Word of God. Yet they are also both the Spirit of God and both are announced through the Holy Spirit. It is in particular the identification of Jesus with the Spirit of God that proves that he is filled with the spirit, and this is an opportunity for Islamic theology to see the function of Jesus in a different light – as the content of God's message.

This is a Qur'anic signal that God did not pledge Himself in the Qur'an alone. To what extent can we Muslims acknowledge Jesus of Nazareth as God's self-commitment without of course deifying Jesus? To my mind, this question raises an urgent question for contemporary Islamic theology. The Qur'an's suggestions of such recognition seem very plausible to me. By equating Jesus at the same time with the Word and with God's Spirit, the Qur'an uses the terminology Christians have adopted for the theology of the Trinity. By binding the terms 'Word' and 'Spirit' to Jesus, the Qur'an scotches any possible speculation about a social trinitarian theology.

My third point involves a prevalent opinion among Muslims that although Jesus received his own revealed scripture, the Christians allegedly corrupted it. The Qur'an does indeed say that a *kitāb* or the *'injīl* was revealed to Jesus. We saw earlier that the word '*kitāb*' (pl. '*kutub*') means not only 'book(s)' but also 'divine teaching'. The Qur'an's call for Muslims to believe in God's *kutub* – a tenet of the Islamic faith – is actually a call for people to believe that God gave His commitment in a variety of forms.

Muslims often ignore Jewish and Christian holy scriptures, or challenge their divine dignity with the argument that they are nothing more than falsified versions of the original holy books of the Jews and the Christians. These people point to passages in the Qur'an such as Q 3:78, which mentions the falsification of scripture. As we have discovered during our research, however, this Qur'anic criticism is explicitly targeted at a specific Christian or Jewish grouping. The lie therefore resides not in the scripture itself, but in its deliberate falsification by the relevant grouping. The Qur'an is obviously not very interested in naming these groupings, as it is concerned with something more fundamental – namely, warning its audience about a conscious instrumentalisation of the holy scriptures. Yet this danger also lurks for the Qur'an. The greatest manipulation of the holy scriptures is when one religion claims sole possession of God's truth.

One other sensitive topic is the issue of Jesus's Crucifixion. Our findings on this subject make the debate about the death of Jesus significantly less sensitive for Muslims. As we have demonstrated, the Qur'an emphasises that it was not the Jews who crucified Jesus. It contradicts their claim to be responsible for the Crucifixion. Yet the Qur'an does not deny the death of Jesus, merely underlining that he did not succumb for good to the hatred of his opponents. Like the martyrs who were killed on God's path, Jesus too should not be considered dead. This conclusion invites us to cease drawing a sharp dividing line between Islam and Christianity about Jesus's Crucifixion. In the preceding chapter about functional equivalents, we noted that the God of the Qur'an is also a compassionate God, who is moved by human distress. Muslims' recognition of Jesus's Crucifixion does not mean that they believe in a salvation through God's suffering on the cross. This is one of the many gaps in the Qur'an that leaves room for interpretation and speculation, while simultaneously diverting from the thinking of the two more ancient and related religions.

The fifth point I would like to raise briefly here concerns the Qur'an's emphasis on the similar contents of the Qur'anic message and Jesus's message. It is striking that the central theme of the Qur'an – mercy – first features prominently in the Qur'an in relation to Surah 19, i.e. in a surah exclusively devoted to Mary and Jesus. The proclaimer of the Qur'an is clearly making an effort here to stress the continuity of the central message of the two religions – God's mercy. I encounter God's mercy in the Qur'an but also in Jesus, for both are defined as mercy itself.

It can hardly be a coincidence either that the third and fifth surahs, which concentrate exclusively on Jesus of Nazareth, describe the relationship between God and humankind in terms of love. And so one can find evidence in the Qur'an that the relationship between God and humans is defined as one of love. The Qur'an thereby invites believers from both religions to strive, regardless of the enduring differences between their two faiths, after the same essence of their two messages and to place it at the centre of their dialogue.

The final point I would like to explore is the Qur'an's emphasis on its inclusive spirit, which our reading of the Qur'anic Jesus highlights. We have seen that the Qur'an never criticises Christianity or Judaism *per se*, only ever specific groupings and specific positions within them; otherwise, the Qur'an offers no shortage of praise and recognition for the two religions. We also encounter this inclusive spirit of the Qur'an in the late phase of Muhammad's activity, i.e. when his political power was at its peak. We have already referred to the oft-cited passage at Q 5:48. This explains that, in the Qur'an's view, a variety of different beliefs is in accordance with God's salvific will. The Qur'an criticises Judaism's and Christianity's exclusive vision of salvation and supports the diversity of religions. It rejects any kind of hierarchy of religious groups. As a Muslim theologian, I interpret this as a clear rebuttal of Islam's current claims to be the only route to salvation. The Qur'an obviously urges Muslims to enter into dialogue with other religions and worldviews with a willingness to learn from them.

Contrary to the widespread view that the proclaimer of the Qur'an indulges in anti-Christian rhetoric, we have shown that the Qur'an adopts a Christological title by referring to Jesus as a 'servant of God'. At the same time, the Qur'an categorically rejects any form of redemptive power of ritual sacrifices. The title of 'servant of God' is therefore freshly cast and placed in its wider biblical context again. And as we have noted, passages such as Q 5:116 and Q 9:29 do not refer to social trinitarian theologies, but are intended as rejections of any form of deification of humans, which can escalate to a point that erodes all faith in God. The target of this Qur'anic criticism is clearly a version of Christianity that has utterly lost faith in God. We are not entitled to lump all such critical statements by the Qur'an together and see all of them as critical of Christianity. As we have seen, the Qur'an expresses, during the same historical period, both searing criticism of (Q 9:29–31) and the highest recognition (Q 5:83–84) for Church officials.

One of the most important findings of our research is the Qur'an's willingness to confirm some of the central principles of Christology. At the same time and in the same breath, however, it alerts us to aberrations of Christian theology that we regard as having lasting significance.

The Qur'an does not, however, explicitly engage with some theological issues relating to Christology including the Trinity, the Crucifixion and Jesus's atonement for the sins of humankind. Nor does the Qur'an undertake any interpretation of the title of Messiah used in Christology. These 'gaps' in the Qur'an leave room for interpretation, but also for speculation and new theological emphasis.

If it was the Qur'an's intention to distance itself from Christianity and to reject its substance in polemical fashion, then one is entitled to wonder why the proclaimer of the Qur'an does not shrink from using the main Christian titles for Jesus. By calling Jesus the 'Word' and the 'Spirit of God', the Qur'an gives grounds for seeing Jesus as more than just a passive message-bearer. What the Qur'an does dismiss, however, is any form of deification of Jesus.

Our book should have demonstrated that the proclaimer of the Qur'an does not mean to reject Christianity as a whole. That is because it is obvious that Christianity is not interested in the deification of Jesus but in the belief that God's Word becomes experiential reality in Jesus Christ. This is not about a human being elevated to divine status, but about God doing the opposite and showing His affection for humans – an idea to which the Qur'an repeatedly attests, even if Islam gives priority to other images and other paths to bear witness to this affection. The result, though, is a productive distinction between the two religions rather than an irreconcilable standoff. Our book – entirely in keeping with the Qur'an – aims to be the first step in a fresh definition of the relationship between Islam and Christianity based on a willingness to learn, engage in dialogue and promote peace.

Bibliography

Abu l-Fida', Isma'il Ibn Kathir al-Qurashi al-Dimashqi, *Tafsir al-Qur'an al-'azim*, ed. Muhammad Bayyumi, vol. 5, Cairo 2008.

Adshead, Kate, 'Justinian and Aphthartodocetism', in Stephen Mitchell / Geoffrey B. Greatrex (eds.), *Ethnicity and Culture in Late Antiquity*, London 2000, 331–6.

Al-Amidi, Sayf al-Din, *Abkar al-afkar fi usul al-din*, vol. 1, Cairo 2004.

Andrae, Tor, *Der Ursprung des Islams und das Christentum*, Uppsala 1926.

Anwar, Etin, 'Ibn Sīnā's Philosophical Theology of Love. A Study of the Risālah fī al-'Ishq', in *Islamic Studies* 42 (2003) 331–45.

Arkoun, Mohammed, 'Islam', in *Encyclopaedia of the Qur'an* 2 (2002) 565–71.

Asghar-Zadeh, Darius, 'Menschsein im Angesicht des Absoluten. Theologische Anthropologie in der Perspektive christlich-muslimischer Komparativer Theologie' (*Beiträge zur Komparativen Theologie*; 29), Paderborn 2017.

Aslan, Reza, *No god but God. The Origins, Evolution and Future of Islam*, New York 2005.

Ayoub, Mahmoud, *A Muslim View of Christianity. Essays on Dialogue*, ed. Irfan A. Omar, Maryknoll, New York 2007.

al-Azmeh, Aziz, *The Emergence of Islam in Late Antiquity. Allah and His People*, Cambridge 2014.

Bangert, Kurt, 'Zeitgenössische Zeugnisse. Haben Koran und Islam judenchristliche Wurzeln?' in Bangert, *Muhammad. Eine historisch-kritische Studie zur Entstehung des Islams und seines Propheten*, Wiesbaden 2016, 587–652.

Al-Baqillani, Muhammad, *Tamhid al-awa'il wa-talkhis al-dala'il*, ed. 'Imad al-Din Haydar, Bayrut 1987.

Bauckham, Richard, *God Crucified. Monotheism and Christology in the New Testament*, Cambridge 1998.

Bauer, Karen, 'Emotion in the Qur'an: An Overview', in *Journal of Qur'anic Studies* 19 (2017) 1–30.

Bauschke, Martin, 'Jesus – Stein des Anstoßes. Die Christologie des Korans und die deutschsprachige Theologie' (*Kölner Veröffentlichungen zur Religionsgeschichte*; 29), Cologne 2000.

——, *Jesus im Koran*, Cologne 2001.

Bell, Richard, *The Origin of Islam in its Christian Environment*, The Gunning Lectures, Edinburgh University 1925, London 1968.

Berger, Lutz, *Islamische Theologie*, Vienna 2010.

Berkey, Jonathan P., *The Formation of Islam. Religion and Society in the Near East, 600–1800*, Cambridge 2003.

Blois, François de, 'Naṣrānī (Ναζωραῖος) and ḥanīf (ἐθνικός): Studies on the Religious Vocabulary of Christianity and of Islam', in *Bulletin of the School of Oriental and African Studies* 65 (2002) 1–30.

Bobzin, Hartmut, 'The "Seal of the Prophets": Towards an Understanding of Muhammad's Prophethood', in Angelika Neuwirth / Nicolai Sinai / Michael Marx (eds.), *The Qur'an in Context. Historical and Literary Investigations into the Qur'anic Milieu*, Leiden 2011, 565–83.

Bonhoeffer, Dietrich, *Prisoner for God: Letters and Papers from Prison*, ed. Eberhard Bethge, tr. Reginald H. Fuller, New York 1959.

Boumaaiz, Amina / Feininger, Bernd / Schröter, Jörg Imran, '"Bin Ich nicht Euer Herr?" (Sure 7,172). Aspekte zum Menschenbild im Islam', in Katja Boehme (ed.), *'Wer ist der Mensch?', Anthropologie im interreligiösen Lernen und Lehren*, Berlin 2013, 101–43.

Boutroux, Emile, *Nouvelles études d'histoire de la philosophie*, Paris 1927.

Brock, Sebastian, *Die verborgene Perle. An der Schwelle zum Dritten Jahrtausend*, vol. 2, Rome 2001.

Buchegger, Jürg H., *Das Wort vom Kreuz in der christlich-muslimischen Begegnung. Leben und Werk von Johan Bouman*, Basel 2013.

Bürkle, Horst, 'Jesus und Maria im Koran', in Günter Riße / Heino Sonnemans / Burkhard Theß (eds.), *Wege der Theologie an der Schwelle zum dritten Jahrtausend*, Paderborn 1996.

Cillis, Maria De, *Free Will and Predestination in Islamic Thought: Theoretical Compromises in the Works of Avicenna, al-Ghazali and Ibn 'Arabi*, London 2014.

Çinar, Hüseyin Ilker, 'Maria und Jesus im Islam. Darstellung anhand des Korans und der islamischen kanonischen Tradition unter Berücksichtigung der islamischen Exegeten' (*Arabisch-Islamische Welt in Tradition und Moderne*; 6), Wiesbaden 2007.

Cragg, Kenneth, *Jesus and the Muslim: An Exploration*, London 1985.

Crone, Patricia, 'The Book of Watchers in the Qur'an', in Haggai-Ben Shammai / Shaul Shaked / Sarah Stroumsa (eds.), *Exchange and Transmission across Cultural Boundaries. Philosophy, Mysticism and Science in the Mediterranean World*, Jerusalem 2013, 16–51.

Danz, Christian, *Grundprobleme der Christologie*, Tübingen 2013.

Dassmann, Ernst, *Kirchengeschichte I. Ausbreitung, Leben und Lehre der Kirche in den ersten drei Jahrhunderten*, Stuttgart 1991.

Dockter, Cornelia, *Geist im Wort. Zur Bedeutung Jesu Christi in Christentum und Islam* (unpublished).

Donner, Fred, *Muhammad and the Believers. At the Origins of Islam*, Cambridge 2010.

Dostoevsky, Fyodor, *The Brothers Karamazov*, part II, tr. David McDuff, London 1993.

Draguet, René, *Julien d'Harnicasse et sa controverse avec Sévère d'Antioche sur l'incorruptibilité du corps du Christ. Etude d'histoire littéraire et doctrinale suivie des fragments dogmatiques de Julien* (Syriac text with Greek tranlsation), Louvain 1924.

Eißler, Friedmann, 'Jesus und Maria im Islam', in Christfried Böttrich / Beate Ego / Friedmann Eißler, *Jesus und Maria in Judentum, Christentum und Islam*, Göttingen 2009, 120–205.

El Kaisy-Friemuth, Maha, *God and Humans in Islamic Thought. 'Abd al-Jabbar, Ibn Sina and al-Ghazali*, New York 2006.

Erder, Yoram, 'Idris', *Enyclopaedia of the Qur'an* 2 (2002), 484–6.

Esbroeck, Michael van, 'The Aphthartodocetic Edict of Justinian and Its Armenian Background', in *Studia Patristica* 33 (1997) 578–85.

Essen, Georg, 'Die Freiheit Jesu, Der neuchalkedonische Enhypostasiebegriff im Horizont neuzeitlicher Subjekt- und Personphilosophie' (*ratio fidei*; 5), Regensburg 2001.

Farağ, Muhammad, A conversation between Muhammad Farağ and Nasr Hamed Abu Zaid, *Al-Badil* (2008); https://rowaqnasrabuzaid.wordpress. com/2008/04/12/ (14. 02. 2018).

Finster, Barbara, 'Arabia in Late Antiquity. An Outline of the Cultural Situation in the peninsula at the time of Muhammad', in Angelika Neuwirth / Nicolai Sinai / Michael Marx (eds.), *The Qur'an in Context. Historical and Literary Investigations into the Qur'anic Milieu*, Leiden 2011, 61–114.

Fischer, Hermann, *Friedrich Daniel Ernst Schleiermacher*, Munich 2001.

Fisher, Greg, *Between Empires. Arabs, Romans and Sasanians in Late Antiquity*, Oxford 2011.

Frend, W. H. C., *The Rise of the Monophysite Movement. Chapters in the History of the Church in the Fifth and Sixth Centuries*, Cambridge 1972.

Jabr, Mujahid Ibn, *Tafsir*, ed. Muhammad 'Abdassalam Abul-Nail, 1989/1410.

Ghaemmaghami, Ayatollah 'Abbas Hosseini, 'Einheit und Vielfalt im Gottesgedanken', in Muna Tatari / Klaus von Stosch (eds.), *Trinität – Anstoß für das islamisch-christliche Gespräch* (*Beiträge zur Komparativen Theologie*; 7), Paderborn 2013, 171–93.

Ghaffar, Zishan, 'Jesus redivivus – Der koranische Jesus im Kontext von Prophetologie', in Thomas Fornet-Ponse (ed.), *Jesus Christus. Von alttestamentlichen Messiasvorstellungen bis zur literarischen Figur*, Münster 2015, 149–62.

Gramlich, Richard, *Muhammad Al-Gazzalis Lehre von den Stufen zur Gottesliebe, Books 31–36 of his major work introduced, translated and explained*, Wiesbaden 1984.

Griffel, Frank, 'Muslim Philosophers' Rationalist Explanation of Muḥammad's Prophecy', in Jonathan E. Brockopp (ed.), *The Cambridge Companion to Muḥammad*, Cambridge 2010, 158–79.

——, 'Philosophy and Prophecy', in Richard C. Taylor / Luis Xavier López-Farjeat (eds.), *The Routledge Companion to Islamic Philosophy*, London 2016, 385–98.

Griffith, Sidney H., 'Syriacisms in the "Arabic Qur'an": Who were "those who said Allah is the third of three" according to al-Ma'ida 73?', in Meir M. Bar-Asher *et al* (ed.), *A Word Fitly Spoken. Studies in Medieval Exegesis of the Hebrew Bible and the Qur'an*, Jerusalem 2007, 83–110.

——, '*Al Naṣārā* in the Qur'an. A Hermeneutical Reflection', in Gabriel Said Reynolds (ed.), *New Perspectives on the Qur'an. The Qur'an in its Historical Context 2*, London 2011, 301–22.

——, 'The Melkites and the Muslims. The Qur'an, Christology, and Arab Orthodoxy', in *Al-Qantara* 33 (2012) 413–43.

——, 'The Poetics of Scriptural Reasoning: Syriac *Mêmrê* at Work', in Jeffrey Wickes / Kristian S. Heal (eds.), *Literature, Rhetoric, and Exegesis in Syriac Verse* (*Studia Patristica*; 78), Leuven 2017, 5–25.

Grillmeier, Alois, *Christ in Christian Tradition. Vol. 1: From the Apostolic Age to Chalcedon*, tr. John Bowden, 2nd revised edition, Louisville, KY 1988.

——, *Christ in Christian Tradition. Vol. 2/2: The Church of Constantinople in the Sixth Century*, with Theresia Hainthaler, tr. John Cawte & Pauline Allen, Louisville, KY 1995.

——, *Christ in Christian Tradition. Vol. 2/4: The Church of Alexandria with Nubia and Ethiopia after 451*, with Theresia Hainthaler, tr. O.C. Dean, Louisville, KY 1996.

——, *Christ in Christian Tradition. Vol. 2/3: The Churches of Jerusalem and Antioch from 451 to 600*, ed. Theresia Hainthaler, tr. Marianne Ehrhardt, Louisville, KY 2013.

Guillaume, Alfred, *The Life of Muhammad. A Translation of Ibn Isḥāq's Sīrat rasūl Allāh*, Karachi 1967.

Hainthaler, Theresia, 'La foi au Christ dans l'Eglise éthiopienne. Une synthèse des éléments judéo-chrétiens et helléno-chrétiens', *Revue des sciences religieuses* 71 (1997) 329–37.

——, 'Christliche Araber vor dem Islam. Verbreitung und konfessionelle Zugehörigkeit. Eine Hinführung' (*Eastern Christian Studies*; 7), Leuven 2007.

Hajatpour, Reza, *Mehdi Hairi Yazdi interkulturell gelesen*, Nordhausen 2005.

——, *Vom Gottesentwurf zum Selbstentwurf. Die Idee der Perfektibilität in der islamischen Existenzphilosophie*, Freiburg 2013.

Haldon, John F., *Byzantium in the Seventh Century. The Transformation of a Culture*, Cambridge 1990.

Harnack, Adolf von, 'Dogmengeschichte' (*Grundriss der Theologischen Wissenschaften*; 4/3), Freiburg 1893.

——, *Lehrbuch der Dogmengeschichte. Vol. 1: Die Entstehung des kirchlichen Dogmas*, Darmstadt 1964.

——, *Das Wesen des Christentums. Hg. u. komm. v. Trutz Rendtorff*, Gütersloh 1999.

Hebblethwaite, Brian, *The Incarnation. Collected Essays in Christology*, Cambridge 1987.

Henrich, Dieter, 'Selbstbewusstsein. Kritische Einleitung in eine Theorie', in Rüdiger Bubner / Konrad Cramer / Reiner Wiehl (eds.), *Hermeneutik und Dialektik. Aufsätze I: Methode und Wissenschaft – Lebenswelt und Geschichte*, Tübingen 1970, 257–84.

Hoppe, Rudolf, 'Jesus – das Paradoxon Gottes. Überlegungen zu Botschaft und Wirken des Nazareners', *Impulse* 60 (2001) 2–6.

Horovitz, Josef, *Koranische Untersuchungen*, Berlin 1926.

Hurtado, Larry W., *How on Earth did Jesus Become a God? Historical Questions about Earliest Devotion to Jesus*, Grand Rapids 2005.

Ibn Sina, *Avicenna's De Anima* (Arabic Text), ed. Fazlur Rahman, London 1959.

——, 'Kitab al-Shifa'': *al-Ilahiyat* VIII 7 (= Ibn Sina, Kitab al-shifa' : al-Ilahiyat. Bd. 2, eds. Muhammad Yusuf Musa / Sulayman Dunya / Sa'id Zaid, Cairo 1960 [ND Qom 1983]).

——, *al- Ta'liqat*, edited and introduced by 'Abd al-Rahman Badawi, Cairo 1973.

——, *The Metaphysica of Avicenna (Ibn Sina). A Critical Translation-Commentary and Analysis of the Fundamental Arguments in Avicenna's Metaphysica in the Danish Nama-i 'ala'i (The Book of Scientific Knowledge)*, ed. Parviz Morewedge, New York 1973.

Ibn Sulaiman, Muqatil, *Tafsir Muqatil b. Sulaiman*, ed. 'Abdallah Mahmud Shihata, Beirut 2002/1423.

——, *al-wujuh wa al-naza'ir fi al-Qur'an al-'Azim*, ed. Hatim Salih al-Damin, Damascus 2006/1427.

Ibn Taymiyya, Taqi al-Din, *Minhaq al-sunna al-nabawiya*, vol. 3, ed. Muhammad Salim, Bulaq 1904.

——, *Sharh al-isfahaniya*, Riyad 1995.

Ibrahim, Zakariyya, *Mushkilat al-hurriya*, Cairo 1972.

Imbach, Josef, *Wem gehört Jesus? Seine Bedeutung für Juden, Christen und Moslems*, Munich 1989.

Jawad, Haifaa, 'A Muslim Response to the Christian Theology of Religions', in Elizabeth Harris / Paul Hedges / Shanthikumar Hettiarachchi (eds.), *Twenty-First Century Theologies of Religions. Retrospection and Future Prospects*, Leiden 2016.

Jedin, Hubert, *Kleine Konzilsgeschichte*, Freiburg 1978.

Kaegi, Walter E., *Heraclius. Emperor of Byzantium*, Cambridge 2003.

Kermani, Navid, *God is Beautiful. The Aesthetic Experience of the Qur'an*, London 2015.

——, *Wonder Beyond Belief: On Christianity*, tr. Tony Crawford, London 2017, 44.

Khorchide, Mouhanad, 'Eine Frage der Lesart. Islamische Positionen zum religiösen Pluralismus', in *Herder Korrespondenz Spezialheft 2* (2010) 17–20.

——, *Islam ist Barmherzigkeit*, Freiburg 2012.

——, 'Anstöße zu einer Theologie der Barhmherzigkeit', in Khorchide / Milad Karimi / Klaus von Stosch (eds), *Theologie der Barmherzigkeit? Zeitgemäße Fragen und Antworten des Kalām*, Münster 2014.

Kister, Meir Jacob, 'The Massacre of the Banū Qurayẓa. A Re-examination of a Tradition', *Jerusalem Studies in Arabic and Islam* 8 (1986) 61–96.

Klein, Wassilios, 'Art. Propheten/Prophetie', in *Theologische Realenzyklopädie* 27 (1997), 474–5.

Kofsky, Aryeh, 'The Miaphysite Monasticism of Gaza and Julian of Halicarnassus', in *Orientalia christiana periodica* 78 (2012) 81–96.

Koutzarova, Tiana, *Das Transzendentale bei Ibn Sina. Zur Metaphysik als Wissenschaft erster Begriffsund Urteilsprinzipien*, Leiden 2009.

Kreuzer, Georg, *Die Honoriusfrage im Mittelalter und in der Neuzeit* (Päpste und Papsttum; 8), Stuttgart 1975.

Krings, Hermann, 'Freiheit. Ein Versuch, Gott zu denken', in Krings (ed.), *System und Freiheit. Gesammelte Aufsätze* (Reihe: *Praktische Philosophie*; 12), Freiburg 1980, 161–84.

Krötke, Wolf, 'Vorösterlicher Jesus – Nachösterlicher Christus. Dialogische Perspektiven in der Christologie', in Klaus von Stosch / Mouhanad Khorchide (eds.), *Streit um Jesus. Muslimische und christliche Annäherungen* (*Beiträge zur Komparativen Theologie*; 21), Paderborn 2016, 155–66.

Kuschel, Karl-Josef, *Festmahl am Hermelstisch. Wie Mahl feiern Juden, Christen und Muslime verbindet*, Ostfildern 2013.

——, *Die Bibel im Koran. Grundlagen für das interreligiöse Gespräch*, Ostfildern 2017.

Lammens, Henri, 'Les chrétiens à la Mecque à la veille de l'hégire', in Lammens, *L'Arabie occidentale avant l'hégire*, Beirut 1928, 1–49.

Langenfeld, Aaron, 'Das Schweigen brechen. Christliche Soteriologie im Kontext islamischer Theologie' (*Beiträge zur Komparativen Theologie*; 22), Paderborn 2016.

Lawson, Todd, *The Crucifixion and the Qur'an. A Study in the History of Muslim Thought*, Oxford 2009.

Lecker, Michael, 'Did Muḥammad conclude Treaties with the Jewish Tribes Naḍīr, Qurayẓa and Qaynuqā'?', in *Israel Oriental Studies* 17 (1997) 29–36.

Legenhausen, Hajj Muhammad, 'Jesus as Kalimat Allah, the Word of God', in Mohammad Ali Shomali (ed.), *Word of God*, London 2009, 129–56.

——, 'Appreciating Muslim and Christian Christologies', in Klaus von Stosch / Mouhanad Khorchide (eds.), *Streit um Jesus. Muslimische und christliche Annäherungen* (*Beiträge zur Komparativen Theologie*; 21), Paderborn 2016, 59–79.

——, 'Mulla Sadra's Critique of Apophatic Mysticism and Pantheism', Bernhard Nitsche / Klaus von Stosch / Muna Tatari (eds.), *Gott – jenseits von Monismus und Theismus?* (*Beiträge zur Komparativen Theologie*; 23), Paderborn 2017, 309–21.

Lerch, Magnus, 'Selbstmitteilung Gottes. Herausforderungen einer freiheitstheoretischen Offenbarungstheologie' (*ratio fidei*; 56), Regensburg 2015.

Luxenberg, Christoph, *Die syro-aramäische Lesart des Koran*, Köthen 2004.

Madigan, Daniel, 'God's Word to the World: Jesus and the Qur'ân, Incarnation and Recitation', in Terence Merrigan / Frederik Glorieux (eds.), *Godhead Here in Hiding. Incarnation and the History of Human Suffering*, Leuven 2012, 143–58.

Markschies, Christoph, 'Hellenisierung des Christentums. Sinn und Unsinn einer historischen Deutungskategorie' (*Forum Theologische Literaturzeitung*; 25), Leipzig 2012.

Menke, Karl-Heinz, *Fleisch geworden aus Maria. Die Geschichte Israels und der Marienglaube der Kirche*, Regensburg 1999.

——, *Jesus ist Gott der Sohn, Denkformen und Brennpunkte der Christologie*, Regensburg 2008.

——, 'Gott sühnt in seiner Menschwerdung die Sünde des Menschen', in Magnus Striet / Jan-Heiner Tück (eds.), *Erlösung auf Golgota? Der Opfertod Jesu im Streit der Interpretationen*, Freiburg 2012, 101–25.

——, 'Das heterogene Phänomen der Geist-Christologien', in George Augustin / Klaus Krämer / Markus Schulze (ed.), *Mein Herr und mein Gott. Christus bekennen und verkünden,* Freiburg 2013, 220–57.

——, *Das unterscheidend Christliche. Beiträge zur Bestimmung seiner Einzigkeit*, Regensburg 2015.

Menzel, Volker, *Justinian and the Making of the Syrian Orthodox Church*, Oxford 2008.

Merklein, Helmut, 'Studien zu Jesus und Paulus II' (*Wissenschaftliche Untersuchungen zum Neuen Testament*; 105), Tübingen 1998.

——, 'Jesus, Künder des Reiches Gottes', in Walter Kern / Hermann J. Pottmeyer / Max Seckler (eds.), *Handbuch der Fundamentaltheologie. Vol. 2: Traktat Offenbarung*, 2nd improved and updated edition, Tübingen 2000, 115–39.

Metz, Johann Baptist, 'Theologie als Theodizee?', Willi Oelmüller (ed.), *Theodizee – Gott vor Gericht? With articles by C.-F. Geyer et al*, Munich 1990, 103–18.

Middelbeck-Varwick, Anja, *Cum aestimatione. Konturen einer christlichen Islamtheologie*, Münster 2017.

Mimouni, Simon Claude, *Le judéo-christianisme ancien. Essais historiques*, Paris 1998.

Mohagheghi, Hamideh, '"Tötet sie, wo ihr sie trefft." Eine Auslegung zu Q 2:190–195', in Mimouni / Klaus von Stosch (eds.), *Gewalt in den Heiligen Schriften von Islam und Christentum (Beiträge zur Komparativen Theologie;* 10), Paderborn 2014, 73–91.

Müller, Klaus, 'Wenn ich "ich" sage. Studien zur fundamentaltheologischen Relevanz selbstbewußter Subjektivität' (*Regensburger Studien zur Theologie;* 46), Frankfurt 1994.

Nagel, Tilmann, *Islam: Die Heilsbotschaft des Korans und ihre Konsequenzen*, Westhofen 2001.

Nebes, Norbert, 'The Martyrs of Najran and the End of the Heryar. On the Political History of South Arabia in the Early Sixth Century', in Angelika Neuwirth / Nicolai Sinai / Michael Marx (eds.), *The Qur'an in Context. Historical and Literary Investigations into the Qur'anic Milieu*, Leiden 2009, 25–60.

Neuner, Peter, 'Ekklesiologie I. Von den Anfängen zum Mittelalter' (*Texte zur Theologie. Dogmatik;* 5.1), Graz 1994.

Neuwirth, Angelika, 'Mary and Jesus: Counterbalancing the Biblical Patriarchs. A re-reading of *sūrat Maryam* in *sūrat Āl 'Imrān* (Q 3:1–62)', in *Parole de l'Orient* 30 (2005) 231–60.

——, *Studien zur Komposition der mekkanischen Suren. Die literarische Form des Koran – ein Zeugnis seiner Historizität?*, Berlin 2007.

——, 'Imagining Mary – Disputing Jesus. Reading Surah Maryam and related Meccan Texts within the Qur'anic Communication Process', in Benjamin Jokisch / Ulrich Rebstock / Lawrence Conrad (eds.), *Fremde, Feinde und Kurioses. Innen und Außenansichten unseres muslimischen Nachbarn*, Berlin 2009, 383–416.

——, *The Qur'an and Late Antiquity. A Shared Heritage*, tr. Samuel Wilder, Oxford 2019.

——, *Koranforschung – eine politische Philologie? Bibel, Koran und Islamentstehung im Spiegel spätantiker Textpolitik und moderner Philologie*, Berlin 2014.

——, 'Zur Jesaja-Rezeption im Koran', in Florian Wilk / Peter Gemeinhardt (eds.), *Transmission and Interpretation of the Book of Isaiah in the Context of Intra- and Interreligious Debates*, Leuven 2016, 373–91.

——, *Die koranische Verzauberung der Welt und ihre Entzauberung in der Geschichte*, Freiburg 2017.

——, *Der Koran. Vol. 2/1: Frühmittelmekkanische Suren. Das neue Gottesvolk: ‚Biblisierung' des altarabischen Weltbildes*, Berlin 2017.

——, *Der Koran. Bd. 2/2, Handkommentar zu Q 17* (unpublished manuscript).

Nickel, Gordon, '"We will make peace with you": the Christians of Najrān in Muqātil's "Tafsīr"', in *Collectanea Christiana Orientalia* 3 (2006) 171–88.

Nöldeke, Theodor, *Geschichte des Qorāns, Zweite Auflage, Erster Teil, Über den Ursprung des Qorāns*, Leipzig 1909.

Nossel, Alfons, 'Der Geist als Gegenwart Jesu Christi', in Walter Kasper (ed.), *Gegenwart des Geistes. Aspekte der Pneumatologie*, Freiburg 1979, 132–54.

Oeldemann, Johannes, *Die Kirchen des christlichen Ostens. Orthodoxe, orientalische und mit Rom unierte Ostkirchen*, Kevelaer 2008.

Pannenberg, Wolfhart, *Grundzüge der Christologie*, Gütersloh 1966.

Parrinder, Geoffrey, *Jesus in the Qur'an*, London 1965.

Parsania, Hamid, *Existence and the Fall. Spiritual Anthropology of Islam*, tr. Shuja Ali Mirza, London 2006.

Plessner, Helmuth, *Mit anderen Augen. Aspekte einer philosophischen Anthropologie*, Stuttgart 1982.

Powers, David S., 'The Finality of Prophecy', in Adam J. Silverstein / Guy G. Stroumsa (eds.), *The Oxford Handbook of The Abrahamic Religions*, Oxford 2015, 254–71.

Pröpper, Thomas, *Erlösungsglaube und Freiheitsgeschichte. Eine Skizze zur Soteriologie*, München 1991.

——, *Evangelium und freie Vernunft. Konturen einer theologischen Hermeneutik*, Freiburg 2001.

——, *Theologische Anthropologie*, 2nd vol., Freiburg 2011.

al-Qurtubi, Abu 'Abdallah Muhammad b. Ahmad al-Ansari, *al-Jami' li-ahkam al-Qur'an*, ed. Hamid Ahmad al-Tahir, Cairo 2009.

Radscheit, Matthias, 'Table', in *Encyclopaedia of the Qur'an* 5 (2006), 189.

Rahman, Fazlur, *Prophecy in Islam*, London 1958.

Rahner, Johanna, *Creatura Evangelii. Zum Verhältnis von Rechtfertigung und Kirche*, Freiburg 2005.

Rahner, Karl, 'Jesus Christus', in *SM* 2 (1968), 900–57.

——, *Foundations of Christian Faith: An Introduction to the Idea of Christianity*, trans. William V. Dych, London 1978.

al-Razi, Fakhr al-Din, *al-Tafsir al-kabir aw mafatih al-gaib*, ed. Hani al-Haj, Kairo 2002.

Renz, Andreas, *Der Mensch unter dem An-Spruch Gottes. Offenbarungsverständnis und Menschenbild des Islam im Urteil gegenwärtiger christlicher Theologie*, Würzburg 2002.

Rizvi, Sajjad H., *Mullā Ṣadrā and Metaphysics: Modulation of Being*, London 2009.

Robin, Christian Julien, 'Ḥimyar, Aksūm, and *Arabia Deserta* in Late Antiquity. The Epigraphic Evidence', in Greg Fisher (ed.), *Arabs and Empires before Islam*, Oxford 2015, 127–71.

Rubin, Uri, 'Prophets and Prophethood', in *Encyclopeadia of the Qur'an* 4 (2004), 289–307.

Samuelson, Francine E., 'Messianic Judaism: Church, denomination, sect, or cult?', in *Journal of Ecumenical Studies* 37 (2000) 161–86.

Shamshiri, Babak, *Tarhi naw dar insanshinasi-i islami*, Tehran 1395/2016.

Schäfer, Peter, *Jesus in the Talmud*, Princeton 2009.

Schedl, Claus, *Muhammad und Jesus. Die christologisch relevanten Texte des Korans*, Freiburg 1978.

Schelling, Friedrich Wilhelm Joseph, *Philosophie der Offenbarung. Ausgewählte Werke*, vol. 2, Darmstadt 1974.

Schiller, Friedrich, *Aesthetical and Philosophical Essays*, trans. Nathan Haskell Dole, Boston 1902.

——, Correspondence with Gottfried Körner. Letter dated 19th February 1793, *Schillers Briefwechsel mit Körner*, Berlin 1859, 41–3.

Schmoldt, Hans, *Das Alte Testament*, Stuttgart 2004.

Schmucker, Werner, 'Die christliche Minderheit von Nāǧrān und die Problematik ihrer Beziehungen zum frühen Islam', in *Studien zum Minderheitenproblem im Islam* 1 (1973) 183–281.

Schöller, Marco, *Exegetisches Denken und Prophetenbiographie*, Wiesbaden 1998.

Schoen, Ulrich, 'Gottes Allmacht und die Freiheit des Menschen. Gemeinsames Problem von Islam und Christentum', With an introduction by K. Hock and with an updated postface (*Christentum und Islam im Dialog*; 2), Münster 2003.

Schöndorf, Harald, 'Warum musste Jesus leiden?', in *Zeitschrift für katholische Theologie* 124 (2002) 440–67.

Schoeps, Hans-Joachim, *Theologie und Geschichte des Judenchristentums*, Tübingen 1949.

Schreiber, Stefan, *Die Anfänge der Christologie. Deutungen Jesu im Neuen Testament*, Neukirchen 2015.

Secretan, Charles, *La Philosophie de La Liberté. Cours de philosophie morale fait à Lausanne*, Lausanne 1849.

Shahid, Irfan, *Byzantium and the Arabs in the Sixth Century*, vol. 2/1, Washington, DC 2002.

Shoemaker, Stephen J., 'The Reign of God Has Come. Eschatology and Empire in Late Antiquity and Early Islam', in *Arabica* 61 (2014) 514–58.

Sinai, Nicolai, *Fortschreibung und Auslegung. Studien zur frühen Koraninterpretation*, Wiesbaden 2009.

——, 'The Unknown Known: Some Groundwork for Interpreting the Medinan Qur'an', in *Mélanges de l'Université Saint-Joseph* 66 (2015–2016) 54–61.

——, 'Der Koran', in Rainer Brunner (ed.), *Islam. Einheit und Vielfalt einer Weltreligion*, Stuttgart 2016, 132–66.

al-Shirazi, Sadr al-Din Muhammad ibn Ibrahim (= Mulla Sadra), *al-Hikma al-muta'aliya fi l-asfar al-'aqliya al-arba'a* (= al-Asfar), vol. 1, ed. Rida Lutfi and Muhammad Rida Muzaffar, Qom 1387/1967.

Sirry, Mun'im, *Scriptural Polemics. The Qur'an and other Religions*, Oxford 2014.

Specker, Tobias, 'Das Kreuz – der trennende theologische Skandal', *ThPQ* 161 (2013) 243–52.

Stosch, Klaus von, *Gott – Macht – Geschichte. Versuch einer theodizeesensiblen Rede vom Handeln Gottes in der Welt*, Freiburg 2006.

——, 'Der muslimische Offenbarungsanspruch als Herausforderung komparativer Theologie. Christlich-theologische Untersuchungen zur innerislamischen Debatte um Ungeschaffenheit und Präexistenz des Korans', *ZKTh* 129 (2007) 53–74.

——, *Offenbarung (Grundwissen Theologie)*, Paderborn 2010.

——, 'Komparative Theologie als Wegweiser in der Welt der Religionen' (*Beiträge zur Komparativen Theologie*; 6), Paderborn 2012.

——, 'Streit um die Erbsünde?' in Jürgen Werbick (ed.), *Sühne, Martyrium und Erlösung? Opfergedanke und Glaubensgewissheit in Judentum, Christentum und Islam*, Paderborn 2013.

——, *Einführung in die Systematische Theologie*, Paderborn 2014.

——, 'Jesus im Koran. Ansatzpunkte und Stolpersteine einer koranischen Christologie', in Stosch / Muna Tatari (eds.), *Handeln Gottes – Antwort des Menschen* (*Beiträge zur Komparativen Theologie*; 11), Paderborn 2014, 109–33.

——, 'Gott wird Kind. Das Gottes und Menschenbild der Inkarnationstheologie', in *ThPQ* 162 (2014) 380–89.

——, *Trinität (Grundwissen Theologie)*, Paderborn 2017.

——, *Herausforderung Islam. Christliche Annäherungen*, Paderborn 2017.

Strecker, Georg, 'Art. Judenchristentum', in *TRE* 17 (1988) 310–25.

Strotmann, Angelika, *Jesus von Nazaret (Grundwissen Theologie)*, Paderborn 2012.

Stroumsa, Guy, *The Making of the Abrahamic Religions in Late Antiquity*, Oxford 2015, 59–71.

al-Suyuti, Jalal al-Din, *al-Itqan fi 'ulum al-Qur'an*, ed. 'Isam Faris al-Harastani, vol. 1, Beirut 1998/1419.

al-Tabari, Abu Ja'far Muhammad b. Jarir, *Jami' al-bayan 'an ta'wil al-Qur'an*, ed. 'Abdullah b. 'Abd al-Muhsin al-Turkiy, Cairo 2001/1422.

Tabataba'i, Seyyed Muhammad Hussein, *Tafsir al-mizan*, vol. 18, Tehran 1987, 19, 59.

Tardy, René, *Najrân. Chrétiens d'Arabie avant l'islam*, Beirut 1999.

Theissen, Gerd / Merz, Annette, *Der historische Jesus. Ein Lehrbuch*, Göttingen 2001.

Trimingham, J. Spencer, *Christianity among the Arabs in Pre-Islamic Times*, London 1979.

Uthemann, Karl-Heinz, 'Kaiser Justinian als Kirchenpolitiker und Theologe', in *Augustinianum* 33 (1999) 5–83.

Vahdat, Farzin, 'Mehdi Haeri Yazdi and the Discourse of Modernity', in Ramin Jahanbegloo (ed.), *Iran Between Tradition and Modernity*, Lanham 2004, 51–70.

Velden, Frank van der, 'Konvergenztexte syrischer und arabischer Christologie. Stufen der Textentwicklung von Sure 3', in *Oriens Christianus. Hefte für die Kunde des christlichen Orients* 91 (2007) 164–203.

——, 'Kotexte im Konvergenzstrang – die Bedeutung textkritischer Varianten und christlicher Bezugstexte für die Redaktion von Sure 61 und Sure 5, 110–19', *Oriens Christianus. Hefte für die Kunde des christlichen Orients* 92 (2008) 130–73.

——, 'Die Felsendominschrift als Ende einer christologischen Konvergenztextökumene', in *Oriens Christianus. Hefte für die Kunde des christlichen Orients* 95 (2011) 213–46.

Vries, Wilhelm de, 'Die Gründe der Ablehnung des Konzils von Chalzedon durch die altorientalischen Kirchen', in Rudolf Kirchschläger / Alfred Stirnemann (eds.), *Chalzedon und die Folgen. 1. Wiener Konsultation mit der Orientalischen Orthodoxie. Dokumentation des Dialogs zwischen der armenisch-apostolischen und der römisch-katholischen Kirche sowie des Dialogs zwischen chalzedonensischer und nicht chalzedonensischer Orthodoxie. FS 60. Geburtstag v. Bischof Mesrob K. Krikorian (Pro Oriente*; 14), Vienna 1992, 124–31.

al-Wahidi, 'Ali ibn Ahmad, *Asbab nuzul al-Qur'an*, ed. Kamal Basyuni Zaqlul, Beirut 1991/1411.

Watt, William Montgomery, 'The Condemnation of the Jews of Banū Qurayẓah', in *The Muslim World* 42 (1952) 160–71.

Wehnert, Jürgen, 'Ebioniten', in *LThK* 3 (1995) 430–1.

Weichlein, Raphael, *Gottmenschliche Freiheit. Zum Verhältnis von Christologie und Willensfreiheit bei Maximus Confessor*, Saarbrücken 2013.

Wellhausen, Julius, *Reste arabischen Heidentums*, Berlin 1897.

Wensinck, A. J., 'Muhammed und die Propheten', in *Acta Orientalia* 2 (1924) 169–70.

Werbick, Jürgen, 'Von Gott sprechen an der Grenze zum Verstummen' (*Religion – Geschichte – Gesellschaft*; 40), Münster 2004.

——, 'Ist die Trinitätstheologie die kirchlich normative Gestalt einer Theologie der Selbstoffenbarung Gottes?', in Magnus Striet (ed.), *Monotheismus Israels und christlicher Trinitätsglaube (QD* 210), Freiburg 2004, 70–92.

——, *Gott-menschlich. Elementare Christologie*, Freiburg 2016.

——, 'Vergöttlichung Jesu? Die koranischen Jesus-Deutungen als Herausforderung zu christlich-christologischer Selbstreflexion', in Klaus von Stosch / Mouhanad Khorchide (eds.), *Streit um Jesus. Muslimische und christliche Annäherungen (Beiträge zur Komparativen Theologie*; 21), Paderborn 2016, 255–69.

Der Wiener Altorientalendialog, *Kommuniqués und gemeinsame Dokumente, Fünf Pro Oriente Konsultationen mit den Altorientalischen Kirchen*, vol. 1, Wien 1977.

Wiesel, Elie, *All Rivers Run to the Sea: Memoirs*, tr. Marion Wiesel, New York 1995.

Wittgenstein, Ludwig, *Culture and Value,* ed. G. H. von Wright, tr. Peter Winch, Chicago 1980.

Wolf, Hubert, *Krypta. Unterdrückte Traditionen der Kirchengeschichte*, München 2015.

Yazdi, Mahdi Ha'iri, *Hiram-i hasti: tahlili az mabadi-i hastishinasi-i tatbiqi*, Tehran 1980.

Zahniser, Mathias, 'The Word of God and the Apostleship of 'Īsā: A Narrative Analysis of Āl'Imrān', in *Journal of Semitic Studies* 37 (1991) 77–112.

al-Zamakhshari, Mahmud Ibn 'Umar, *al-Kashshaf 'an Haqa'iq al-tanzil wa-'uyun al-aqawil fi wujuh al-ta'wil*, ed. Ahmad b. Muhammad b. al-Munaiyir, vol. 1, Cairo 2012.

Zellentin, Holger Michael, *The Qur'an's Legal Culture. The Didascalia Apostolorum as a Point of Departure*, Tübingen 2013.

Zirker, Hans, *Islam. Theologische und gesellschaftliche Herausforderungen*, Düsseldorf 1993.

Reference text

Unless stated otherwise, texts from the Qur'an are quoted from M.A.S. Abdel Haleem's translation (Oxford University Press 2008).